JOHN FREEMAN'S LETTERS

MACMILLAN AND CO., Limited
LONDON · BOMBAY · CALCUTTA · MADRAS
MELBOURNE

THE MACMILLAN COMPANY
NEW YORK · BOSTON · CHICAGO
DALLAS · ATLANTA · SAN FRANCISCO

THE MACMILLAN COMPANY
OF CANADA, LIMITED
TORONTO

JOHN FREEMAN

John Freeman's Letters

Edited by
Gertrude Freeman and Sir John Squire

With an Introduction by
Walter de la Mare

London
Macmillan & Co. Ltd.
1936

COPYRIGHT

PRINTED IN GREAT BRITAIN
BY R. & R. CLARK, LIMITED, EDINBURGH

CONTENTS

INTRODUCTION

DREAMERS whose delight is in the past and zealots for progress seldom see eye to eye, but both may lament that, owing to what needs no flattery—the pace and pressure of modern life, its fever and its fret, there is nowadays little time and leisure left for the writing of letters. Letters, that is, which would have been deemed worthy of acceptance by our grandmothers who thought nothing of an epistle consisting of hand-made paper a yard square festooned with the closest calligraphy in black ink, and this criss-crossed in red. Those inhuman boons of social intercourse, the postcard, the telegram and the telephone, have, it is said, made all such outpourings of heart and head superfluous, and may soon put an end to what is perhaps the easiest and happiest and most intimate and the least mercenary of the arts.

However that may be, it was an art very dear to John Freeman; and this volume, even though it consists of only a brief selection of his Letters, reveals his mastery in it. Wholly impulsive and happy-go-lucky what he says may appear to be, but he seldom fails to say it well and fittingly. There is style, grace, arrangement, afterthought. "I have a lover-like palate for phrases", he confesses, and scores of such little felicities as, "bright as the bright light of a dream" and, "rankling praise", or *obiter dicta* such as that quoted by Sir John Squire in his vivifying introduction to *Last Poems*, "Some men know at last, more than half unconsciously, how their mind's made, and let it move where it will. Which is the elementary forgotten wisdom of the world"; and, "Happiness depends of course on such simple small things, and carries with it the sense of such simple great things",

are not assuredly the reward of an eye or mind negligent of
the "object". Postcards, it is true, were not taboo, but he
usually took full advantage of their ha'porth of space. He
now and then solicits a telegram, but rejects mere "news"
in a letter as little short of an insult to its recipient, and
pleads for what he himself bestows in such variety and
abundance—gossip, a gossip welling up out of a mind rich
in reflection, knowledge and sensibility. And if gossip has a
soul, it certainly does not resemble that of wit.

In consequence, his letters flow along like a brimming
brook through English meadows; rippling and shimmering,
yet often as placid as they are profound; eloquent of their
source yet seldom suggestive of any pressing or particular
object, aim and destination. He pined, positively hungered,
to receive letters; they were for him—as sympathy, presents,
cheques, publicity, scandal may be for others—a chronic
craving; and he no less delighted in answering them. The
postman who alone can ignore the modern unfranciscan
fiat—No beggars, no hawkers, no circulars—was never to
him a demon in a double-peaked cap whose knock is
anathema, but a wing-footed Mercury from the quieter
recesses of Olympus. After browsing in these leisurely,
lively and peaceable pages, we might, then, easily assume
that earthly existence for their writer had been a perpetual
dolce far niente.

Nothing could be further from the truth. Whatever of
the *dolce* his life may have contained—and his letters suggest
how much and how sweet it was—he seems never to have
been idle except when asleep; and then he was dreaming.
Day-dreaming, of course, as all good pedagogues agree, is the
most active kind of living of which the human mind is
capable. He lived in fact a *double* life; served two mistresses
in widely separated establishments. If either ever heard of the
other, secure in her conviction that she herself had wholly

appropriated Dr. Jekyll, she must immediately have accused her rival of harbouring a Mr Hyde. The names of these mistresses were Commerce and Poetry.

Of Poetry we hear much, but never a word to her discredit. She might perplex, torment, evade, elude and seem to have jilted him, but never once does he utterly despair of this impossible She; never once by one iota fail in his allegiance to her. Yet nothing he knew better than the meaning of

> His soul shall taste the sadness of her might
> And be among her cloudy trophies hung.

But of his dealings with his other and less capricious, but in certain respects no less exacting mistress, we hear astonishingly little. The word "treadmill" occurs only once; only once the statement, "figures I hate"; and both thus lightly refer to the fact that when he was only thirteen years old he became a little something in the City, a little something that gradually expanded in range, complexity and responsibility until he found himself supreme overseer of a hive numbering some seven thousand bees whose honey consisted of millions of insurance contracts, and whose labours included the dispensing of millions of pounds of solid gold. What this hive thought of the activities of its queen bee in the Gardens of the Hesperides is not related. The first drafts of his odes at any rate, we may safely assume—in his minute, queer, attractive, long-legged script—were never to be found on notepaper headed "The Liverpool Victoria Friendly Society".

Bees of a literary turn have been known to frequent the City, not less busy perhaps at times, but infinitely less able and conscientious. Other English authors, too—though few of them have been poets—have doubly triumphed over a similar destiny—Charles Lamb, Anthony Trollope, Walter Bagehot, Austin Dobson, Walter Leaf. But very few, I fancy, having begun so low, climbed so high, or remained so amazingly mute about it.

In a Memoir prefixed to Walter Bagehot's *Literary Studies* —leagues distant from his work as editor of *The Economist*— "I have sometimes", says R. H. Hutton, "felt somewhat unreasonably vexed that those [including the Chancellor of the Exchequer of the day] who appreciated so well what I may almost call the smallest part of him, appeared to know so little of the essence of him,—of the high-spirited, buoyant, subtle, speculative nature in which the imaginative qualities were even more remarkable than the judgment, and were indeed at the root of all that was strongest in the judgment— of the gay and dashing humour which was the life of every conversation in which he joined,—and of the visionary nature to which the commonest things often seemed the most marvellous, and the marvellous things the most intrinsically probable. To those who hear of Bagehot only as an original political economist and an illustrious political thinker, a curiously false image of him must be suggested— that, possibly, of 'the dreary professors of a dismal science'."

In John Freeman's case, and every word of the first sentence, from "high-spirited" onwards, is no less true of himself, it is the readers of his books and the lovers of his poetry who will share his "essence" and the true image of him, but may remain completely unaware of his highly practical and organizing faculties, not so seldom to be found associated with imaginative qualities as is generally supposed. And for reasons which he was never apparently tempted to share, even his letters will little enlighten them. When any mention of the City occurs, it is merely by the way; no tears, maledictions, or despair, and—even more remarkable—not a syllable of self-congratulation. He might be referring merely to the chronic ailment of the indolent when he casually confesses, "I am tired". "I am tired, but wanting to talk, and afraid to postpone writing until I am not tired." "What a happy letter I could send you—if I had the brains"—the brains which, though he does not say so, were as likely as not reposing wearied out on the dissecting tables of the actuaries.

Not by any means that he was contented with his tether. "The thought of your western solitude makes me envious, for it can never be mine. I have to stick to London"—a London which otherwise *as* London, with its music and music halls, its life and leaven, he delighted in no less than Samuel Johnson or Charles Lamb—"I have to stick to London as faithfully as London adheres to me." Again:

> But I doubt if you read poetry, nowadays. Probably you've changed: you devote your days to golf and your nights to bridge.
> —While I who might have been Milton, am only Selfridge. Instead of Odes on Immortality, I am concerned with Expectation of Life. Instead of working at Letters, I compel others to work: my heart is vowed to Idleness, but my profession is all Industry....

And again:

> You speak of the office. Things move very happily—they *move*. Not a jar, not a murmur, breaks the fair concord which all creatures make in the Board room now; we are all doves, cooing one to another, and the voice of the turtle is indeed pleasant to hear. A week ago I returned from our Convention at Blackpool— a strenuous affair, of course, but so entirely satisfactory that one doesn't mind the stress. Never was such a gathering in our Office, with 350 people thoroughly satisfied and hopeful. The only trouble is the list of engagements for the future, an insidiously growing number; but these I shall—do you say "wangle"?

There can be no question then that he enjoyed an ample satisfaction in having achieved what he achieved so well. Nevertheless, and no less naturally, he often pined for the wings of a dove, to flee away into all that England meant for him, and be at liberty, if not at rest. His poems indirectly tell how much. But no; it was never to be. "I can brag", he writes, "of my absolute idleness. For months I have written nothing; two poems this year and one—I think one only—

short story. Why does vacuity extend thus through all one's being, and leave one as sounding brass or tinkling cymbal? Worries of my daily job perhaps account for it, but I hate to think of being so much at the mercy of these externalities." "Wangle!" "Externalities!" "Nevertheless I should go on writing till all the seas gang dry, though I don't go dry except as the result of my bread and butter burdens, alack."

Even if Hercules himself were appointed poet laureate his labours in other spheres would neither palliate nor add lustre to his ventures into verse or prose. Nevertheless it would be unjust to Freeman, in some degree even as a letter writer, and wholly as a man of character and energy and devotion to duty (a term nowadays as remote from popular affection perhaps as "work" itself) if his "treadmill" were ignored. In spite, then, of the abundance of what follows, one may excusably regret the absence of a specimen or two of his official and professional letters and reports, accomplishments certainly no less arduous or less valuable in their own sphere than his other writings in theirs. Although, too, Sir Richard Whittington, decked and weighted with his chain of office, does, as we have seen, ever and again smile, or refrain from smiling, at us in these pages, nowhere shall we enjoy a single glimpse of the youthful Dick—perched up in his first teens on an office stool, his Cheshire cat on his shoulder.

Because, indeed, like the legal ascetics who die intestate, this indefatigable Man of Business usually refrained from dating his letters ("Thursday", "Saturday" rather suggesting eternity than time), we first meet him in this volume in 1920, as a man of forty, and not until much later in it are we introduced to him as a comparative boy of twenty-five. For earlier beginnings we must, at present at any rate, go to his poems, his *Memories of Childhood* in particular, and there share the early griefs, afflictions and raptures, concerning which, *except* in his poems, he was habitually reticent, if not silent.

No reader of his poems, from first to last, could fail to realize their pervasive gravity, the intensity of feeling, the torment of spirit so frequently expressed in them. In a playful expostulatory little discourse of 1907 (one of a group of letters addressed to two "dear ladies" and showing him not only trying his literary wings and preening his poetic feathers but already critically and comprehensively aware of such writers as Montaigne, Emerson, Balzac, Ruskin and Dostoevsky), he is discussing autobiography. "I think of Swift," he says, "and wonder what sort of *Praeterita* he would have left us:—that breaking fire of indignation, wrath and dusky passion:—sudden flame of tenderness; sadness over all. . . . Swift surely must have found the past only too intolerably poignant for speech." It is a summary, and perhaps he himself was aware of it even then, that might be no less truthfully applied to himself.

The first of his *Twenty Poems*, his first collection, which was published in 1909, is entitled "Prayer to my Lord":

> Lord, there are words that were not meant for Thee
> In this poor morgue of petty imagery!
> Things that sore need yet are not worthy Thy righting,
> True things writ false, conceived with heart unsighting;
> Intent for "this", yet plainly shewing "that",
> Utterly failed of the mark I flung them at. . . .
>   Oh! since the hand is Thine, the tongue, the head,
> And all that daily avoids the imminent dead,
> Call the words Thine too; so their only praise
> Be that, all-worthless, they yet gained Thy grace.

It is followed by "Happy Death":

> Bugle and battle-cry are still,
>   The long strife's over;
> Low o'er the corpse-encumbered hill
>   The sad stars hover.

It is in vain, O stars! ye look
    On these forsaken:
Awhile with blows on blows they shook,
    Or struck unshaken.

Needs now no pity of God or man. . . .
    Tears for the living!
They have 'scaped the confines of life's plan
    That holds us grieving.

The unperturbed soft moon, the stars,
    The breeze that lingers,
Wake not to ineffectual wars
    Their hearts and fingers.

Warriors o'ercoming and o'ercome,
    Alike contented,
Have marched now to the last far drum,
    Praised, unlamented.

Bugle and battle-cry are still,
    The long strife's over;
Oh that with them I had fought my fill
    And found like cover!

Such poems as these reveal the deepest tone and temper of his mind, the inmost places of his heart. Whatever reticence there may be in his letters, then, concerns, as we shall see, far less his writings than what those writings are about. It was not "Joy" moreover, which he had in plenty, but Life itself whose hand for him was ever at its lips "bidding adieu". For sixteen years, owing to a heart that never failed him in any other respect, he was under sentence of death. Not a single reference or even hint of this, I think, occurs in the following pages. Letters more intimate but not included here may well have spoken of it, but concerning first and last things he was profoundly reserved. Strangely so at times. I remember in the summer of 1928 sitting one late evening with him in his lodgings at Lyme Regis, a lighted oil-lamp on the garish tablecloth at his elbow. We had been idly gossiping together through the narrow sea-haunted streets, and I dropped some trivial speculative remark about the mystery of time. A slow flush spread over his face, followed by a glance of the deepest dismay. "I prefer", he said with suppressed emotion, "not to speak of it."

It is what a man, who has learned how to use them, *means* by his words that is of moment of course; and it may be that this open and perpetual menace both deepened and sharpened the meaning of all his work, just as the divination of it perhaps gave to that of Emily Brontë, Keats and Katherine Mansfield a similar edge. A man on his way to his execution, remarks Dostoevsky somewhere, is singularly observant of all that he encounters on the journey.

A reviewer once charged Freeman with an "excessive choiceness", and with being afraid of the commonplace; whereas, "The Lord in heaven knows the commonplace is the only thing I am not afraid of and feel at home in". A similar choiceness—and he early went to school to Coventry Patmore and Alice Meynell—is present in a brief list of his favourite composers: "My admired Beethoven, my adored Mozart, my awful Bach"; and elsewhere, in buoyant doggerel, he crowns Handel with praises which even Samuel Butler would approve.

By and large, whether in epics or comic songs, giblets, scenery, pictures or friends, he preferred and delighted most in the best, and was not to be fobbed off, in principle at any rate, with anything short of it—an inclination which one might have *assumed* would be common to us all. And no doubt his staff in the City were well aware of this little prejudice. "I want things simple . . . yet enjoy them when complicated and enriched with all manner of variety. Nothing pleases me like a green hill or a grey stone, and the mere sparkle of water sends me crazy as it falls down between green grasses. But I yield. . . ."

"No man should dare to write below his best", is an astringent aphorism, but he habitually practised what he modestly preached, and it is all the distance that elegance is from a natural grace from a mere precious fastidiousness. This may account in part for his distrust and contempt for the merely clever. He seldom defends himself, but not the least enlightening of his letters in respect to the practice of his mind is that to a friend who, no doubt with the most considerate intentions, has complimented him on being precisely that.

His eight- or nine-hours working-day over, he could return home — home to those two "angel imps", his daughters, who shine like wild flowers whenever he speaks of them; though, alas, there are no family letters here—to friends, talk, books and to the Muses. How in this 'leisure' he managed both to read so widely and to write his many books, not one of them other than a labour of love, which implies an infinitude of care, is a mystery left unexplained, but one not perhaps inexplicable. His delight in so doing is copiously illustrated. "Business", said Bagehot, "is more amusing than pleasure." And even in his infancy perhaps Freeman came to the same conclusion. He was never a professional writer; he remained an amateur, but scorned the amateurish. And "bread and butter" is none the less appetizing if it fails to taste of ink. Publishers then, royalties, words *per diem*, fees, the printers' devil, and all lamentations concerning them figure very little here. Thus he had the advantage, not necessarily of course of being able to do better work, or so much, but of choosing his kind and taking his time over it. Nor do his letters tell us when and how and where he fell in love with Poetry—the faculty for it, like that of music, being innate—only what unwearying delight

it conferred, and the fervour and fidelity of his passion.
They range from brief and urbane epistles to a stranger, and
acknowledgments of circumspect gratitude for a sympathetic
review, as free from vanity as from a mock humility, to
screeds pages long, resembling that culinary masterpiece
probably of Chinese origin—a turkey stuffed with a goose
and that with a capon and that with a fat pheasant, and so
ad infinitum.

Wise, witty and never heedless criticism, spontaneous
excursions of as much insight as sagacity into the relation
of poetry to metaphysics, to philosophy, to psychology, to
music, to free verse, vie with impulsive talk upon any theme
his fancy cares to follow, and in pursuit of any hare a correspondent has chanced to raise. He is revising proofs, he tells
us, with particular attention to his *a*'s and *e*'s and *i*'s for the
sake of verbal harmonies and to counter "the casual and
gross discord into which I'm betrayed like any rabbit". "I
hear stories, I *hear* prose"—prose, that jade of jades who
won't be seduced and won't be obstinate: and all this is in
relation to the "persistent quenchless desire" he had "to
write well, no matter how ill I write". This indeed was the
ideal that made him a formidable and exacting as well as a
just and candid critic—even in gratitude for a "presentation
copy". That dubious puff, the pre-view, was not as yet in
fashion. And he could no more talk about books and keep
life out than a flower can refrain from becoming a seed. In
fact he deplored Literature in letters. He was disappointed in
Edward Thomas's because "they are mainly upon purely
literary subjects", rather than wholly self-expressive. Again,
"I didn't mean to write of Literature. I am not Stevenson,
I meant to write gossip." Even then though, pen in hand,
he could no more elude the enticement of books than a
moth the flame of a candle, friendship was his dearest solace,
and talk one of its richest rewards.

B

He was that kind of solitary who delights, much more than the merely social and sociable being can, in the company he loves—in his friends and fellow-devotees; and in these he was uncommonly rich. Not in order to chatter, argue, soliloquize, bandy stories or simply mix, but to talk with them, anywhere and anywhen (except possibly in business hours). Talk, either through long quiet evenings into the night, or at their Mermaid or Triple Tun, the Tibbald (together with reading, meditating, walking, eating and drinking, listening to music, enjoying melodrama, but not acted "plays" or sex-drama—and keeping tryst—flowers, birds, waters, *trees*—with that ageless and lovely young goddess, Nature, whom Science makes hoary and the poets ever more golden), was his liveliest and lifelong satisfaction. He was, too, a consummate listener. "For it's my weakness to be pleased."

In days, distant now, alas, I had the happiness of sharing many such talks, *tête à tête* for the most part. And what the postman then exchanged between us were little more than assignations and *billets doux*. We often pow-wowed the moon into her zenith, if not the sun down the sky. Later, space severed us; and worse, one of us became a wretched correspondent. Seeing then that he could not always be talking, letters were the next, and a hardly less excellent, best. Let at any time a discerning friend pipe but a single note of the genuine decoy, and Freeman seems never to have failed to respond copiously and in kind.

He was convinced, too, that by far the most fertile subject for a letter worthy of the name is its writer—an "eager egotism". "Forgive all nonsense for the sake of the pea in the bladder." There have been admirable letter-writers chiefly intent on edification, or love, or politics, or public affairs, or the addressee, or the musical glasses, or the domesticities, or birds. But it is who is saying it, even when a Cleopatra, a dogma, a bee-boy or a hermit toad is the theme, that is more vital than the thing said. And so: "I will give you a song of Myself"; and so: "This strikes me as an indecent letter—full of me and none of you; but it is the kind I shall be very glad to receive in reply—all of You". For what you are about to receive may *you* make me truly thankful. "Coleridges are rare, but surely it is not impossible to learn that the one eternal subject is the personal, the one inexhaustible well is self, no matter what the bucket. And there can be but one authentic discovery." This in 1905; and this nineteen years afterwards: "I'm naturally idle and thirst for activity; lazy, and forced to be doing; slow-witted, and continually stirred to attempt the things I love. Well! And if this letter isn't sufficiently sprinkled with *I's*, pray write a better and yet more egotistical one yourself."

Even then though this indefatigable egotist, who, unlike George Meredith's hero, has as many "legs" as a centipede, had only the crannies of a jealously guarded leisure with which to endow his friends—"Give me but the parings of your time, give me but twenty-five hours a day"—his letters are full not only of stuff as original as it is substantial, but of high spirits, gaiety, enthusiasm, humour—now dry, now sweet, now exuberant, and always within call of its sister, imagination; and last, but by no means least, a delicious zest for nonsense.

I remember no fellow-creature whose habitual expression was so placidly sedate and even solemn as his, or one who more enjoyed laughing. He was tall, inclined to the angular, leisurely in movement, and stooped a little, his face being surmounted with beautiful brows, beneath which gazed out, as bland as a child's, ruminative eyes of a peculiarly ardent blue, the like of which I can only twice recall. As one might assume from his books and from his style, that gaze was neither penetrating, keen nor analytical. An habitual meditativeness and prolonged inward imaginings had, as it were, stilled and deepened it. They were comprehending rather than apprehending eyes. Attired for an evening talk at times as the occasion deserved in a brown velvet jacket, his gold eye-glasses hooked with a tiny chain, beneath hair sleek, fair, and unusually thick, over his ear—a sedate tribute perhaps to his chair of office in the City, he spoke, as he wrote, with a certain punctilio, slightly drawling his words when he was most persuasive, his voice, like Shelley's, rising in pitch when he became fervent, provocative or challenging.

His favourite wine, as he lyrically mentions here and there, was sherry. And, while its bouquet by no means precluded body, his conversation resembled it—rather than, say, a tawny port or a heady champagne, or—well, absinthe. His smile was tinged with the pensive, though not with melancholy. As for his laughter—a slow, condensed chuckle —even in memory it reminds me of nothing so much as real turtle soup, and it was no less palatable. Now and then it reached the irrepressible stage and became an incantation, spiriting one back to one's nursery and to that *elixir vitae* from the well of Nature, a fit of the giggles.

A most winning satisfaction over the pleasure he is both giving and receiving in his letters is perhaps their sovereign charm. And ever and again it is not solely John Freeman, the poet or the critic or the friend or boon companion, or the gay or grave or ironic or genially abusive gossiper whose presence we are in, but a John Freeman disporting himself in a Harlequin domino of his own devisal. He is, as it were, indulging in make-believe, but without the least dissimulation. He may be elucidating the episode entitled "Literature on the Rocks", or discussing—as Henry James fastidiously and into a ninth dimension discussed the gift of a dressing bag—a mysterious azalea or the disappearance of a fountain pen, or mocking at pundits doomed to the sententious because burdened with duties at a public dinner; and the raillery, the rhetoric, the banter surprise and amuse him no less as he watches them magically appearing on his own notepaper than they will, he knows, amuse the friend who will share them.

"I have a difficulty", he confesses, "in confining my pen to literality, and always want to tell lies." What man of imagination has not shared this craving for a sort of personal fiction, for a release from the merely expected, for a leaven in the sheer sad lump of Fact? Day in, day out, moreover, Freeman faced figures. What wonder he loved to indulge in the little more that gilds the much, the *higher* mathematics.

One friend in particular, J. W. Haines—the friend of many poets—had the secret of easing this want. Some of the longest and therefore the best of these letters not only begin with "dear Jack" but keep reiterating it. It is as if somehow Prince Hal had dressed up as Falstaff simply because nothing would satisfy his exuberance but to double his part.

Much of all this, and a great deal more than there is space to mention, is surely past the divination of even the most heedful reader of his books. Letters such as these, in Mr Edward Marsh's words, are "one of those queer encouraging counter-currents which impede the modern trend towards barbarism". Apart from the ghastly threat of such a trend, discerning readers of Freeman's poems and prose, who may at present preen themselves on being fit because they are few, will steadily multiply. And if work so vigorous and delicate is not in itself invitation enough, here is a wealth of wit and wisdom which should lead to its living waters scores of others, who can surely need no other persuasion, let alone any compulsion, to drink.

WALTER DE LA MARE

September 22, 1935

CONRAD AIKEN

TO CONRAD AIKEN

MY DEAR AIKEN

Your letter was a great pleasure, even though it did so kindly rob me of the fun of hunting for your meaning through the mazes of a handwriting so much better than my own. I'm afraid I still can't give you clearly my impressions of your poetry beyond this—that in reading *Senlin* I became more sharply aware than before of a special "appeal"; and I don't mean that the characteristics that made it weren't in *The House of Dust*, but only that I hadn't been so conscious of it until I pondered over *Senlin*. The appeal I speak of was the appeal of music; that is to say, that just as, when I listen to music, music that I admire or love, my mind is set going at a new pace, touching new islands in wilder seas, so *Senlin*, instead of giving me one sharp definite picture or sound, provoked a multitude of pictures or sounds, or rather I was sensible of these sounds and aspects flowing about me as I read. Hence it seemed that I could only speak correctly of the poems as a musical subject; the music not being associated with the sounds of your verse (you have paid but small attention to that "artificiality") but with the effect of your pictures on my sensations. But when I have laboriously said this I have still to say that I doubt whether we are thinking of the same thing when we think of poetry. You have chosen a field of enormous possibilities, enormous difficulties, a field which no great poet has hitherto explored. The fascination of it is obvious, and one danger seems obvious to me also, namely, that a kind of poetry may result which is profoundly psychological but expressing such intuitions—or

3

such deductions—as prose can very well express. Don't think this is meant uncivilly; think rather that I see that bargain as a bad one which involves the losing of poetry and the gaining of psychology. For I am in the midst of my old difficulty—that the subtle extension of psychological apprehensions needs more and not less form than many other kinds of poetry. Quite simply, poetry means to me creation, while group-psychology seems to be—not analytic only, but at any rate not a creative activity. I think a fine and eternal poem may be born of a psychological fingering of human minds; but I don't see how it can be made except by means of the images, the sounds, the colours of poetry used in such a way as to *present* rather than describe.... You must forgive my unphilosophic way of trying to say these things:— I don't conceive of poetry except as poetry achieved, that is in terms of Form. In the words of the Apostle, "God giveth it a body"; and until the poet has given his divined or imagined world the body of a world, his poetry can neither satisfy himself nor capture others. I don't presume to say this to you as you, but as indicating my difficulty about those modern and younger writers whose feet may be trembling upon the edge of a new land, but whose ardours have not very deeply caught me up.

But what you say of *St. Bartholomew* confirms me in thinking that we look from opposite ends of the earth at this Idea of poetry. In that poem I am not "describing"—I am presenting a vision of a changed world, and also the atmosphere in which that world is born or that vision brought to me. Unconsciously but (as I now see) quite definitely I was moved to the presentation of that vision not directly or nakedly, but washed and shimmering in an aura which is as essentially a part of the whole as the light is of the world. That elaboration of picture, that artificiality as it seemed to you, was a *vital* part of the whole; although I freely admit that in the presentation of the aura I speak of, I had little *deliberate* activity. And now as I see the complete vision (which all the time, of course, was but disengaging itself slowly from murk and tangles) I see it in a shimmering suspension of light and heat.—But I won't labour this. Far pleasanter is it to thank you for what you've done for *St. Bartholomew* in spite of your own austere judgment, and to say that *The Red Path* accompanies this and a shorter poem *The Wounded Bird* which you are to take quite literally as the transcription of a dream. Each of them is available for U.S.A., but I want to say that I've an uneasy sense of burdening you with responsibilities which only a miraculous good nature might accept. But at least I shall hear from you again and perhaps you'll send back what U.S.A. doesn't want.

I've met Lindsay twice: that is to say I've talked a little and listened much; and you'll know how impressive his *Congo* etc. can sound. I should have written before but I've been away, carrying your letter down to a lonely village in Gloucester but doing no more than think over what you said and ponder upon *Senlin* and the differences which my letter may only show as seeming deeper than they are. No matter! I've been looking lately at the Collected Poems of Edward Thomas and de la Mare, but without the time to brood over them as I should like; for I'm wrestling with a longish narrative poem (in the strictest of forms—the couplet) which obstinately resists my devoutest efforts to close it briskly.

Renewed thanks.   Ever yours

JOHN FREEMAN

ANERLEY
16th. January, 1921

MY DEAR AIKEN

I had been hoping to have another long metaphysical and delightful letter from you, and indeed I'm somewhat conscious of giving the occasion in remarks (already answered by you) concerning the "moral" of your last book, a moral—absurd term! which I fancied was supported by *Senlin*. I assume that my last letter reached you, for with it I sent *The Red Path*, which partly prompts my present writing. But first I will say that I've been glad to come upon your traces in magazines now and then, and to see references to your work which show that critics and reviewers, if bemused, are at any rate interested. And that's all to the good. I've heard of you too through Armstrong,[1] with whom I've had several opportunities of talking, and who is being consistently remarked as the sole valuable contributor to a volume of Cambridge poets: a tribute, too, based not merely upon the splendid *Buzzards*. Possibly faint echoes of these things reach your young continent. At this moment the only poetry talked of is Wilfred Owen's, whose *Strange Meeting* (not his best poem yet very fine and powerfully imaged) was published somewhere before you left these shores,—and John Clare's, whose hitherto uncollected poems have just been issued and welcomed.

Do you happen, by the way, to be an authority on the Works of George Moore? I'm writing again on him, and should like any crumbs that fall from the table of your meditations. Prose being my preoccupation at the moment, I'm dry, or nearly dry, of verse; but lately I finished a kind of pastoral called *The Harp* on which I'm inclined to rest all my hopes. At any rate, it will go into my next book, and as the publisher wants it to be prepared for this Spring, I'm wondering how the question stands with *St. Bartholomew* and *The Red Path*. I'm not certain about the Spring, and indeed am half inclined to defer the book until the Autumn; certainly I shall, if otherwise the publication of the two poems in America were to be jeopardised.—

[1] Martin Armstrong.

A line from you, then, will probably settle the matter for me.

I've meant to write this many times during the past month or so, but you see it doesn't grow by delay. Nevertheless I'll sum up all the unsaid in good wishes.

Ever yours

JOHN FREEMAN

ANERLEY
28th. May, 1921

MY DEAR AIKEN

I'm a bad correspondent, and scarce one out of a dozen letters carried in my head ever gets on to paper. I've been very busy, very tired, bothered with illness at home and family bereavement, wanting to write to you but putting it off until the hour was more fortunate. But that hour doesn't come. As soon as I'd finished *Punch* I swore I'd write to tell you precisely how and why I'd liked it; and that letter, too, I believe, remained unwritten. You in the idyllic quietness of U.S.A. won't understand this old-world fever, and will say it's like gnats over a swamp; and you will be right.—And tell me, please, at this point why it's easier (apart from all the accidents I've mentioned) to write to you at 25,000 miles distance, than to the man next door, or de la Mare round the corner? . . . As I said, our busy, healthy swamp will be incomprehensible to you, for you've only seen it by glimpses as of a photographic shutter, when even swift movement seems still and lifeless.

Is *Punch* your best? I'm inclined, but not quite persuaded to think that it is, for it's queer, changeful, life-like in strangeness, with a level of style which does not shut out passages of beauty; or passages of beauty which don't diminish the general effect of the style. I can only speak generally of my impression, which that philosophical rogue himself first of all—a philosophical creation, I mean, breathed into human correspondence—and then, scarcely less vivid, of his women. Curious that a sense of colour should wreathe over all the poem, or sense of richness and not at all of meagre philosophy:—I mean, I think, that it's a most *human* poem. Else I should not get that sense of colour and warmth and movement. Isn't the style itself better than anywhere else? Purely as style the quatrains are the best, but that passage, if I may venture, seems to me too sharp an innovation upon the tone of the rest. It proves that the author can write easily in the strictest as well as the laxest lyrical form: but does it prove anything else? But I hesitate to cavil at anything beautiful, and am only inclined to say that it's beautiful and therefore appropriate. I should like to see it reviewed over here, and know how such a poem affects our metaphysical critics who care little about the poetry if only the metaphysics be right—or wrong.

To resume gossip: I can only gossip of myself and say that part of my "business" has been an article for the *Quarterly* on Maurice Hewlett's English poems (*The Song of the Plow*, etc.) and another, nearly finished, on Chesterton for the *Mercury*. I'm meditating a Lecture in November on *The Other World*, meaning your and my other world, and Keats's and Blake's—not Conan Doyle's and Oliver Lodge's. The subject attracts me, but I haven't yet begun to write the Lecture and shall probably regret bitterly the audacious choice of a high theme. Meanwhile my book on George Moore is suspended for revision—deliberately put aside so that I can come to it again in the autumn and look at it both more narrowly and more largely. —O and a matter that may interest you is that a week ago I read *The Wounded Bird*, *The Red Path* and another long narrative to a Balliol group. The Oxford intellects seemed interested, more particularly since it was the first occasion of anything but lyrics being

read to them. Once before Bridges read English hexameters
(his own) and told Balliol that that was the only measure for
narrative poems; meaning, of course, that narrative poems
had never been written. Well!

And by the way, I've not heard anything more about
Firuski and his Chap Book. If difficulties cloud the prospect,
I shouldn't like you to be bothered to death, and would
simply include *The Wounded Bird* and *The Red Path* in my
autumn book. Soon I shall be handing the copy to my
publisher, and if you can let me know something within the
next few weeks I shall be very glad.

At this point someone hands me *The Boston Evening
Transcript*, containing an article headed with my name. It is
an article which gives me at once pleasure and humiliation—
pleasure easily accountable, humiliation too obscure to be
explained. Or I'll say that humiliation is not the word, but
some other term which will embrace a touch of misgiving,
a hint of doubt, and threepenny worth of amusement. Do I
guess rightly that you are the anonymous author—bene-
factor, rather? The man who gave the paper to me said that
the review was worth a fortune to me. The writing seems
like yours, save that the praise may pardonably weaken my
admiration for your critical-philosophical "distinguishing-
ness". I'm proud really, to read such a notice, and an inch
prouder if you wrote it. Ever yours

JOHN FREEMAN

ANERLEY
1924

DEAR CONRAD

Cathy asked me to address her letter to John, and I
couldn't write the name without wanting to send an idle
line to you. Not that I'm idle, for my bread-and-butter has
been particularly crusty of late and leaves me little energy,

but since you never come up now, and as yet I've not been able to come to you—though still "expecting"—I must scribble. I had a short Tuesday—Saturday with Robin [1] last week: Ely, Peterboro, King's Lynn, Norwich and Bury St. Edmunds; and I've seldom been happier than in lingering among Norman miracles and—as delightful—the humbler miracles of domestic architecture surviving from a time when it was easier, or certainly commoner, to make useful things beautiful, than now. And two river saunterings—I dreaming while Robin rowed—made the time fleet carelessly, between meadows of gold and meadows of green: or embayed under flowering willow that smells so rank and green and vital. I wish you had been there—unless it had made you melancholy, though some melancholys are pleasant in their influence, in their touch of a distant past upon a present that seems hardly less distant.

My pen lags, being tied to Melville proofs and finding room for endless correction—a's and e's and i's and the rest all sounding their teasing bells and demanding another harmony, or any harmony rather than the casual and gross discord into which I'm betrayed like any rabbit. I'm still wanting to go on with a Madame Tussaud poem which is half done, and X and Y and Z are still to be started. No matter: *Prince Absalom* will be a handsome quarto and is printing. Haven't I reason to be pleased?

I still boast of the author of *Bring! Bring!* Perhaps I shan't read it again for years, but I find phrases or *airs* in it haunting me with an astonishing beauty. I *hear* stories, I *hear* prose, and the hearing of *Bring! Bring!* is a delight. When this music echoes and prolongs itself I think it must indeed be true and individual.

I babble and I'll stop. Write more, and write more prose. To think that you, who deny yourself images in what

[1] Dr Robin Flower of the British Museum.

you are pleased to call critical prose, should be able to breathe up images as a fish breathes up bubbles! Down, Envy!

My love to Jessie and the infants three. Ever

J. F.

ANERLEY
Nov. 3rd., 1924

DEAR CONRAD

It was rude of me to send your book back without a note, but I didn't expect to be able to write a note; but as I'm sitting at home with a headache and thinking of Winchelsea, and too restless to do whatever I ought to do, I've chosen this instead. I caught a brief glimpse of Martin and heard that you were back again, not much the worse for the week-end storm which set us all thinking of you. Perhaps we shall be lucky enough to see you before you go to America again. All I've seen of you is the Anthology which I bought for a friend last week, took down to him and scarcely looked at myself. That was in Oxfordshire, where I saw what was better (it seemed) than American poetry, namely, woods that were a great flame, bright as the bright light of a dream, and once (in the sunset) red as a virginia creeper. I walked and sauntered and scribbled, playing again the game of the best novels, the best poems and sending people hastily to their note books to remember *Moby Dick*; and talking of Wordsworth and so on.

A fortnight ago I saw Fletcher,[1] who was anxious to try the Q.R. with an article on E.A.R.: but the Q.R. quite curtly declined, saying they (the assistant editor) had read E.A.R. I fancy Fletcher was disappointed. My own disappointment was reserved for another occasion. When Jessie was here a few years ago I read her a new story of my own,

[1] John Gould Fletcher.

C

The Gold Coast, which she seemed mildly to like. I liked it much more, gave it to Squire[1] and said it was pretty good. He returned it saying it's exquisitely written but too indefinite in its ending. My anger rose at his praise as much as at his rejection: if it is exquisitely written, why not print it? if the end is indefinite, that's not my fault—the "solution" is no clearer to the boy of the story than to its writer. It reminded me of your beauty that he returned! Probably the headache which is sprawling through this letter, is caused by that rankling praise.

I should have added a line here for Jessie, but she wrote a letter to me a few weeks ago, expressing such (mock) annoyance at something I'd quite innocently said that I'm rather afraid of provoking further misunderstanding. Besides, her letter seemed to promise silence for the future. But give my love to John and Jane: Jane fairly won Flower's heart.

Did you discover the track of *Sleep Pretty Wanton?* Pray don't write merely to acknowledge the book: I hate "acknowledgment" letters.
                                                    Ever
                                                                    JOHN

                                                            ANERLEY
                                                        Sunday. 1925
DEAR CONRAD

I hope you are all right now, after the excision of a false quantity, and that you've nothing to fear or do but contemplate.

I looked up Milton: I was right (or was it you?)—it is *Eyeless in Gaza* etc. Did you check your own proofs for *Senlin?* There are a couple of misprints—small things, but your own now and for ever. I liked *Senlin* better now than years ago, though without comparing the versions. Maybe it's my taste has improved, my tongue grown healthier

---

[1] Sir John Squire.

(excuse the range of metaphor at this conjuncture): maybe you've improved the poem by your revisions.

Well, I've been to Pirandello's *Henry IV*. I think I've never been to a theatre before, just as, on reading Dostoieffsky (even for the hundredth time) you feel you've never read a novel before, and that there are no novels but his;—Allah is great and Mahomet is his Prophet. That's how I felt with Pirandello. The nuisance is I can't be sure whether part of the impression isn't Henry IV's, I mean Ernest Milton's, rather than Pirandello's; but against this I set the fact that the author easily loses as much by the rest of the cast as he gains by Henry IV. I never go to theatres and don't know what acting is: but I think I know what it isn't. Unluckily I can't be sure whether Pirandello didn't intend them to be as repulsive as they are, and whether they (the rest) aren't after all played with inconceivable sureness and skill. Pity my confusion: I'm at the mercy of my prejudices—and am candid about them.

My Lord! I'm writing again. I don't mean letters but verse, the long or longish poem I spoke of on Monday. It's for children and I ease my conscience by saying children of all ages. I think one of the episodes will be in Skeltonian verse, if I can manage it decorously.

I hope Joan's measles are diminishing properly. Do you know Robin's youngest girl has them, or it? My love to all at Jeakes.

Affly.

J. F.

JESSIE AIKEN

TO JESSIE AIKEN

DEAR JESSIE

I sit down at once to write what should be, in your expectation, a letter of thanks but is a letter of perplexity. A tea-cosy for me, a cigarette box for Gertrude: I'm thankful, of course, but am teased and humiliated. And I can't think that you didn't mean it so;—somehow or other I must have offended you, though in so clumsy and thoughtless a way that I'm stupidly ignorant even yet. Was it—no, surely not. Then was it when Jessie said—but she couldn't mean *that*. . . . And so on, and my poor head tingles.

You'll have no difficulty, then, in believing that my perplexity is profound, but since I can't solve it I must needs ignore and dismiss it, and take your gift quite simply, gladly and proudly, and so (don't you see?) disarm you of whatever revenge you have subtly pondered. It is kind of you, and the kinder being so superfluously and wantonly thoughtful, as if I didn't know without that how—I never could speak one undisconnected sentence: fill in the rest please. Won't you? well, then, I mean, as if I didn't know already how more than—more than commonly, and beyond *our* poor insularity of thought, you—you what? No, I can't write the sense I can't talk.

I came home faintly hoping that your departure had been deferred, and that I should have had a long, long evening listening to you. I think, too, I should have liked to interpose Jane between my chest and Cathy's exuberant affections. But I don't repine and am glad you stayed a whole week in this neglected suburb—dejected suburb, now. Gertrude says she dropped a dim and timid hint, suggesting that if you are tired or tiring of being alone at Winchelsea, when days are short and evenings long, you might care to come up again, with John and Jane. I can be bolder and say that even though you are ravenously busy and would be bored by coming, you would be blessing our children by bringing yours here before Conrad's return. Maybe the four could be got to bed earlier in the dark evenings, and leave you free for conversation or what do you call it, disquisition. At any rate I make the suggestion quite the reverse of timidly and infinitely far from hopelessly. My love to Conrad when you write to him, and emphatically to John and Jane.

Ever

J. F.

I *do* like the cosy, but much more the kindness: though you'll smile at my being so simple.

ANERLEY
October, 1922

DEAR JESSIE

I have been puzzled in asking myself whether your letter needed an answer or not. Does the etiquette of correspondence permit, or demand, an answer, and is it better to fail by neglect than by effusive excess? I shrink from the latter, but may I not be shrinking morbidly? At any rate, I shall get rid of that particular spectral misgiving by writing, whatever other fault I decline into.

Well, the real puzzle follows, namely, what did you mean by saying that you weren't using a hook, when there's no possible reason for a particular remark save a prehensile one? The remark, as you will very well remember, was about yourself, "so depressingly agreeable". I chuckled over that phrase, I positively gargled it until my throat was smooth and my tones became bell-like. I have a lover-like palate for phrases, and I enjoyed that one gratefully—for a week, and then began tardily to suspect the significance. Depressingly

agreeable, that is merely abstract; but to whom is the depression imparted—there is the concrete. (Forgive me if I
blunder in trying to write like a civilized westerner, and not
an uncivilized easterner; pity the oriental who would be an
occidental.) Is it yourself that you so agreeably depress, or is
it your audience: which have you on mind? Are you thinking
of those dreadful midnight hours when one lies and rues the
follies of the day—the mean acquiescences, the paltry com-
promises, the smirking civilities? Or is it that you fear that
this persisting and invariable agreeableness, this courageous
smilingness, of which you know you have the absolute
secret, this that you would call esoteric mollificatoriness
(forgive me again) is depressing to your no less courageous
and no less ambiguous audience? I can't pursue this obstinate
questioning without approaching the confines of the im-
polite; but since I am genuinely perplexed you will understand that the largest hook still dangles meatless before my
eyes.

I had hours of talk on Friday, and was only sorry that
Martin couldn't join Haines and me and talk of Shelley and
Keats, and how to write a critical article for Squire on
Edward Thomas (which Haines is asked to do) and so on.
Martin was dining with "one of these American poets", to
use Davies' phrase, Krembourg, and so we missed him. But
it was amusing. We sat for three hours at the Trocadero,
then for an hour on the Embankment, then for an hour
somewhere else; and the longer we sat the sprightlier became
Haines' tongue—not unaided, I fear. When I left him, very
late, he had reached dazzling heights of tributary brightness;
I have, it seems, no conception of my influence upon the
younger writers, who don't so much like as respect and
FEAR me; I am almost the only person who can write such
articles and (I think he said) stories as—well, see how the
paper blushes. Nothing was more delightful than to watch

his temperature rising, and nothing more amusing than to see people near looking with curiosity at me while they listened to Haines, and trying to reconcile what they heard with what they saw. If only my head would turn I should be happy.

Why do I tell you all this? Because you are not here, and it would be amusing if you were. But when one is so depressingly unagreeable, and the depression is infectious, my only chance to talk to you is to write to you. And besides, if you were here I should be reduced to listening, which may be interesting but is decidedly ignoble.

Yours

JOHN

MARTIN ARMSTRONG

TO MARTIN ARMSTRONG

ANERLEY
Monday
[No date]

DEAR MARTIN

You have indeed made a fine poem. I can't conceive of a bad sherry, and so you've had an advantage in your subject, since even a bad painting of say a beautiful Leg must give more pleasure than a good painting of a thick Leg in which only the abstract beauty of Leg may be inferred. I envy you—but most the subject. Why do you so persistently anticipate my subjects?

I don't see how you can get the sailing ship in—and yet: the ship, the rolling sky, the gently rolling casks, the gently rolling supercargo with a perpetually rolling belly, enjoying at once satiety and anticipation and showing us (if it needs) that you can't have too much of a good thing: a sailing ship, slipping slily through the Panama Canal (to make the shortest passage through dry America) touching at the no more vexed Bermoothes (unless you don't call there, and then vexation would be exasperated), and at length floating swanlike up the Bristol Channel and spewing its year-old maturity into the sacred cellars of Denmark Street. It *was* my subject. Is Sherry more to you than to me? But it's your poem and to make a poem is to make a thing—sherry: and so you become Confederate with Time, Summer, and the Creator of the Grape.

Thinking of your subject after you left today I recalled (I don't know why) Arnold's

"Shy traffickers, the dark Iberians came".

They must be the modern bootleggers, don't you think?

23

And torn between admiration and envy, gratitude and hate,
I remain, Sir,
Yours inveterately
JOHN FREEMAN

ANERLEY
27th. Decr. [1926?]

DEAR MARTIN

Your letter came an hour ago, so welcome that I must say so at once. It is the only letter, except one from Haines, that I've had for days, and since I ought to answer his, and since it's a change of posture to sit at a machine, and since I'm sure the crash of the machine and the roar of speed are a help to Composition, I'll trouble you to forgive a type-written letter. It is written in the middle of the holiday-time as we call it, a time which I characterised yesterday, in a letter, as justifiably devoted to overeating. Perhaps it is the only time when sheer overeating is religiously justified. Hermits (though you know more about their habits than I do) and Indian fakirs and American Vidhejas and other ascetic persons might feel justified in gorging, had they the equivalent of our Christmas. Don't people overeat in Pick-wick Papers, and isn't that supposed to be the Epic of Christmas? Agamemnon I take it is but the great Feaster and Achilles the sulky stomach, Hector is surely the roast beef, Hector the embodied Appetite and Helen—why, anything; for Helen doesn't matter in the Iliad. Anyone might be Helen to Homer. Hasn't it struck you that Helen and Paris are indifferent figures? Well, we ate on Christmas day im-moderately, and yesterday more moderately, yet still with a kind of dying fury. I was in some difficulty for I was un-supported by any other man. Allan and a Scots friend of his came yesterday but couldn't be beguiled into staying to supper. Perhaps they had sniffed comparative meagreness

and weren't hungry enough to eat except for sheer volup-
tuousness. Not like our cat, our true Roman, who ate, sicked,
ate and sicked again in a perfectly heavenly zest of appetite.

"Teach me to eat that I may dread
Supper as little as my bed—"

eagerly, bravely, emetically. But alas, age comes and with
age prudence, and shamefacedness, and wives and daughters
of an incredible delicacy. Would that I had more courage.
We are going to my sister's to lunch, and my sister is married
to a parson, and he can number all the vices, of which drinking—not over-drinking but mere drinking—is easily first.
I lack courage, and would fain stay at home with the heroic
kitten. But I lack courage even for that.

Forgive this tragic nonsense, and tell Cape that someone gave me several volumes of the Travellers' Library.
He will be pleased and will drink again. I shall hope to see
you at the Tibbald later on this week, or if you want to eat,
I mean to really eat (infinitive and all) I will come with you
to the Horseshoe.   Ever

                                            J. F.

                                    Tuesday
                            16th. July, 1928

DEAR MARTIN
    He cometh not! and maybe if I saw you I shouldn't
know you. Have you grown a beard? Are you bent, blear,
sour? Do you dribble your drink and beslaver your waistcoat? I do: It's years since we met: I really do and you can't
be much more decent.

    I thought of you all of a sudden, a brief pricking thought,
when I crossed Great Ormond Street yesterday and again
when I read *Miss Thompson* to all the eighteen-year-olds at
St. Paul's school in the evening. *Miss Thompson*, of course,
was delighted in by all her potential nieces and grandnieces:

I announced and repeated your name in a great voice—but you didn't hear me: the applause meant for you fell upon me, as though I were you, as though I could write *Miss Thompson*. For a moment I knew what human glory is, as I stood there smiling and blushing in your coat. Forgive me, or forgive yourself for making the usurpation easy.

I hope your absence—from my point of view—has been worth while; I hope that verse and prose have flowed from you like waters from a Mountain. From me the trickle has approached inexistence, inconspicuousness. I've written some lyrics and the second part (nearly) of a longish poem which you could or would see. And you'll be aware that my *Collected Poems* (really selected) are out: I spend all my time rubbing my belly—to read and read again the sweet dear phrases of reviewers. I ought to have sent you the book: I ought to send it. But I doubt if you read poetry, nowadays. Probably you've changed: you devote your days to golf and your nights to bridge.

—While I who might have been Milton, am only Self-ridge. Instead of Odes of Immortality, I am concerned with Expectation of Life. Instead of working at Letters, I compel others to work: my heart is vowed to Idleness, but my profession is all Industry.

Write when you can—I mean when you can't.

Affly.

J.

ANERLEY
Sunday. [9/9/28?]

SIR

We shall be at the Knight's at about 9.30, very much hoping to see you. We can give you a lift at least part of the way home, for we are using Elijah's 2nd. hand chariot, with room to spare.

I shan't be at lunch tomorrow, but eating my raven's provender elsewhere.

J.

ANERLEY
Sunday. October, 1928

DEAR MARTIN

Your book and letter smiled broadly at me when I returned from Lyme Regis on Thursday. I read the letter at once, and the book I've read to-day. I ought not to have read it to-day, I ought to have reviewed two books about Blake. You despise reviewing and it must seem insulting to you that, in a novel, you say so, and yet I leave the novel for some reviewing. The novel shows also an inadequate esteem for offices where men do work and groan; yet I leave the novel unread, so that I might do a day's work in an office. Unworthy, then, am I to receive your gift, but glad nevertheless; and indeed, nobody can be so grateful as the utterly unworthy. How hard it must be to tip a millionaire, yet how welcome to me were any tip!

Must I indeed be frank? Of course I like the book, for I find it hard not to like *where* I like. A friend can never get more than friendly thanks from me. Ask me not for honesty, for why should there be honesty between friends? Reserve that acidulous draught for enemies, rather. But for me, honesty has no power. My judgment suffers when I read a friend's book: I can't see it pure, but under a slight intoxication. How, then, can I be frank?

Honestly (or rather dishonestly), however, though I like the new novel, I'm not sure whether liking is allowable. Isn't it a "stream of consciousness" novel, and isn't the method a little facile? If Jerome K. Jerome weren't already resting in the bosom of Abraham I'm certain he would write a sequel to his famous masterpiece—*Three Men in a Boat on the Stream of Consciousness*. And yet I'm bound to admit

D

(grudgingly) that you've done wonders with the method, by using two streams and keeping them parallel. And I'm bound to admit also the poignancy of the story which your method hardly diminishes, and the extreme success of your woman. Only—and this is the gist of my demur—the stream runs thin here and dry there, and the extraordinary minuteness of your relation of journeys in London—and mind—is oddly contrasted with the vagueness of other circumstances, or one at least, namely, the nature of Chris's occupation. Is he a lawyer, untrained, or an estate agent, or a financier, or a gentlemanly insurance agent? What *precisely* has occupied him for seven years and made his existence unbearable?— But apart from this I am interested in the fact that Spenser's philosophy didn't help him—I presume you mean Edmund Spenser; and I wonder whether Herbert Spenser's *Fairie Queene* wouldn't have been better. And again, I am dishonestly glad that your morality is so splendid. "To learn to live worthily in the present is the Only Way." Here is the real thing.

Dear Martin, forgive this mockery and, as the hymn says, pity my simplicity. I like reading every word of yours because it is yours and that is the chief reason of my pleasure in the new novel. But I want to be able to say that I hate you but can't help admiring everything you write. Is it that you are not meant for the psychological novel? Is it that you should leave it for those inferior Beasts of Swift's imagination who are not so much born as damned into the world? I suggest this with hesitation, for I don't presume to say what kind you *should* write. But right or wrong, you've certainly employed a style of developing ease and fitness. It's like a sea lapping a shore, idly but with hints of power adequate to any burden of ships or office of storm.

Please send a wire to say I'm forgiven for looking this horse in the belly.

We had a very good holiday. The Ingpens spent three weeks of the month with us, and Bergen and Meyerstein came down as well for parts: de la Mare also turned up for a couple of nights to see the Ingpens. And I went over to see H.M.T. and Murry. Do you know, Martin, clever people are always astonishing one. I expect to be dumbfoundered, but hear of nothing but the price of potatoes and the ordinary scandals of the Hush-Not Press. I suspect they save their wit for their Editors.

Don't I wish I'd seen you when you were in town, and don't I wish for another chance. Frost dined with me on Friday and will be coming down here. Won't you meet him here or in town? There'll be more talk of potatoes.

Affly.

J.

P.S. Don't forget to wire.

ANERLEY, S.E.20
Tuesday

DEAR MARTIN

I am overwhelmed, I will never joke again. My conversation shall be yea and nay and blunt as a Quaker's. I will not lie, I will not pursue fantasies or fantoms (as you spell them). I will not squander the remnant of minute intelligence in prevarication. I will never ask you to wire again, lest you wire again. I see I have hurt your feelings, in supposing you to lack the Magnanimity of great minds. How could you be imagined to lack it? It's a smallness in me to suppose a smallness in you.

And economically looked at, my fault is huge. I have supposed my uneasiness to be worth a shilling—*your* shilling. Martin, it isn't. Aspirins would have cost no more, and would have spared you trouble. In the old blissful days of the sixpenny telegram I might not have scrupled, and aspirins were not invented then. But a shilling wire, when a penny card at most would have sufficed—I am abject.

IT IS A MAGNIFICENT BOOK.

· Take your revenge on these my latest verses: tear them up, burn them, and tell me you have done so. They are *genuinely* bad and I send them because I know they are. If I had anything worse I should send it.—Stay! If I had anything better, better than my best, it would still serve: you could still look down contemptuously on the man who made you waste a shilling on easing his remorse.

I lunched with Ellis on Monday: he had been eating onions; he must have been eating onions for weeks past. He pressed and then persuaded me to go with him to his new flat in Charlotte Street, where he wants to work. He is busy with a man on a play. I asked him innocently if it would be produced and he said very probably it would—as if it were already accepted by a whole troupe of rival Managers. But then he added that it wasn't written yet! He is full of unwritten masterpieces. He has been employing a Secretary to decipher his notes and conduct his correspondence! so idleness breeds industry.

Affly.

J.

ANERLEY, S.E.20.
[No date]

DEAR MARTIN

If all the pens that ever poets held were mine, they could not even hint at my humiliation and contrition.

But as for the Postmaster General, may perdition seize him, moths get into the feathers of his cocked hat, bees into his wife's bonnet, adventurers into his daughter's affections and worms into his intestines.

And may I be forgiven.

Affly.

J.

ANERLEY, S.E.20
Friday. February, 1929

DEAR MARTIN

I am not worthy of a shilling wire. A 1½d letter, even an express letter—yes, but a shilling wire is extravagant.

Which is as much as to say that a weekend is now impossible. Or stay! it is possible that at Easter, say from the Thursday to the Bank Holiday we shall spend a few days in Sussex, Midhurst has been suggested by one friend—is there a really first-class hotel at really third-class prices? If we go to Midhurst, or some other near place, I could come over to see you, as a prelude to a week-end later.

At present, alas! my mind is all on shop. If I came now I should call you "Gentlemen". Suggesting anything I should add, "Is there any Amendment?" I should ask you to pass a Resolution, instead of the salt. I should move a vote of thanks to you instead of saying I'd had a delightful time. If you disagreed with me I should mechanically rule you out of order—as indeed you must be.

But a little later, if I may, I will come like a shot or like a cannonade.   Ever affly.

J.

P.S. re *a New Anthology:*
Scene: a Committee.
I: You must have new names, never mind the old ones.
A LADY: We simply *must* have Martin Armstrong.
EVERY OTHER LADY (*together*): Oh yes—Martin Armstrong, Martin *Armstrong*!
I: Pray who is Martin Armstrong?

ANERLEY
Sunday. 15/3/29

DEAR MARTIN

I was delighted by your letter and even more by your Quintessence, the two little poems. They came when I was finishing *Juno* and wondering if I should write to you about

it. I'd much rather come down to Winchelsea and talk about
it and a dozen other things, and I was thinking yesterday,
as I stood in the woods near here and wishing for the sun
and primroses, how much better it would be at Winchelsea
fighting the rampant primroses. And again this morning,
Gertrude found an advertisement in the *Observer* that told
of an elegant old cottage at Winchelsea for £590, which set
us all thinking and wishing. By pawning everything and
raising a mortgage on the tortoise (as a rarity) I might find
£500, but then couldn't furnish the place, and so, mournful
but prudent—and prudence is profoundly mournful—we
dismissed the matter from our conscious Minds.   And yet I
don't know why you should be in Winchelsea, in Spring,
and not I. Have I not desires, appetites and virtue? True
I can't write novels but—scarcely less persistent than a
novelist—I can read them; and I can write verse and sundry
prose and find pleasure in browsing upon words, phrases,
rhythms and sounds. Yourself, saving the novels, can do no
more—only better. You have even done better than much
of your best in the writing of the stories in *Juno*, though I
have a malicious and envious pleasure in thinking that the
prose of the stories is sometimes better than the stories. See
what it is to have a mean and grudging mind. But the grudge
fails utterly sometimes e.g. when I read the last story of all
and refuse to believe that it was written by the putative
owner of that smiling face which adorns—yes, entirely
adorns—a page in *T.P.'s Weekly*.

I've not heard from Conrad, not a line lately from Bergen,
and Fletcher has sent me only a grumpy disillusioned letter,
threatening rather than promising a speedy return. But I saw
Mottram for half an hour, and he told me how the Gaumont
people had stumbled upon *Spanish Farm* for a film. They had
prepared the picture for *Roses in Picardy* and unnamed the
Film, when they thought a story to hang it on should be

obtained. Literary advice they have none—their talk is only of captions and amperes and publicity, and their dilemma was awkward until the little office typist said, "I've been reading the story you want!" and showed them *Spanish Farm.* Without a moment's delay or hesitation they wired terms to Mottram, who is quite able to look after Mottram, and with a little stiffness on his part (I fancy) the thing was done. But I fancy not even a large cheque can soften the title of *Roses in Picardy* as a substitute for one's own title. Never mind, make love to your publisher's typist, your agent's typist, your own typist—and touch the Heart of Humanity and a large cheque.

I shall see you perhaps, when you are an old man and preparing your Definitive Edition. Meanwhile . . .

Ever

J. F.

P.S. I've written a longish article on the Prose of Winston Churchill.

ANERLEY

August, 1929

DEAR MARTIN

—To explain I must apologize and to apologize I must explain.

Last week, in Norfolk, I got a letter you sent here a month before. It had been re-directed to Inverness where, in pursuance of business, I was spending a lordly week-end; it missed me there, and the infernal imbeciles—who had my address—kept it a month before handing it over to the G.P.O. The G.P.O. opened it, read it, admired your style, and sent it back here. We were then on holiday in Norfolk, but the maids sent it on. This time, despite the utmost clearness in the re-direction the G.P.O. insisted that I was at Thundersley, Essex, although letters were constantly reaching me at "Trunch, Mundesley, Norfolk". At length, having read it again for the improvement of his style, the P.M.G. sent it to me last week.

Alack! I couldn't answer it. I was beginning my third

"temperature"—cause unknown. I've wasted four weeks holiday and am still on my back, wondering how flies hang on to ceilings and if that's to be my future mode of progression. I'm trying to get the dentist here, and if I lose my teeth without avail, I suppose my toes will have to follow (on a theory of superfluity) and then my ears, fingers and ——! Seriously, I've not been well for a long time, and now can't get released until I am.

Now if your weeks' old letter was a delight—as it was— guess how pleased I was with this morning's virgin. I'm grateful, but sorry Adcock bothered you. Some time ago I was urging him to do you proud: the time had come, I said, when . . . etc. He asked me to do it. I demurred, and said it ought to be done by someone who etc. Noyes was standing near, and when he urged me again it seemed there was a risk that if I didn't hurt your feelings Noyes would, for Adcock thinks much of him. (By the way he talks very intelligently.) So I said Yes. For a month the article has been done, save for the flowers at the end, for which I depended on the new volume; and not until I got here on Saturday evening (here means of course bed—*bed*, you understand, Martin—BEDevilled) did I learn from Adcock that the book was really out, but unprocurable. I'd arranged that Gertrude should spend this morning 'phoning to various booksellers for a copy, but your parcel came just when my temperature had been reported normal, after the usual night's rise. I was proud and elated.

Forgive this dismal letter. Don't read my article, but read this copy of verses made at Trunch a fortnight ago.[1]

Affly.

J.

P.S. You'll see there's no chance for me and a week-end for some little time.

[1] *Last Lines.*

HENRY BERGEN

TO HENRY BERGEN[1]

ANERLEY
22nd. December, 1925

MY DEAR BERGEN

I was delighted to get your long letter, and to realise that already, like Ruth, you feel sick for home amid the alien corn foods. I had expected a letter somewhat impatiently, and was rewarded with your comments upon your blood relations and spiritual antagonists, the American People. And to-day Eddie read to our table your fresh letter, which betrays a somewhat more genial regard of your local situation.

Here life runs as sweetly and smoothly as ever. Eddie still scowls at whiles, still sympathises with every murderer, still tries to conquer his native love of the theatre, and still writes verse. And Flower still laughs, and still distils something new from the latest Museum acquisition—this time from the Wilkes papers, or rather from the papers of Martin, a forgotten rival. Aiken, soon after his return from America, had to come up to town for another operation, the first apparently having been bungled by American surgeons. He is at Fitzroy Square, and I go to see him whenever I can. He will be there a fortnight yet, and so will have a subdued Christmas.

And I? I have been working half idly, at reviews mainly. *Solomon* is done, and those who have seen it think it easily my best poem—Aiken is very strongly of this opinion. So I feel boastful, for he's a difficult critic. And if you have seen the Christmas number of YOUR *Saturday Review*, you will have found my poem on Madame Tussaud's—a truly

[1] Henry Bergen, Editor of Lydgate.

cheerful subject for a Christmas number. Else I'm dry—no prohibitionist could wish me drier. My mouth is dry—"lean thirst lolling my cracked tongue"—and I shall never write verse again—until I start again. You may be interested to know meanwhile that Prince Absalom has a rival—a Liverpool poet sent me a typed copy of his poem on the same subject, treated like mine in something of the Greek way. He's only fourteen and a half, and has just written gratefully in answer to my acknowledgment. If you see Frost you may discover what he thinks of my article on him in the *Mercury*. It isn't an extravagance of praise, but a cool estimate—for Frost is worth that kind of serious consideration which is reserved ordinarily for the glorious dead. You are luckier than most—you haven't to die to be appreciated. The Tibbald is scarce what it was since you were gone. Talk languishes now and again; something odd strikes us, and we turn to tell it to you—and you are gone. A question of food, or pots, or printing, or the Underground, or clothes, or English, or what-not—and you are gone; the jest dies on our lips, a mere commonplace phrase is staggered forth, our lips move awry. Only one good thing has been said for weeks, and I said it. It related to your infamous Wycherley, another of whose bawdy plays has been produced by some of the societies devoted to the Sabbath exhibition of dull bawdy. We scorned it, and then fell to imagining how it might be produced; and then I said (remembering you, and remembering Eddie) that the proper setting would be just a plain scene hung all round with cuckoo clocks, all striking at odd times and keeping up a reiterated *cuckoo, cuckoo!* We laughed furiously, and Eddie shocked all the room with his prolonged shrieks. That day, for a moment, we lived. "Yet seemed it winter still, and you away!"

One other experiment in forced mirth will be made, if our present resolution holds good. We shall once again go to the pantomime. Think of us then chasing the shadow of merriment, while you, far away, chase commas and bandy jokes with niggers.

But all in this house join in wishing you nevertheless a happy new year, which is the purpose of this present writing.

Ever yours

JOHN FREEMAN

P.S. The other night I saw G. M., who was well, but O as dogmatic as a leech—guess whether merely human, or yet more purely animal.

ANERLEY
17th. January, 1926

DEAR LORD BERGEN

(I think that was your style) Your letter came last night and brought a beam of kindly Fire into a frozen world. Truly frozen: it is colder here than at Dedham, for our temperature is only one degree above zero. Snow lies unmelting. A week ago the Thames Valley was flooded, and the river three miles wide; now 'tis ice everywhere. There are dozens of street accidents daily, and it is of course great fun to see harmless old ladies falling on the ice in Holborn and breaking their legs. The laughter of the policeman is heard in the land, and the ambulance men shake their sides. Nobody goes anywhere, nobody does anything. We haven't even been to the pantomime yet, but we shall go soon and drink your health in the adjoining bar.

Do not attempt to discourage me—I should go to America if I could. I would lecture anywhere and everywhere, and denounce your Wycherley (though I suspect his name could not be uttered in Select Provincial Circles) and your Sinclair Lewis (not having read him), and praise Melville and Kipling's *Jungle Books* and *The Brook Kerith*. Which reminds me that I saw G. M. before Christmas, and told him the story of the Balkis episode in my new poem (two chapters), and shocked him by saying that the episode would not take more than 700-1,000 lines. He *declared* it couldn't be done in less than 30-40 thousand and entreated me to reconsider my ways. He sees the thing as a prolonged wandering narrative, like *Eloise and Abelard,* but I as a dramatic lyric.

Come back as soon as you can. Eddie is hard at work on his third novel; *The Pleasure Lover* comes out soon, and he is still entertaining. Aiken is back at Rye, cured I think. Fletcher has turned up at the Tibbald once or twice lately, and Ellis has appeared unaccountably and then disappeared. —Thank you for a sight of the American press: it's always wonderful. I read it when I can with a stupefaction in which envy plays a part. I envy this daily growth of genius—poets and other Immortals coming up like spring weeds. *Prince Absalom* would be a great poem in America, if I put in a negro or two as bodyguards. Here it has been well received —the best reviews have been the longest—the *T.L.S.*, and *The Bookman*: I don't suppose the first edition will be exhausted when you return, but in any case the publishers shall yield up a virgin copy.

And once more, thanks for your letter. I can't repay it: you know already how much a hair-cut costs over here, or an apple-dumpling. You know nearly all about everything. So write again when you've time, remembering that the modern Eden is spelt Anerley.

All here send their love.

J. F.

ANERLEY
13th. June, 1926

MY DEAR BERGEN

Your last letter enclosed snow-pictures. If I had a camera prone to a little—only a little—exaggeration, I might send back pictures of snow-bound Anerley. It is almost cold enough for snow. For weeks we had north wind and repeated heavy rains; for days past we've had south wind and heavier rains. There's a coal strike and we can't have fires; instead we have cold winds, strong winds, fierce sudden rains and occasional blue slits above. You, I suppose, sip soft drinks all day long and play tennis in a dance hall all night long—and Lydgate languishes.

Well, your letter was welcome, but your return will be more welcome. You're wanted back. Eddie has been moody of late, writing with deadly fury, and enduring with malign fortitude the knowledge that no one will print his "lays". But he's getting better and is near recovering his delightful boyish shrill laugh.

Don't mention Doughty. You have no ear, no head, no heart. Stick to Lydgate, and when Doughty has been dead six centuries or so you shall re-edit him. I've been down to see Mrs. Doughty, but I'll not tell you a word. I've been to Oxford to eat and read, I've been to Edith Sitwell's, and I've worked and worked. My *Solomon and Balkis* comes out this autumn, in the same form as *Absalom*: but stick to Lydgate. de la Mare gave me his new stories. I gave him Melville. You can't be interested in Melville: stick to Lydgate. Melville has been welcomed in U.S.A., but not by the myriads that read Lydgate. He's been welcomed here, but we don't read Lydgate in England. Martin Armstrong's new novel is just out and I've not seen it: I shall read it while you read Lydgate. Leach turned up some time ago and I wanted to go to his show, but there was a General Strike and I couldn't get there. I'm afraid it was an unfortunate show for him, since people couldn't face the difficulties of getting through London. Not that you'll care: you'll stick to Lydgate.

Dear Bergen, Lord Bergen, Duke Bergen, you see I'm not in my right mind—I'm tired, my right hand has lost its cunning and I've cut my left. Forgive this nonsense and write again to me.

Affly.

J. F.

ANERLEY
29th. August, 1926

DEAR BERGEN

Another! but I promised to tell you of my visit to Mrs. Doughty, which took place in the spring but which I've not told you of, I think.

I went down to Staplehurst and was met by one of the two daughters with a car which had been acquired for the sake of C. M. D., when he was unable to walk much. Staplehurst is four miles from the house, and the house is a pretty and small house with a large and charming garden. Mrs. Doughty is very kind, simple and friendly, and I gathered that she had devoted her life to the care of the great man who was absorbed in other realities than the common. She shewed me his favourite garden walk (in Winter under the shelter of a noble yew hedge), and spoke of his remembering Eye for flowers. She shewed me his books and notes, his Arabian Inkhorn and Food Bowl, and the cloak which was given him for his rags at the end of his long perilous journey. She detests Eric Kennington's portrait (in the N.P.G.) and showed me an unfinished sketch by his daughter, and several photographs which had caught him smiling; for when he sat he was always shy and awkward, but when he was "snapped" the natural man appeared. He was "wonderful" she said: he never, never raised his voice, and never read a contemporary, saying it would divert his interest. In his last months, unable to work, she had read modern books to him, and he was so much interested that she regretted all the more his exclusion of the moderns, though not disputing his reason.

She spoke of privations which the Civil List and some other life interest had relieved, and I gathered that the family means were narrowed since his death.—His notes were indecipherable: he always carried them with him in a small portmanteau, which was the one thing he never let out of his own hand in travelling. Indecipherable—but she says he knew them all and knew exactly what he wanted and where to find it. For months before he died, and though failing, he had been busy on a second revision of *Mansoul*: I saw it and it is incomplete; I suppose it can't be published. It was his Testament, his answer to the question he perpetually faced— What is *right*, and what is man's place, duty and privilege in the world? He revised untiringly and no pains were too much if it helped him with a single word or phrase. He was conscious (she thinks) of a difficulty for readers in his style, and this revision shewed certain attempts e.g. at removing inversions and making the verse simpler; but it also shewed new inversions introduced!—I saw his Spenser, with every word (it seemed) scored and commented upon: also his Dante, unopened. He didn't care for Dante.

The car had been a great boon, for it enabled him to see more of the country he loved and soothed his last years with a new ease. He seems to have been a happy man, and the lack of recognition of his poems never troubled him. He was making a new language, or rather, restoring an old one, and so was contented.

. . . . . .

I might spin this letter out but I've told you the essentials —some, of course, for *your* eye alone. My article on *C. M. D.* appeared in the August *Mercury*, with a horrid blunder for which I'm responsible and can only plead an enforced haste with proofs and a necessity to cut down the article—which it utterly perplexed me to do.

Well, well! Flower has just started holidays at Frensham

(Hants or Surrey). Eddie is with his family at Eastbourne, Ellis is at Selsfield, Allan comes back from France this week, and in a fortnight Fletcher goes to America to send you back. Armstrong is away and Aiken is at Rye, probably wrestling with proofs of a novel. I dined with Moore lately and found him very well, and charmed with *Urn Burial*. I've just finished the proofs of *Solomon and Balkis*, and I nearly forgot to tell you (or did I tell you last time?—yes, I did) about Melville's daughter, and grand-daughter holding different opinions about my book. See how small a world I live in, that I tell you the same news over and over again; and see how often you are in my thoughts.

Write again, pray, whenever you've a mind to or whenever you think I'd like a letter (which is very often) and above all write to say you are returning soon to England, Home, and Beauty.

Affly.

JOHN FREEMAN

ANERLEY
ENGLAND of course
28th. November, 1926

MY DEAR BERGEN

I won't attempt to answer your letter, though I was amused at some of the names you communicated—e.g. Mrs. Foyer—a doubtful collaborator for an Editor of the defenceless Lydgate; but I will attempt to find out from you when you are coming home. You've been gone fourteen months, after promising but six, and we of the Tibbald, and our wives and mistresses, constantly ask, when is Bergen coming home? The others usually turn to me, for I've been honoured with the largest share of your letters, and I suppose I've provoked them; well, here is another provocation, demanding a prompt answer.

I'll try to give you news—higgledy-piggledy, and much of it true: disentangle the dull truth from the bright invention; the task shall be easy. First, did I tell you that Joy had settled down happily at Oxford—Lady Margaret Hall? I usually tell her, in my weekly chronicle, that I've not heard from you, of whom she asked when I saw her there a month ago. Next, Gertrude has had an operation for appendicitis, ordinarily not a very serious affair but in her case desperately urgent. By dint of telephone and ambulance Father Time—step-father, I prefer to call him—was drummed off the field; the surgeon told me afterwards that a couple of hours later would have been too late. She is in a comfortable hospital not too far from here, and she hopes to be home a week hence to bed for a time. She shows a marvellous patience for a home-loving creature, and seemed not to feel agonies and pangs both major and minor.

Next, I've had inscribed copies of the three Sitwell books. Edith's *Elegy of Dead Fashions*, Osbert's novel *Before the Bombardment* and Sachie's *All Summer in a Day*, a biographical fantasia and a very remarkable achievement. I was pleased at the flattery, for it's my weakness to be pleased. Flatter me and I'll flatter you, inscribe a pot to me "in homage" and I'll inscribe a letter or a poem or a book to you; I'll even begin to believe in the flattery! Show me the man who won't be flattered by flattery!

Eddie has written a hundred and seventeen sonnets—perhaps more. Some are very good, others not. He's used the Sonnet as newspapers use the stop-press column, for anything that strikes him at the last moment. He'll write you a sonnet on a green-grocer, on the dole, on a picture, on anything, or nothing.

Next? There's no next. We've had a vile November, dreadful rains following severe cold; sudden frosts and fog and rains and frost. I'd like to go somewhere—I don't know where—and be warm and idle; but if I went I should want to be home again.

"Home again!" Isn't that a bugle? Conrad is home again, and why not you? If you touch New York, call and see Fletcher at The American Express Co., 65 Broadway. I don't know if he's living in a pigeon-hole there, but that's the address he's given me. I have a letter from him (unanswered), and *I'm writing to you instead of to him!* Someone, apropos of *Solomon*, compares me to Keats: but only to Mercury himself may I be likened.

Affly.

JOHN FREEMAN

ANERLEY
18th. May, 1927

MY DEAR BERGEN

First an apology for typewriting. Next an explanation of my silence. I didn't write before because every week I expected you back, and every week was disappointed; and moreover you had written to Eddie about returning. Well, you really are coming back, and maybe you will be reading this on the boat, between Charleston and ping-pong. And welcome back. The world is sadder for your absence. Never was man so missed. The Round Table has lacked its chairman, its Arthur—but no Lancelot, I. You don't grudge yourself to America half as much as I grudge you. Think!—at one time you were there and Fletcher and Conrad Aiken. Now Fletcher is back, and happier, soon you will be back, and I suppose a year hence Aiken will be talking of returning. I've seen Fletcher once, and talked with him of the two Great Problems of his native land; the colour problem and the Jewish problem. He says that both are insoluble, and both dreadful. He found a sort of blind stimulation in the excitement of New York, but isn't sorry to have escaped with his life, and a little more prosperity than he took with him.

Your last letter was very interesting, particularly because

I've been immersed in America. First in reading *An American Tragedy*, next in writing about Poe. The novel is a remarkable book, quite the best long novel I've read for years. Dreiser is nearly a great man among moderns, so near that it doesn't matter how far. It was Eddie who persuaded me to start the book, but I needed no persuasion to go on.

Then Poe. I've had an enormous book on Poe by Hervey Allen, and have just written a long article on Poe in a great hurry (I didn't want the hurry) for the *Mercury*. You must see the article, for I'd like to know how Poe appeals to you now, and how you think he appeals to the modern American. Also I've lately done a long article on Winston Churchill's prose (the occasion being his War book), as well as others on your friends Aldous Huxley and H. M. Tomlinson. Here's virtue! And some poems as well—here's genius!

I meant to tell you many things but have forgotten them all. My hair comes out in clouds, memory departs from me like small change, feebleness besets me—in other words I'm too tired to send you a letter that isn't all apologies. What will you have? This Eastern air is heavy, men are dull here, they are not psychologists, everyone is commonplace and there's nothing left remarkable. But I want to say again thanks for your letter (it occurs to me, though, that I haven't thanked you yet) and welcome back whether you come alive or dead, richer or poorer, for better or worse.

My wife and Cathy join their Loves to mine, and so would Joy if Oxford were Anerley.   Affly.

JOHN FREEMAN

I've just read your letter for the —th. time. It's a good letter and very good, but you are utterly wrong about Shaw and Galsworthy and all these men and you *know* in your heart that you are wrong and only want to prick my imperturbability.

ANERLEY
23rd. June, 1927

DEAR HENRY BERGEN

He cometh not, they said, as they sat at the Tibbald, those Knights of the Round Table, and saw the Empty Chair and thought of their broken concord. And since you come not, after many promises and long-deluded Expectation, I write to ask why? Or not so much to ask Why, as *When*? Winters have come and gone, Springs have come and gone, and now another Summer has come and already gone again. If you were here we might cherish a general warmth, but wanting you we feel the usual arctic airs of summer. June is cold, blusterous, dull. For a day I left off my pants, and pantless I left the house, pantless—yet decent still—walked the streets still echoing with the steps of de Quincey and his Anne;—for one day! An hour after I left the house the wind changed, the temperature fell from 66 to 25, everyone shivered and everyone, like me, caught cold. For two days I was silent—with rage and laryngitis. And now, as I think, had you kept faith this would not have happened: summer would still be with us and I should not now be panted and shivering, but happy and unconfined.

You must come in July. At the end of that month— which *can't* be colder than this whether you are here or not —we go to Lyme Regis for three weeks. The Ingpens will be there and Eddie will spend a week with us. Don't come home perversely as soon as we leave home. Come early in July. Not next week, for I shall be in Scotland, but between 30th. June and 29th. July you may return; and heaven bless you. Flower is back from Ireland. Eddie may soon be back from the doldrums. He has only just paid a visit to those lugubrious Islands, from which he emits no sound except that of a foghorn: there he sits, cowering, wrapped in an impenetrable mist, feeling the heavy and the weary weight of the world and quite contentedly miserable. He will be back in our cheerful commonplace world when you are home—back with Shakespeare and Mozart and Johnson and Crome and Cobbett and Fitzgerald and Henry Bergen!

A fortnight ago I went to Oxford and saw Joy in her Glory, and walked by the river and up to Boar's Hill and saw Bridges and didn't see Masefield. And I shall never see anyone again until you are back.   Affly.

                                                        J. F.

Your enclosures last time were very interesting, but not very convincing, for I'm certain that such bagatelle could never keep a man in such a Country!

                                            ANERLEY
                                            ENGLAND
                                Sunday, 9th. Oct: 1927

DEAR HENRY

Your letter was very welcome and gave me much pleasure and a touch of pride. I'm glad *your* pride didn't forbid your liking the article. Poets are supposed to sneer at prose and write it only with their left hands—badly enough; but I love writing prose, as a painter may love painting, or a musician music, or a 'bus conductor 'bussing, or a potter potting or an editor editing. But as you know, I can't write rational criticism; I write out of love or admiration or prejudice, and if I condemn I can hardly do more than try to rationalize my prejudices. What I like best, of course, is to mix the author with his work, make a portrait of him as seen in his work, and so produce what may be a likeness or may prove a caricature, but is in any case a lively drawing—or a failure.

But why should I tell you what you know already? To talk of oneself is only to talk of one's limitations; to shut one's mouth may be to pass for a great man. I will shut my mouth. But you remain wise, benignant, forgiving. If

Lycurgus were York or Bath I should be very angry if Silas K. Macklecroft wrote *An English Tragedy* about Alfred Tomkinson and showed a few such things as Dreiser shows everywhere. I should scowl at you and refuse to see the smallest virtue in the book; but you show me the more excellent way.

I'm afraid I can't be at the Tibbald until Wednesday: do try to come then.

Ever

J. F.

WILLIAM BLISS

TO WILLIAM BLISS

MY DEAR BLISS

Your letter was indeed welcome, and half induces me to forgive your long silence, though it only makes it worse since you had so much to say and didn't say it, and have clearly forgotten so much and will never say it. Don't you know that I'm a glutton for letters? I hang nervously on the postman's knock. If ever I cut myself in shaving (and I'd have you to know that I cling honourably to the old straight razor yet, and shall cling till I die) it is because of the tremors of anticipation that run through me when I hear his loud thunder, and the deeper tremors that seize upon me when it is a double knock that tells me he wants, as we used to say as children, "to come in"—like Father Christmas. Thrice welcome then, for it means a parcel, a book, a bundle of books to read and review, books returned or offered with delightful letters from true and adequate friends. Father Christmas staggers here sometimes, but I grow greedy and happy. The letters are brought up, thrust into the room, torn open, fingered fondly, read as apples are eaten or sherry drunken; but what sad mornings of what hollow days are they when no postman comes. . . . I tell you all this not in reproach for the past, though there's cause for that, but in anticipation of a reformation for the future—*your* reformation, I mean. And here I ought to say that I'm not typing this so that you may read it easily, but for the relief of sitting upright to type instead of hooked over a writing board.

You made remarks about family life, that is, children; of

course they are engrossing, teasing, and what not. They are also voracious, and must needs do as Landor did, namely, warm both hands before the fire of life. They, or rather our Elder seems now to live ten lives at once, and to hunger for ten others and then ten more. I was never so much alive at fifteen, or since; my slower wits are contented, as they have always been, with one thing at a time, and the more or less consistent adherence to one grand principle, which no one in the world shares with me, that you can't have too much of a good thing. It is my sole discovery, and almost my sole faith—and indeed what other is necessary, seeing that this is so wide-embracing?

I babble. You too babbled—of the Pyrenees. Mountains are not for me, I cannot manage them, though I so much wish I could.

I've been hoping to see you, and now promise myself a chance on the 23rd, when I expect to be in Oxford. I shan't be very free, but shall contrive certainly to see you either then or the night before. It's a mere matter of business, that is, bread and butter, that takes me there. From there I expect to pay a final visit to an aunt whose house is to be sold the day before and who wants to see me about various things. was there a fortnight ago, may go there again next week-end, and finally on the 23rd. One of the things I've to see about is a small, oldish pipe organ of rather sweet tone, which at present rests, unplayed in a fourteenth-century room, in the lovely old Manor. I like going but rather grudge the time. I've to-day finished writing or rather revising an introduction I've undertaken for a new edition of Johnson's *Tour to the Hebrides*—a favourite book. And my essays which are due in the Spring also call for work, but *not* (you ask the question) a revision of Stevenson. We'll agree to differ still—mainly about definitions. What immediately concerns me is to finish an Essay upon the Essay in English, a presumptuous sort of thing to place as a final piece in my own scraggy, spindly collection. Howbeit. . . .

Do let me know if ever you run up to town. Anerley is not quite impossibly far from Paddington, and Paddington is the next station to Oxford. Men who are undaunted by death and the Pyrenees should not be disardoured by the Great Western and the Suburbs. Men who spur the gilded youth should not despise the guiltless middle-age whose wife has just discovered that his hair is at length thinning. She, I must say, sends her remembrances, and the children often ask about you.   Ever

                                                                J. F.

LOUIS BONNEROT

TO LOUIS BONNEROT

ANERLEY
July 19th., 1927

DEAR MR. BONNEROT

I am ashamed that I haven't written before to thank you heartily for sending me the magazine containing your article on *Solomon and Balkis*, but I need not say how glad I was to find that the poem pleased you so much: I ought to have written at once, especially as it was interesting to see the French view of my contemporaries, but I put off until mood and opportunity came together, and so delayed past all conscience. I wondered how the form would strike a French reader, especially since it was my only adventure outside our cold and sparse Northern landscape, though it came spontaneously enough, of course, and hadn't to be fetched in a cart from your Parnassians' suburb or our Romantics' village. If I could appropriately say thank you for liking it, I might do so, but you will understand why I don't. Since *Solomon* I've given my mind to more or less grave and sombre lyrics, that please me when I write them but may please no one else, though as you know now, I don't disdain pleasing.

I thought you might have to give years to Hazlitt, whom I dote on, but Allan says you are able to turn to Arnold, whom I admire for many things and adore for a few. I hope you share this attitude to one of our purest poets and most English prose writers—most English, for with all his smiling pretensions he was an intellectual John Bull even when he cavilled and depreciated John Bullishness. Above all he was a superbly English poet.—I wish we could meet again and talk as we did that night in Paris, returning after dinner, but

I shan't be in Paris again this year and may have to wait until I can welcome you in England. But pray write again soon and I will prove a more punctual Replier.—Pray give my regards to your wife.

Yours ever sincerely

JOHN FREEMAN

ANERLEY

MY DEAR MR. BONNEROT   30/12/27

I was so very glad to have a letter from you and to read your kind wishes. I think all the neglects and delays have been mine and I ought to anticipate your apology with my own. But I ought to do many things I never shall be able to do: I ought to answer you in French as good as your English, I ought to know as much about French prosody as you know about English; I ought to know as much about Sainte Beuve as you know about Hazlitt. But I am full of ignorance and of incapacities: at best I limp in English of no particular dialect and no peculiar idiom, and answer you in such style as I may and not as I would. I should like to do Hazlitt and Sainte Beuve and Shelley and Verlaine: but vain is wishing—unless it is a Christmas or a New Year wish, which surely is never vain.

Whenever you come over I certainly hope to see you and your wife, and then I can talk more freely about unwritten poems and unattempted essays. But poems have been written this year, mostly short but some rather long; and I hope you will see them. Some may be included in a volume of *Selected Poems* which is being considered now and which may escape shipwreck at the hands of copyright claimants, etc. The selection has been made—partly by myself and partly by the best of friends, J. C. Squire—the publishers approached: the rest is Fate's. I have written little prose—a few essays and reviews—merely for lack of time and true leisure.

All this letter, you see, is "I". This summer holiday was spent in Dorset, upon a lovely serene coast, and comprised a very pleasant visit to Thomas Hardy, and 1928 will probably see me still tied to England. Not that I wasn't glad to see Paris and you, but it becomes harder every year to forfeit English country for the sake of Timbuctoo or Van Diemen's Land. And so our only hope of meeting again and talking far more than previously is for you to come to England and give me fair warning.

A VERY happy New Year to you both.

Yours
JOHN FREEMAN

TRUNCH, NORFOLK
31/7/29

MY DEAR BONNEROT

I was very glad indeed to receive the copy of the *Anglo-Américaine* containing your article. It is not often that a Poet reads such a just and discriminating article upon his work:—I say "just", not because you find things to praise but because you find what I aim at doing in verse. It must be exceedingly hard for one trained in French to appreciate the singularities of English poetry, and I felt flattered and grateful that you should have been at the pains to "listen-in" to my rather dissembled rhythms and slight infractions of normal measures. That's on the technical side. On the non-technical side your article gave me equal pleasure and I thank you sincerely for sending it.

I am here with my family in an old decrepit village in Norfolk, with a large magnificent church, and other large and noble churches scattered over the country around. Roger Ingpen (the editor of the Shelley Letters) and his family are with us and we have a large and pleasant picnic daily.—I wish you were coming to London again: heaven knows when I shall have time or energy for Paris or Amiens! But perhaps Fate will arrange something suitable and we shall be able to resume our talk of modern verse and Arnold and Patmore.

Pray give my kindest remembrances to your wife.

Yours ever sincerely

JOHN FREEMAN

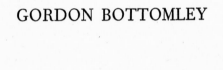

GORDON BOTTOMLEY

TO GORDON BOTTOMLEY

MY DEAR BOTTOMLEY

I've been shamefully dilatory in answering your letter, carrying it with me for nearly three weeks without putting down with this pen what I meant to say. One thing was that I was very glad you were better: perhaps the spring-like weather has been knocking at your door too. I've just been away for two or three days, in Oxfordshire and Kent, and have caught mouthfuls of the mild air at whiles; and to-day has been so warm as to make me happy and incredulous.— February will do for your MS.—I only wish I could find all the writers so compliant. Abercrombie has not written, but I have high hopes based partly (it must be confessed) on his silence.—I've not seen anything in the *Nation* on the Georgian book. Do you refuse any personal application and agree that the book isn't very good? Much of it I can't read, or can't read with pleasure. My own spare minutes have been taken up with making a discreet collection (not discreet enough, I doubt) from old books of verse, and adding an equal batch of new poems for a so-called "collected" edition which is meant to come out as soon as may be. I mention this small item because I remember seeing an announcement of a collection of yours—was it *Plays*?

I do hope you keep better now.

Ever yours

JOHN FREEMAN

MY DEAR GORDON BOTTOMLEY

I am eager to tell you how delightful your letter was and how welcome your praise of *The Red Path*. It has indeed found fit audience, and it's good to know that my first narrative should please you, and that Lascelles too should still find something to praise in it.—And it was a good fortune that gave me two more glimpses of you in your no-garden—though when I got back here I found that fortune exhausted. Joy, my elder daughter, aged eleven, was down with intestinal poisoning, and although the attack is not severe it is obstinate and recurrent; hence my next letter is to the doctor to anticipate his promised visit. She's an admirable patient, humorous, with enormous mental activity that makes the lot of her mother-nurse a little exacting. We're hoping that she'll be well enough to get to the seaside in less than a fortnight, when her holiday is planned.

But it's a shame to repay your letter with this. Tell Lascelles that I lunched with Hodgson [1] to-day and talked of him: Hodgson is better.—Certainly when I see de la Mare I'll urge him to go to Silverdale: I'll speak to him as soon as our small trouble is gone. And you may be sure that I'll seize the slightest opportunity to repeat my visit and show you (I hope) something better and newer than the *Tarred and Feathered* verses. Meanwhile, there's one kindness I want to ask of your wife—that she will send me a print of the photograph of yourself and Lascelles, and me as bad third looming overhead. I'd so like to have some such record—better still to have *as well* a photograph on a little larger scale, of you alone or with Lascelles. Have you anything of this kind to spare?

All kindest thoughts, and may your book come out soon!

Ever

JOHN FREEMAN

P.S. Please don't think that this *necessarily* calls for an answer. I don't want to tax your time in that way, unless it gives you pleasure to write now and then to your friends.

[1] Ralph Hodgson.

Weston-sub-Edge
29th. October, 1919

My dear Bottomley

It is uncivil in me to delay so long in answering your letter, which I've carried about ever since getting it and meant to answer daily. I've been busy versing and occupied in many ways, but I'm none the less ashamed to have to offer excuses. I ought to have acknowledged the photograph at once. The camera has done its worst for me, but at any rate it gives a pleasant reminiscence of you, and a touch of Abercrombie too.

I hope your family anxieties are over, and that there's nothing to prevent your coming south. And I hope we shall meet: else my only chance of seeing you will be the chance of visiting Yorkshire again on business—which may happen in the next month or two. Our family anxieties are a little relieved. My elder daughter is still ill, but a specialist whom we have had to call in last week gave a rather reassuring report—entire freedom from organic disease and simply a form of rheumatism which has the appearance of poisoning without the power thereof.

I'm glad to see your book advertised, especially after Lascelles telling me how good he knew it would be. I take it to be your most considerable book, in size and scope:—God speed it.—I've been sticking to narrative and a kind of long reflective lyric; and some partial evidence of this activity is promised for next spring—collected poems including some unpublished ones. That, and a later book of quite new verse-narratives etc; may break the back of my Muse; but the poor jade does her best.

Pray take this chatter as an earnest of my pleasure in hearing from you. With kind remembrances to your wife.

Ever yours

John Freeman

ANERLEY
16th. May, 1920

MY DEAR BOTTOMLEY

I was so glad to find a letter from you when I got back from my week along and about the Wye, but very sorry that you had had such a bad time. So far as health is concerned your long journeys seem to have been wasted, and even the visit to Hardy, which I envy, wasn't adequate compensation. Perhaps you are now looking back with a smile from a present season of contented energy:—I hope so.

Yes, our elder daughter, Joy, is quite well and at this moment bumping boisterously overhead and exclaiming in the shrillest of voices. She's just come back from tea at de la Mare's and told me of her pleasure at meeting Edward Marsh and an old friend in Locke Ellis; but her special cause of excitement is her twelfth birthday, which falls to-morrow and will find her partly a baby, partly a woman (yes!) and partly a poet, creating things which touch me with astonishment and envy. She's been back at school all this year, and save for nervous agitation has given us nothing to worry about:—oh, except her facility in growing through her clothes.

My book comes out this week. I am told it will "make my reputation" but am doubtful or indifferent. It seems much more important that poetry should be written than this or that writer should be praised for it; and since I know that the probable praise of the *London Mercury* will be outweighed by the more than probable dislike of the *Athenaeum*, I look round quite equably and am content (I think) if Gordon Bottomley and a few other friends who are themselves poets find something to like. To have written a few lines which may enrich English poetry would be a rare honour for any man, and it's an honour to which I'm grateful to have been allowed to aspire, even so vainly.—Enough of this.

I think I understand you about Garnett's article, but the impression you speak of must be so very far from intended that it must be forgiven as an accident. Garnett was, I believe, one of E. T.'s oldest and closest friends, but it is still unlucky that the Letters he prints should be so exclusively "professional" and speak of such a melancholy time and temper.

I look forward to something much better than writing, if I have the satisfaction of calling during the second week in July. All my good wishes, and my remembrances to Mrs. Bottomley.

Ever yours

JOHN FREEMAN

P.S. Do you see Abercrombie yet awhile? If so, give him a remembrance from me.—Joy has just said good-night to her favourite cat with "Good-night, my darling. Your mother will be an aged woman in the morning."

ANERLEY
18th. March, 1922

MY DEAR BOTTOMLEY

I didn't answer your last letter when I should have done, and I write now not by way of answer but greeting, to tell you that I hope you have started this year well and will be able to extend your energies of last year in all sorts of ways. I was glad that you spoke so much of your own ways and work: it's a fault in some friends that their letters are lacking in that eager egotism which is the justification of letters.—I don't know why you should discourage my prose, when you have been devoted to editing someone else's poems. On the whole I have enjoyed the Moore prose effort —and perhaps you have enjoyed your more voluntary and kindly task; and so we need not reproach one another, and I for my part shall feel glad in any case that you don't urge me to forsake poetry for prose. Frankly I get pleasure and a certain touch of satisfaction from trying prose; and if you should read the Moore book I hope you will find evidence of an ear attent, for I've tried not to fail and have taken the task seriously enough in remembering that no man should dare to write below his best. Many of the things I've said you will object to, no doubt, thinking I've been too candid, too querulous, too indulgent—here, there, everywhere; but I want to find that the book makes at any rate one impression —an impression of being written by the ear, from listening to a rhythm, the rhythm into which one's own speech naturally tends to fall. "Naturally"—do you ask what that means here? I don't surely know: a rhythm which is influenced by echoes, perhaps, by tastes acquired from innumerable contacts, but going back farther still: going back, perhaps, to early memories, of the swaying of trees, the flow of hills, the lapse of water. Perhaps, if we could detect it, every good writer has a rhythm which is as exclusively and definitely his own as the nose on his face—a rhythm not amenable to any formal notation, but still discernible as characteristic of the whole writer. And it may be true even of the bad or at any rate insignificant writer; and that is my final hope.

All this is an indecent piece of egotism, which you may magnificently forgive. For the rest, I've finished my promised articles—one on Stevenson for *The Mercury* and one on de la Mare for the *Quarterly*; and I've limped on to a few lyrics, and now wait to see what happens next. Did I tell you I've been frequently meeting Conrad Aiken, the American poet, who is here for some time. Possibly he'll be summering in the Lake district, in which case I should like to give him your address so that he might call and see you. I think you'd find him interesting and stimulating—a specimen, too, of the analytic critic to whom the newest psychology is not less friendly a companion than is the oldest . . . Not such am I, but rather—

"Like one that on a lonesome road
Doth walk in fear and dread":

the frightful fiend of the journey being the Freudian method,
which amuses me so far as I understand it, and dismays me
so far as I don't. Another of our luncheon circle (if two or
three form a circle) is sometimes Martin Armstrong, whose
poems you perhaps know, or know of, and who hails from
your cold salubrious North.

I'm wondering if I shall see you at Silverdale this summer,
I'm hoping to go to Scotland on business, and then I'll break
everything else in trying to break my journey home. But
long before then I shall be hearing from you and getting
your news!

Our family are well, and looking forward to an Easter
fortnight on the south coast. My remembrances to your
wife, please, and all regards to you.

Ever yours

JOHN FREEMAN

ANERLEY
5th. July, 1922

MY DEAR BOTTOMLEY

I don't know if you will really welcome a letter in handwriting so negligent and hasty compared with your own,
but it is long since I saw yours or gave you mine and the
reading of Rosenberg's poems stirs me to do what I've many
times wanted to do and send you these very few lines. I've
heard much of you, for I've spent part of a week with Percy
Withers at Souldern—with huge pleasure, feeling my natural
reserve flow from me like mists from a thicket and getting
into fresh touch with the friends that Withers and I both
knew—you, and Wilfrid Gibson, and Abercrombie.

Chiefly in all this interchange of news I was delighted to
hear such good accounts of your health, and of your

vehement curiosity and fervid restlessness. For myself, I mean of myself, I can only tell you little: I've been busy, a little with verse, more with prose, namely, criticism and more particularly with short stories. I find a difficulty in stopping things: I keep on doing one thing after another, one subject springs up as fast as I cut another down, I grow perplexed by themes and impulses and amid all the persistent quenchless desire to write well, no matter how ill I write. But for poetry, there's no such stir; it comes—goes—comes —and goes for longer absences!

I've just had a couple of hours with Moore, talking of Hardy, a diminished figure in his eyes, Stevenson, still a considerable one, himself, ever a candid attractive one; of morals and aesthetics and my inability to disentangle moral and aesthetic attitudes; and lastly of my Portrait of Moore, which hasn't vexed him but still a little pricks him since it is based not only on admiration, but also upon a solid rock of temperamental opposition. You would have been amused at it all—and especially at our discussion of narrative poetry and the availability of the couplet.—Until to-day I'd not seen him for some time, but have constantly met such bright and particular stars as Martin Armstrong, Conrad Aiken and Robin Flower, and discoursed as Hamlets and Horatios together.

I'm wondering if I can make an opportunity of seeing you. On the 27th. I expect to be returning from Edinburgh, and tease myself with the possibility of a call. Would that be practicable for you? Pray tell me if it would be for the slightest reason and in the slightest degree unseasonable; and anyhow, send me a line soon telling me of yourself. And let me add (what I'd nearly forgotten) that I feel myself your debtor for the Rosenberg poems—as I'll tell you later, perhaps.

Forgive this shameful twilight scrawl.

Ever yours with the kindest of wishes

JOHN FREEMAN

ANERLEY
20th. March, 1923

DEAR GORDON BOTTOMLEY

I rejoiced to read the announcement in my *Times* to-day
about the award of the French prize. It was a particular
pleasure because I'd had you in my thoughts many times
lately, reproaching myself only so lately as last Sunday for
feeling too tired to write you the dullest of letters even, and
for my too long silence. I congratulate you heartily on the
award, which is, I fancy, by no means an insubstantial affair.
And I'm glad it's *Gruach*, for that is surely your best work—
quite truly your most imaginative work. I've never forgotten
the impression I received on reading it hurriedly under your
roof two years ago, and the impression of a later, leisured
reading was simply an intenser pleasure.

Various things conspired to prevent me, unluckily, from
getting to the Old Vic. when your play was on last year, and
thus I was deprived of the pleasure of bringing my wife
and daughter to the theatre, to mark and inwardly digest and
then to see you. And since then I've been atrociously busy
and only now am able to look to the end of immediate tasks
—essays on Patmore and Gosse etc.—and see a little idleness
ahead. But I can't wait to repeat my congratulations, which
come piping hot, and bring also my remembrances to Mrs.
Bottomley.   Ever yours

JOHN FREEMAN

ANERLEY
25th. May, 1924

DEAR GORDON

I've let four months flow by without answering your
letter, welcome though it was. *Then* the cold weather of the
worst winter since oxen were roasted in scores on an icy
Thames, was giving you trouble: now, I hope, the belated
and still very uncertain spring has done wonders for you,

if wonders were needed. I've heard nothing of you, except that you are preparing, as you say, a reprint of your early poems. I'm glad, for you are one of those difficult authors who won't *let* people read them even if they want to, and people, in revenge, soon give up wanting to. Happily this is not your case, though I don't know if you will expect, or win, the popularity of Masefield. It seems to me that your best, your loveliest verse is in certain plays—in *Lear* and *Gruach*—and until these become as popular as *The Silver King* and *The Lights of London* you will miss your part in Fame. And so I'd like to see Constable (who seem not to believe in cheap editions) publishing them at 2/6 or 3/6. They would sell, surely.

I hadn't meant, however, to discuss such mean things, but simply to talk. My own poems are at the printer's, but the date of publication isn't fixed: possibly the autumn, though I'd like them out sooner. My Essays are just out, and I suppose will be denounced for putting Stevenson a little lower than the angels, and Patmore a good deal above them. In most of them, however, I've not attempted formal criticism but a free portrait.

I'm afraid I shan't be passing your door this summer. I went to Edinburgh in March but had to hurry back; but later in the year I may get a chance and will take it. I've fallen into a habit of staying at home for week-ends and find it very hard to break, even if I happen to be away for part of a week. Lately my wife and I spent a short time at Arundel, and found the best of the spring on the downs and by the river at Amberley—a part which I fancy you know. But when Withers is back I shall try to spend a day or two with him, and get news of you through them—perhaps at Whitsun. But time presses me: I'm naturally idle and thirst for activity; lazy, and forced to be doing; slow-witted, and continually stirred to attempt the things I love. Well!

And if this letter isn't sufficiently sprinkled with *I's,* pray write a better and yet more egotistical one yourself. All kind and frequent thoughts, and my remembrances to Mrs. Bottomley.

Yours

J. F.

ANERLEY
14th. December, 1924

MY DEAR GORDON

Many times your last letter has stared reproachfully at me, but I'm not sure whether I've ever answered it or not, for it's dated last May. I've often meant to write, and our recent acquisition of a gramophone for the children's education (that's the pretext) was a reminder of you and your multi-voiced instrument.

I wonder how you have been this long time? One reason why I deferred writing was that I hoped for a chance of calling instead, and only a few days ago I stayed for a few days within fifty miles of you without, alas, getting time to bridge that little distance. I've been very busy for months and months and during the summer and autumn succeeded in writing—I say succeeded, but with such ease and sprightliness of motion that I felt none of the efforts of success—a longish poem *Prince Absalom* on the Greek model; a play if you will. It was a great excitement, breaking up a fear that I might never write again, though that small humming gnat-like fear returns and still stings at whiles. I don't know when it will be published for my collection called *The Grove* must first be got out of the way and that —thanks to infamous delays of infamously bad printers— won't be until next month; but I'm very anxious to see my *Prince* in type, especially since most of those who've read it like it. Now I'm back at prose again and prose is a wicked teasing mistress that won't be seduced and won't be

G

obstinate, and says yea and nay at once, yields and flies and sets Egyptian tasks as her price. Prose is a jade, and won't hear of the amorous or of the midwife.

All this of myself, and in the hope that you will reply of You. I see your collection announced, and I'm very glad. There's so little poetry published now that you will have all the world to yourself. I hear of you at times—I saw Withers some months ago—and I've had Gibson here to talk of your work. But it's a pity that Silverdale is a million miles off.

It's not too soon now for Christmas wishes to yourself and Mrs. Bottomley, which I send very heartily.

Yours

JOHN FREEMAN

ANERLEY
2nd. July, 1925

MY DEAR BOTTOMLEY

I rather fancy the last letter that passed between us went north, not south, but in any case it was a long time ago, and I'd no news of you until last week-end, when I was at Souldern and heard that you were wintering in Scotland and were vigorous enough to delight your own Heart— and mine. And while I was there I read in *Poems of Thirty Years* with a good deal of pleasure at seeing how much you had brought together, and at remembering how much more there is in the plays besides. I shall be one of the few to beat you in quantity at the end of thirty years—I'm not quite at twenty—for neither you nor I have indulged ourselves in a succession of little exiguous books, dripped at the end of a lame pen. Perhaps you never thought to be reckoned as prolific, but it's an added virtue, surely, when it doesn't exclude quality—the quality of *Gruach* and *King Lear's Wife*.

Ambidexterity is my virtue, or failing. I've published a volume of verse this year, a long poem, *Prince Absalom* comes out in the autumn, a prose book on *Herman Melville*, and sooner or later a volume of short stories. There's a boast! Give me but the parings of your time, give me but twenty-five hours a day for this niggardly and common twenty-four, and I'll write another and different volume of poems before 1925 is dead!

It's a long time since we met, and I shan't be within two hundred miles of you this summer—or this year, I fear. Hence a page in your own steady clear hand—so different from this nervous and obscure jotting of scarce-related syllables and disordered phrases—will be very welcome. Silverdale is a long way off and news of you reaches me only rarely and uncertainly.—Well!

I hope you will have a good summer and an active mind. My regards to Mrs. Bottomley, whose kindness I remember very well.

Ever

JOHN FREEMAN

P.S. This strikes me as an indecent letter—full of me and none of you; but it's the kind I shall be very glad to receive in reply—all of You.

PAUL CHARNEAU

TO PAUL CHARNEAU

ANERLEY
15th. January, 1927

DEAR MR. CHARNEAU

I ought to have thanked you before for so kindly sending me the Handbook containing the student's curious essay on J. F., but I do so now very heartily: it has been greatly appreciated in this household. I don't propose to give my corpse for dissection in order to prove the young man's (or woman's, probably) theory, but it is not for me to gainsay it either, and so I will accept it as true.

A copy of my recent book *Solomon and Balkis* will reach you at once, and I should very much like to know how it strikes you. I don't know if you write, or read, reviews in French papers, but if you do, or come across any reviews that seem interesting, I should be glad to see them. And in any case, do write again.

Yours sincerely

JOHN FREEMAN

BRIGHTON
30th. December, 1927

DEAR MR. CHARNEAU

It was indeed a welcome letter that my wife brought me this afternoon, and I was very glad to hear from you. Who shall complain of storms? Your letter is dated yesterday, in Paris: it reaches me *via* London, where we are gathered for the week-end at Brighton, and I am answering it forty-eight hours after you wrote it.

I wish I could read French as easily as you write English; I know the name of Albert Samain, of course, but know nothing more than his name—like a true Englishman. But

I am grateful for your kindness in sending me his poems, and I shall no doubt succeed in extracting something of his virtue, by fair means or foul.

What you say of my long *versus* short poems is interesting. Most people agree with you and only this last summer Thomas Hardy was delicately urging me to write short rather than long poems, saying that the public wanted them short:—a strange reason to be suggested by a writer who has spent his best years in ignoring the public's "wants", and only the fag-end of them in accepting the public's homage! Sometimes I agree with you, but not on principle. I agree when I want to write short poems, but when I hunger after a long poem I scorn the short lyric.

All the same, I hope you will be satisfied in the new year, for there is a prospect of a selection of shorter poems from all my books being issued shortly. Nothing is yet quite definite—except the choice of pieces.

I don't know about Paris in 1928, but I should very much like to see you there or in England. Is there no chance of your coming over? For my own part, locomotion is as burdensome as to the grasshopper—yet no grasshopper I. I am contented to stand in a field and look at a tree, or on a hill and look at nothing except my native earth.

A very happy New Year to you, and *pray* write again soon.

Ever yours

JOHN FREEMAN

LYME REGIS
19th. August, 1928

MY DEAR CHARNEAU

I have not forgotten your kind letter and the book you sent me, though I've not written for so long. I acknowledged the book but haven't written again, and now I write partly with the hope of having another letter from you soon.

As you will see from the address, my holiday this year is being spent in England with my family. We have spent many holidays here, in this small coast town with a neat safe harbour and no shipping. It is indeed a very small town, very ancient, with 15th. century houses built above the stream and walls that were probably built by the monks of Sherborne who once owned all the land.

We lounge, walk, motor and have daily picnics whether the sun shine or the rain fall. Next year, next spring, we may all come to Paris for a week: if we do it will give me the chance of seeing you and Bonnerot again. And there is a possibility that my younger daughter may come over soon for a few months, in order to develop her knowledge of your queer Tongue and enjoy her first taste of liberty; in which case I should bring her.

Other news is small, I have been very busy but not with writing, and the only thing I have published this year is *Collected Poems* (really, Selected), with a portrait by our chief woman artist, Laura Knight.

I don't know whether Macmillans send it to French papers, but German papers give the honour of reviews of other books and I presume the French do also; and so you may have heard of the book.

Please forgive this dull letter and write me a livelier reply.

Yours sincerely

JOHN FREEMAN

E. L. DAVISON

TO E. L. DAVISON

MY DEAR MR. DAVISON

It is kind of you to write so handsomely. I very well remember walking in the Strand with you (and Robert Lynd) last year; I heard your name from an American acquaintance—a Mr. Bergen—quite recently; and, again, I read a poem of yours in the *Mercury* that I much liked. I hope to see more, there and elsewhere.

When one has been writing verse for so many years and publishing for some twelve years, a feeling of great Age descends, and a renewed interest in the work of those who are fortunate enough to be near the beginning of things. And, too, especially am I glad that you don't throw over form in the poem I mentioned, but are content to find your own rhythm in a common form and so make a beautiful effect. One can't drink anything without a cup, even if it be no more than the cup of the hand; nor can one present any beautiful living image without form to give it shape and definition.—But this is pedagogic: I am merely saying things that often come into my head without asking myself whether they are pertinent.

I was very glad to get your letter.

Sincerely yours

JOHN FREEMAN

ANERLEY
Monday [1924?]

DEAR DAVISON

(Please let me un-Mr. you) I'm always doubtful how far one may thank a reviewer for appreciation, if one doesn't hasten equally to thank another for severity, and so, though kindness among reviewers (except when they are too consciously and monstrously young) is common enough, in my experience, I've hardly ever ventured upon a thank you that might be misunderstood. But I should like to say thank you for the appreciation under your name in the *Daily News*. I believe you are right in what you said of the shorter and longer poems *relatively*, and you are right unconsciously in speaking of long poems which may be to come; for I've a longish one to come out soon, that will, if I'm lucky, please you and others. My first book was published seventeen or eighteen years ago, and I'm not sure whether I'm an old or young poet; but I was young enough the other morning to feel a great deal of pleasure in your review, and to say to myself that I'd write and tell you so.

Very sincerely yours

JOHN FREEMAN

WALTER DE LA MARE

TO WALTER DE LA MARE

Anerley
30th. June, 1911

Dear de la Mare

May I give myself the pleasure of calling for an hour on Tuesday next—or Friday if that's inconvenient? I liked immensely your Thackeray article and was surprised to find how many damaging things you contrived to squeeze in. I am afraid they are as just as they are damaging:—one by one all my youthful idols crumble!

Have you seen Thomas' new book—*Light and Twilight?* I've just bought it, remembering the delightfulness—dashed with bitterness, or indignation—of *Rest and Unrest*. It seems as sincere and beautiful a thing as the latter, though I've not read much of it yet.

I hope you are all quite well.

Ever yours
John Freeman

Anerley
4th. August, 1911

My dear de la Mare

Many thanks for your letter: I didn't know your powers extended to cricketing as well as criticking. I shall come by the 1.20 which gets to Petersfield at 3.32. But pray don't undertake the enormous fatigue of walking there and back—unless you do it for a wager. I shall find my way perfectly.

I liked your "Swift" exceedingly. I'm afraid my knowledge of his verse exceeds even my admiration of Gulliver, but it was a delight to read your article, with its beautiful sad conclusion.

Please give my love to all the small angel-imps. I hope your wife hasn't neuralgia this time.

Ever yours

J. F.

ANERLEY
21st. September, 1911

MY DEAR DE LA MARE

So much of this little volume seems to me to owe whatever merit it may have to your wise criticism, that I can hardly venture on a proper apology for the book's "thinness". If you hint at any repudiation, then there is so much that, but for you, would have scrambled in, that the book as it stands is none the less your debtor. Pray accept it, then, with as much good will as you can summon up.

And will you kindly forward the enclosed copies, and so further oblige.

Yours with kind regards to all

JOHN FREEMAN

ANERLEY
18th. November, 1911

MY DEAR DE LA MARE

Here is the acute, the sensible, the most admirable "Nation". I'm sorry I haven't yet seen a review of the Mulla Mulgars. My wife and I think it a happy and delightful thing: already Joy sings of Dubbuldideery. I won't attempt to say another word about it now, but will talk of it when I see you.

Will you, for a change, come here one evening? Wednesday next, if it suits you will be very convenient. Pray do, if you can, and as early as you please.

I have here the *E.R.* with Wells' story for Mrs. de la Mare (to whom kindest regards from us both), but have not managed to get it "carted" yet. I hope she is not impatient.

Ever yours sincerely

JOHN FREEMAN

CHARLES DOUGHTY
and
MRS DOUGHTY

TO CHARLES M. DOUGHTY

ANERLEY
26th. January [1925?]

Dear Sir

Will you permit me to ask a question with regard to the vocabulary and syntax of *Mansoul* and its predecessors among your poems? Your note in *The Dawn in Britain* identifies "its Anglecism, or linguistic horizon" as nearly that of Spenser's days. But it seems to me—a quite unskilled reader—that the style is much earlier than that of Spenser's time, and that such a phrase as "to cheese him a bright make" (page 150) or "hulverscrogs" (page 154) may bear a more precise definition than that suggested by the note to *The Dawn in Britain*. And I should very much like to know—pleading my general ignorance in excuse—the principles upon which your construction and punctuation are based; if you would be so good as to give me a brief indication.

Perhaps I should add that although I am about to write a short article on your work, including a review of *Mansoul*, I do not propose to make public use of any answer which you may care to send me. In the meantime, may I say how greatly and how long I have admired your poems, and how glad I am that the new volume gives me another opportunity of saying so?

Believe me

Faithfully yours

John Freeman

TO MRS DOUGHTY

ANERLEY
25th. January, 1926

DEAR MADAM

Will you forgive me for venturing, at this sad moment, to express with the utmost respect my deep sympathy with you in the loss of Mr. Doughty?

As a silent tribute of admiration I stood in the chapel at Golder's Green to-day, and this letter is meant to complete that tribute to the greatest poet and prose-writer of our day, and not less to the character which demands a reverence for those who still live.

Please pardon this intrusion from one who knew Mr. Doughty only in books, portraits and letters.

Very truly yours

JOHN FREEMAN

VIVIAN LOCKE-ELLIS

TO VIVIAN LOCKE-ELLIS

ANERLEY
17th. July [1919?]

DEAR ELLIS

I am a pig

(*a*) for keeping your poem longer than I promised and

(*b*) for letting the ms. get touched by a leaky bottle in my bag, whereby my too-perishable pyjamas suffered more than your imperishable verse.

I'm sorry on both accounts and hope you will forgive me for mauling your pages.

As to the delay, I didn't want to let the poem go without a careful re-reading, for which purpose I took it with me to Edinburgh without finding a leisured mind. I was unwilling to use it as an opiate for sleepless nights, and found even Conrad ineffective in that way. But here it is. It has lovely passages, and one, on the last page (Oberon) containing a repeated rhythm and a "whence stench" which I found rather too noticeable. Shall I say that I found most of the parts greater than the whole? I didn't collapse from amusement or delight when I read your passage about Hats, and indeed generally felt uncertain about the value of your fable. But what pleased me enormously—as always with your poems—are those lines and phrases in which there is shewn the very perfection of poetic "style", using the phrase in its highest and most liberal sense. The two closing lines are an instance, and that other two—

"Or late fowl travels on the shadowy mere
Towards her reedy island and her nest."

I can't tell you what pure, profound satisfaction I draw from such things—they please me more than the Complete Works of many nice poets.

All of which you probably know.

I hope you will turn up Monday, Tuesday, Wednesday, Thursday *and* Friday next week. I stayed a night with Gordon Bottomley and saw Abercrombie and fifty miles of sea and mountains at one glance, under a sunset of living fire and straight soft rays across eternal blue.

All due messages to your wife.   Ever

J. F.

ANERLEY
29th. July, 1919

DEAR ELLIS

I promised to send you this poem when it was done, and should have sent it before but that the copy was basely "lost" by a rival bard whom I scorn to betray. Let me have this copy back please, to restore my faith in human beings, and to confirm it in your critical gifts. I'm working desperately on another, which also you shall see soon, if you wish to and if you can stand shocks. For I've forsaken lyrics and now write simple "shockers".

If you've our present weather I'm sorry for you—arctic airs, Wolverhampton skies, Liverpool draughts. But I've been hopping about—twice staying with Abercrombie at Silverdale and calling on Gordon Bottomley. G. B. talked of you and would like to know you: I stimulated his inadequate curiosity. Flower has had a week of solitary walking about Surrey, and isn't much the better for it: Hodgson hasn't turned up lately, has been ill and is now (I believe) all right again. That's all the news—except that my poor Joy is abed with a form of intestinal poisoning, and that we're hoping she'll be well enough to go convalescing to Worthing in about two or three weeks' time, when the holiday is planned. She rests her body and exercises her mind—and the result is her mother's mental exhaustion.

I hope you and your wife are having a really nice holiday. Do write—poetry, I mean, not letters.

Ever

J. F.

WORTHING
24th. August, 1919

MY DEAR ELLIS

I was glad to hear from you and to know that your long holiday—time encroaching upon Eternity, as the Scots judge told the windy advocate—has been so successful. I think I'd prefer Cornwall to Worthing, but Worthing is better for pushing a bath-chair—my favourite occupation at present. Joy occupies the chair, and at present shews no sign of forsaking it for locomotion by her own legs. . . . Her progress is disappointingly slow, so we are tied to a level mile or so, but as the weather is wretched we don't much mind, but read Shakespeare and Hardy and think of the poems that ought to be written. I've finished the one I spoke of and will shew it to you, but when I've completed my present impossibility I think I shall have to stop altogether. I'm writing no lyrics, and nobody wants anything but lyrics from me; and so my sub-title for next year's book is likely to be "Last Poems".—This is only half a jest, or less than half—a mere wry glint of a jest, a jest round the corner, a jest expiring of an aspic's tooth. I'm dry; and dry or not I'm tired of writing little gasps of rhyme to be edged into the corner of a paper when the prose runs out;—then when these gasps are collected to be told that I'm writing too much, or too obscurely, or will never be popular, and so on and so on. Damn the criticism of poetry: it's vexation enough to write at all, but now it seems that even that vexation (of which, because it's constant, one becomes queerly fond) is vanishing—why or whither I don't know or guess.—But this is stupid.

It's good to hear you've been writing: at least Flower and I will be able once more to marvel at the deafness and blindness of any editor who does not pounce upon the lyrics.— All my regards to your wife.   Yours

J. F.

ANERLEY
9th. September, 1919

DEAR V. L.-E.

I had a hope that last night you'd find nothing better to do than to come here and relieve me of this letter-writing. But you didn't come, or you came and hammered so indifferently that we, enskied but not sainted, couldn't hear your weak fists.

Here are your two poems, then. *The Wind of Carne* delights me—the last verse is unapproachably beautiful. I can't imagine out of what hidden cave you drag so easily such exquisite things. I wish you'd *write* me a copy of this poem. The other I like only a little less. May I say there are two tiny questions which have occurred to me? The construction of the second stanza is a little formal—don't you think?

"The trees, whose feet . . .

.   .   .   .   .   .

Make of earth's native forms, whose fresh robes
    shiver", etc. etc.

And do you agree that the last two lines might better start otherwise than:
"The least . . .
The rest . . ."

Envy's acute eye can find, or pretend, no other flaw than

these. It's a beautiful measure, too, that you've invented. I wish you'd send them to Squire for his new Monthly, or let me tell him what gems he can have by asking you. I hope you'll be up soon, and here, or at the Express, or both. I may not go there infallibly while Flower's away, but would be sure to go there if you were coming up.

Ever

J. F.

P.S. *Winds of Carne*—2nd. verse, last line. Do you get the full value of your middle rhyme here?

ANERLEY

4th. October, 1919

DEAR ELLIS

I was glad to have your letter, and especially glad to read what you say of the poem. It's seldom that the jam's so exquisite when there's no pill: and when the writer of "Dread Distance of thy chanced slumber keep" talks of style, I feel proud, or amused. I've included *Beechwood* in the MS. of *Poems New and Old* which I've just handed to Ingpen for next Spring certain.   It's the Collected Poems with some 1100 lines of new.

Your suggestion of a day or two of my week with Flower to be put in at Selsfield has a wine-like glow: I hold it to the light and dote on it. I mentioned it to Flower when I wrote to him. I don't know if he'll be able to get home quite easily: he's due to return now, I think, and perhaps I shall see him on Monday.—I've wished you had a job in town, or something that took you to W.C.1 between 1 and 2.30 each day.

Pray tell your wife that if I should get down to Selsfield there wouldn't be any Bolshevism on my part. This strike has re-indurated me: I'm a rhinoceros of a Tory again.

Ever

J. F.

ANERLEY
20th. November, 1919

MY DEAR ELLIS

I hope you are expecting this Doughty. If there's one thing for which you're to be envied, apart from your quarry and thistle-wood and radiator and poetry, it is for your first reading of *Arabia*.

Joy seems immensely better for her week-end. My wife has just been saying how noticeable it is that she doesn't now mope and slack, but dances, runs, hops and behaves with something of her old extravagance.

I wish you'd add to your kindness by letting me know when you're likely to bring your wife to town again, so that you may dine here one evening soon. I think I could make any evening convenient, but should like to know in time to ask de la Mare.

I've handed Squire my *Beechwood* and the other poem *Disappearance* as he wants longish poems for his *Mercury* and may print one of these. I rather hope he does.—Flower is in excellent form, especially to-day when the Imagist Richard Aldington turned up and discussed the *Times* reviewer of his translations from the Greek—I mean Aldington's things, which are rather sharply handled by the reviewer.

Ever

J. F.

ANERLEY
SPRING. 1920

DEAR ELLIS

I'd love to come but am afraid I can't. I'm not quite well, and am expecting my doctor to pay me a demi-semi-professional visit to-night or to-morrow night; if he doesn't come to-night I shall be obliged to stay for him to-morrow night. If it should be possible I would 'phone you in the morning—possibly before you get this; but if not, do come in on Sunday for as long as you can. And does your wife come too?

By the way, I suppose you know that Robin has to-night gone to Dublin for his lectures? He was very cheerful about it, and adjured Hodgson and me to "look our last on all things lovely"—himself.

As to the poem, send it to Squire, or better still call and see him with it. He wants poetry, and I'm desperately anxious that he should print yours : I speak as his friend in this, rather than yours, but the *L.M.* is really a very good paper for poets.

If I don't come, many thanks for the suggestion, and more regrets that I can't.

Ever

J. F.

LYME REGIS
21st. August, 1920

DEAR ELLIS

A similar card goes to Robin to tell him what I tell you, viz: that this is a queer small pleasant place with great scenery. I've fallen into a family habit (which was going strong when I got here) of going for drives up high hills and looking down from pre-war encampments upon all south England. I was so sorry not to see you last week: perhaps after all you'll renew your season for the sake of Lincoln's Inn and the Express. "Yet seems it Winter still and you away"—Winter here, truly, in August; for we've cold winds and little sun.

I ought, by the way, to explain this address to a fellow Dissenter. This part of Lyme Regis is called Jericho. Why? —Because the Baptists once ruled the town and practised their unholy rites of total immersion in the river which flows beneath these windows and gurgles at the falls. Hence the stream was called Jordan, this cottage Paradise, the next

Bethel. The large house Jordan House and the whole quarter, as I said, Jericho.

I hope you are well. Joy is, I believe, having a good time near Ostend, apparently running up and down the dunes all day, and all night grieving over the local treatment of dogs. She was going to write to your wife (to whom all our regards) but has probably forgotten. Soon she goes on to Brussels and is getting excited about that.

Haines tells me he is ill.

Ever

J. F.

Anerley
13th. March, 1922

Dear Ellis

Do you know Wordsworth—"Why art thou silent? Is thy love a '*plant*'?" Or to speak without slang, why haven't you been visible except to the eyes of imagination? I don't know whether you are coming up any day this week, but I wonder and hope, because the following week I expect to be away right up to and possibly after Good Friday, and so shan't see you if you happen to come up then. I speak simply selfishly in saying this.

This household, including myself has had a visitation of "flu" during recent weeks, but all's well again. I hope you're finding fewer difficulties with your play than I am with my *Moore*. Truly of making of books there's no end!

All our Sabbatic remembrances to you both.

Ever

John Freeman

HUGH I'ANSON FAUSSET

TO HUGH I'ANSON FAUSSET

DEAR FAUSSET

Yes, you should live in London—but not in London; in some discreet, dull suburb, say in the South East, where men flock to town in the morning (as I do) and back at night, and the whole place sleeps between whiles—one quiet gentle general snore of all the Dull. *There* rents are low, if anywhere, there deaths are few, distraction seldom comes and is easily avoided, schools flourish and church-bells ring all round. *There* are the warm blessed recesses of humanity, near yet remote. For a few pence you may get to town, for fewer into the country. . . . Bless the Lord, O my soul, that suburbs are built for the easy disguise of poets, the refuge of the indigent, and a perpetual asylum from the fashionable and the freakish. Here, too, even writers of books may be met: some in this house to-night; some, I hope, one night next week or the week after. Which brings me to my point, namely, that you might try and make your visit coincide with the occasion of our next "evening". I'll write as soon as I can upon the exact date; but whether you come then or later—and I'd very much like you to meet one or two people —please count upon a bed here.

I've not read your Donne, but want to very shortly. I've a volume of poems due at any moment. *The Grove*, and I've lately finished *Prince Absalom*, a poem after the Greek model (though Greekless I), which Armstrong doesn't much like, Aiken does, E.S. adores it and I even like myself. I wonder what you'll make of it.

I hope you'll be able to come: we could accommodate your

wife too, if you could put your family into a Hygienic Baby
Farm for a night.

Ever yours

JOHN FREEMAN

ANERLEY
Oct: 1925

DEAR FAUSSET

I'm glad I extracted a letter from you, but sorry to hear
of your anxieties and loss. If there's any compensation following for you, I shall be glad again, especially if it means that
you work more lightly and with the power to pick and choose
as you will.—You've had a teasing subject in Coleridge:
I hope you've admitted how tedious his prose can be—
when it isn't pure genius—and how lovely his blank verse.
Your industry is heroic: it's a valuable quality, and I've had
perforce to indulge myself in it for years and years and years,
wishing more and more that I could be idle and finding
idleness more and more impossible and the fond thought of
it unceasing. Thank goodness, at the moment I've nothing
to do—stay! except a *Mercury* on Robert Frost, a review of
several poets, and an address at Brighton and London
University. But this is comparative idleness, after a gush of
real activity—of which I told you.

You see I boast, and it's as well to boast of something
precise and measurable, such as industry, instead of something distant and incalculable such as—no matter what.

What I want to say is that I hope you will be up soon:
I shall drop you a line next time anyone comes here to a
meal, in the hope that you may be in town at the same
time and so come down again. Meanwhile the *Tibbald* is in
Theobald's Road, where several people will welcome you,
including

Your humble servant

JOHN FREEMAN

P.S. If *Prince Absalom* comes your way I should be very

glad to know what you think of it: it is my first dramatic poem—maybe the last, since its successor is Narrative.

ANERLEY
13th. Jan: 1926

DEAR FAUSSET

I'm disappointed at not seeing you in town this winter, and I attribute it to S. T. C. and his influence: he rays disappointments, and this is one of them, like a billiard ball hit at several rebounds.—Which of course is nonsense.

But I hope you will be up soon. Meanwhile it may be that it's you I have to thank for an excellent review of *Prince Absalom.* in the *T.L.S.* I don't know whether I ought to wish it was yours: it would be pleasant to know you thought so well of it, but then it would be almost as pleasant to know that someone else, quite unguessed, had thought so well of it. Between the two reflections I crouch and purr.—It's the next poem that will call forth critical superlatives—I think I told you of *Solomon and Balkis*, the finest subject in the world.

But let me not boast. Let me rather hope that your Coleridgean journey hasn't landed you in Bedlam, or hasn't (another "secondary" effect) confused you into narcotic insensibility. Coleridge is at times the finest of poets and at times the worst of prose writers: a spendthrift of sense, a dreamer of nonsense, an intellectual polygamist to whom all his wives are equal and all seductive and all save the first (poetry) are mortal in their offences. But I needn't talk of Coleridge to you.

You are kindly remembered here. If you come not soon you will find Joy—the elder of these young slips—at Oxford: she starts at L.M. Hall in October.

Yours

JOHN FREEMAN

ANERLEY
2nd. Jan: 1927

MY DEAR FAUSSET

I'm very glad to have a letter with Wishes for the season and I'll return them by saying that I hope that nothing will ever induce you to go to Tokyo. And yet, perhaps, you wouldn't be less in London, or that better part of it Anerley, than you are now; but there would be a risk. You couldn't breathe in a gimcrack place, and your lectures on *The Philosophy of Michael Arlen* wouldn't compete with the films. England's better, even Newbury or Chichester or wherever! Better England and a book on Tolstoi, which is badly wanted—especially since whatever you say of him nobody is likely to agree with you and your reviewers will be the worst of reviewers—the men, or women, who would like the chance of writing books on Tolstoi.

I hope I shall see you soon: our family here would like to, and Joy would be able to compare—quite silently—Oxford and Cambridge.—My wife is getting better, though slowly. The body is never so jovial as the surgeon who gouges lightly into it.

Yours ever

J. F.

ANERLEY
May [1927?]

DEAR FAUSSET

I wonder when we shall meet again? I'd been going to say this several times lately and was at last persuaded to write—in spite of business and idleness—by hearing *Shenandoah* sung in the room where you sung it once to delighted Infants. I suppose you are never in town, and I don't know even where you are living now, whether at Newbury, where I send this, or at Chichester, or by the long wash of Australasian seas whither you have departed hastily and

furtively to cultivate fruit and the Muse. I suppose you are
not a ghost, nor a criminal puzzling the police as well as me,
nor a nephew that one can't find for all the advertisements
for something to his advantage? I wish I could find something to my advantage, for on Saturday I lost something
very much of another kind: I lost a ten-shilling note, one of
the kind of which Patmore unwittingly sang:

"Notes few and sad and fine."

It was an old note, much worn, the green getting dirty, the
brown dingy, the King's effigy less kingly than ever: it was
mine, it is—whose? A bus conductor's, I fancy, or a char-
woman's. They may need it even as much as I do, but their
surprise at finding it can't equal my vexation at losing. It
must be on their conscience, as its loss is on my temper.—
But I don't want to make a song about it, though if I could
make a song about it I should get the money back and a
little more: I mean I don't want to worry you about it, for I
don't suppose that *you* snatched it from me or picked it up
from my feet, at the shop in Oxford Street on Saturday
morning.

But this is trifling—not that I can belittle the loss of a
ten-shilling note, but that I didn't mean to communicate my
despair to you; and all I wanted to say was that I hope when
you've time and inclination in equal—if small—measure,
you will send me a line to say all's well with you, that you
will be in Anerley or town soon and so on. If you come to
town you may meet Armstrong, but not Aiken for he's in
America, and others you know. There was another thing,
but I've half forgotten it: a man named Kerr, a friend of a
friend, is publishing a second book of verse soon. My friend
asked me to look out for it, but I've forgotten all about it
except the author's name and that I met him once, and that
if I liked the book I meant to ask if you could look out for

it: but all this has gone from me with my green and brown note.

Forgive all this foolishness.   Yours

J. F.

ANERLEY
June 1928

MY DEAR FAUSSET

I've not heard a word of you for so long that I've often wondered where you are. I know you left Newbury centuries ago but I've never had your new address and so have delayed writing; and even now I'm reduced to sending this through Withers.—A shameless rudeness to him, for I owe him a letter.

You see that my address is the same and my heart in the same place: nearly everything is the same. I've been about more than usually this year, in pursuit of bread and butter, and seized the chance of a car-tour to shew my wife some of the places I like—mostly cathedrals, Peterboro', Lincoln, Norwich, Ely, Durham, churches galore, and perhaps better still a hundred old towns and villages. A hundred is an exaggeration, but I mean sufficient to root me—and her— still more firmly in England instead of spending week-ends in Ashanti and a honeymoon in Ur of the Chaldees. Between whiles I've written poems and published the best or worst of them in papers and a Collection.

I really think this dull chronicle is all my news, though it conceals more than it reveals—I don't mean conceals anything particularly disgraceful or unhappy, but that behind the dullest story there's God knows what excitement, perturbation and the rest. And even if your story is no more exciting on the surface, I'd be glad to hear it, above all if there's a chance of hearing it from your mouth, either here or in town. Do write, then, or come and spend a night here, only warning me so that I can hurry back from Wigan, or Halifax, or Birmingham; though until August I'm not likely to be away very much.

Always yours   JOHN FREEMAN

A. E. FRANCIS

TO A. E. FRANCIS

ANERLEY
Tuesday. 1922

DEAR FRANCIS

I'm so sorry: I wish you could come on Thursday. The day had to be fixed rather arbitrarily, and couldn't be altered to next week since my family are dispersing for a few days; but I devoutly hope I shall be luckier next time—soon, that is.

It is kind of you to promise me a book of Essays—please inscribe it—and I look forward to reading it. I've heard of John Dennis but haven't read his book.—Neither have I read the books of the spurious J. F. which you reproach me for *not* writing: I believe the reproach would be sharper and juster if I had written them. But I'm not a novelist: apart from short stories, which I hope to publish soon, the only fiction I can sustain is Appearances, and *Keeping up Appearances* might well stand for title of an autobiographic novel, of the kind that X. Y. and Z. are so fond of writing. I shall not write even *that*, or at least not as a novel; its realism would be incredible.

But though I don't write novels I had a happy Easter. I spent a couple of days with a favourite Aunt at Charlton Kings, near Cheltenham, and on Saturday found myself at Tewkesbury, full of admiration of the domestic architecture and the Abbey. Beautiful as the Abbey is I think the red brick and timbered houses pleased me more, in the warm bright sunshine. If you know Tewkesbury you will understand this: if you don't you can't, unless you know Chichester well.

But I'm interrupted, and must stop, for I'm being what

Joy calls garrulous. I'm very glad to hear that Mrs. Francis is mending and hope that all will be well now.

Sincerely yours

JOHN FREEMAN

ANERLEY
Tuesday. [1926 ?]

DEAR FRANCIS

A thousand thanks for your forgiveness of my stupid careless way, and for your restoration of my shoe. You realized the dimensional, I mean the spatial or physical difference between your shoe and mine; I realized the immaterial, immeasurable difference. My left foot breathed out the native threatenings and slaughters; my right was shod with the preparation of the gospel of peace. My left foot was heavy iambic, my right was gay anapestic. My left foot moved in lewd Charlestonian step, my right in a Mozartian minuet. My left foot was gross and ribald, my right—alas, it could not be constrained into that Attic lightness, I could *not* wear your shoe.[1]

Ever yours

JOHN FREEMAN

ANERLEY
4th. December, [1927 ?]

MY DEAR FRANCIS

Your letter came last night, and delighted me. I sent a

[1] Mr Francis and John Freeman had been staying at the same hotel and had agreed to breakfast together before leaving. Mr Francis did not come down until John Freeman was about to leave to take train to Cornwall. He explained his late arrival by exhibiting his feet, one shod in its own neat shoe the other in one several sizes too large, saying despite search and enquiries the fellow could not be found. Expressing sympathy John Freeman left the indignant Mr Francis to buy other shoes and went on to Cornwall, only to find when unpacking late in the evening that the boots of the hotel had carelessly placed one of Mr Francis' shoes with his and he had packed them without noticing.

typed letter last time because it was purely an official one, and I type this myself because of the relief from crouching over a pen and because you will find it easier to read than my rude uncultured hand.

I don't care if it still rains in Rome, for here it is awful. Since last Saturday week, that is eight days ago, there hasn't been a pin-point of sun in this devoted city. We have had an inch or two of rain, a mile or two of fog, persistent cold, and inspissated gloom. It is damp or drizzling now, and I see no good in going out of doors and getting on to my Sunday morning hills. And so I can't pity you, all my pity and sympathy being pre-empted. *Pity me.*

You speak of the office. Things move very happily— they *move.* Not a jar, not a murmur, breaks the fair concord which all creatures make in the Board room now; we are all doves, cooing one to another, and the voice of the turtle is indeed pleasant to hear. A week ago I returned from our Convention at Blackpool—a strenuous affair, of course, but so entirely satisfactory that one doesn't mind the stress. Never was such a gathering in our Office, with 350 people thoroughly satisfied and hopeful. The only trouble is the list of engagements for the future, an insidiously growing number; but these I shall—do you say "wangle"?

I have had two pleasant experiences lately. One was a theatre. You know I don't like theatres, but I took Cathy to our local theatre to see Maria Marten or the Murder in the Red Barn, a century old melodrama which has been revived lately at the old Elephant and drawn the west end to the south east, and is now on tour. I enjoyed every moment, down to the last scene in which the handsome villain is hanged in front of your eyes. Give me melodrama, and keep your sex dramas. There was a comic element rather violently intruded now and then, but I could laugh at that; and there was a really human element which touched virginal eyes like mine, which seldom see a play.—The other event was the dinner of the Elian club, at which Edmund Blunden, back from Japan, spoke of Leigh Hunt, and Chesterton and Squire and Birrell followed. Leigh Hunt has suffered in the mind of posterity (do you realise that *we* are posterity for the dead?) because of Dickens and Skimpole, and these speakers in various fashion dusted his image and restored it to something kinder than Dickens shewed it.

I haven't yet thanked you for the gloriously coloured cards. In spite of the colours the places must be attractive, but I can understand nevertheless that you want to be home for Christmas. You are not a good expatriate, happily, and I've never heard you say—as some fools of Englishmen do when they have spent six months in Paris—how much better are things abroad. The only excuse for "abroad", surely, is that it makes you want to come home again. I hate the cheap Cook's cosmopolitanism, which seeks to deny its nation in order to belong to all nations. I've been looking at an essay of Galsworthy's, in which he wants to promote cosmopolitanism by means of a second and universal language—English—so that all men shall be members of a family and there be no more wars. Aren't there quarrels in families? Don't brothers rise up against brothers and especially against brothers in law? Haven't you derived some slight part of your excellent livelihood from composing family differences? These kind-hearted idiots are amusing.

I must stop. I have Joy's weekly letter to write. I have a lecture to write, for I have promised to go to Liverpool University next month, in place of de la Mare who is ill again. I have a hundred things to do, and such a strong disinclination to do any of them that it was a pleasure to say to myself, First of all I'll do as I like and write to Francis. If you are back for Christmas we may meet—we must meet soon after, and perhaps you will dine with me at our club,

Mr. Dods having seen me this week and satisfied himself
that I appear to exist. More than this who can say of another
or of himself? But if I exist, then I am

Yours (if you exist)

always, with the kindest messages from all here and my
remembrances to Mrs. Francis

JOHN FREEMAN

ANERLEY
October, 1928

DEAR FRANCIS

    I've been going to write this a hundred times, and all
the more when I heard from Henri, that your wife was not
so well. I am extremely sorry for this, and can but say that
I devoutly hope that Italy will do her good, and an Italian
winter prove kinder than summer anywhere else.

    Forgive my not writing before. I've often postponed
your letter until I had got mere necessitous letters out of the
way; and then I've been tired. Sunday is my day for letter-
writing, walking, eating, receiving (sometimes), family occasions and so forth; it's a day I love for its little businesses,
but it's at least twenty-four hours too short. I confess I could
sometimes have written by going without lunch or supper,
or not listening to the Lener people on the gramophone, or
getting up earlier and doing without the country; but then
you would only have had the present dull letter a few days
or weeks earlier, and perhaps a few weeks duller. Consider,
then, that my apology is made, and I will presume that it is
accepted.

    Shall I boast? Since I last saw you (that was the year after
Trafalgar, you remember) I've been really busy, here, there
and everywhere, with a corrugated brow labelled, No ad-
mittance except on business. Friends now cut me, police-
men follow me, duns try to keep pace with me; I become

K

evasive, almost legendary. A hard life, as you say, only
sustained by an iron sense of duty. I've been writing a little,
reading all I can (and no doubt more than I can understand),
and remain as well as the Cherub that sits up aloft; I reflect
his Cherubicity. These last few days have seen me immersed in the Diaries of two wives, Dostoyevsky's and
Tolstoy's. They are strange books, by strange creatures. If
you have the chance of reading them abroad, seize it and
reflect upon Femininity. Their husbands were men of pro-
digious genius, and the diarists themselves had a kind of
genius—one for quarrelling and loving, one for loving and
sinking into resentment. D's wife makes you charmed with
her gaiety and affection, so frank, impervious to mishaps;
Tolstoy's is the victim of suppressed fear and a kind of fond
antagonism. If from my own long experience I may give
you acceptable counsel, it would be, Never keep a diary of
anything but your expenses (which you keep already); certainly not of the expense of spirit in a waste of shame, which
is what Mrs. Tolstoy recorded so diligently and painfully.

Do you ask for more news? I tell you all I can. Joy is very
happy in the first term of her last year, but I know she looks
forward sorrowfully to the end of Oxford. I saw her and her
tutor lately, and am going up soon to lecture to the English
Club on a subject of which, believe me or believe me not,
I know nothing; to wit, the Difference between Prose and
Poetry. I can only attack my contemporaries, whose friends
will be present and laughing at the discomfort of their critic.
It is all the worse for me because I have resolved not to read
my lecture but to speak it from notes; and although I have
done it many times, I have only learned how badly it sounds.
Happily the audience will have dined before they listen: God
give them a good dinner and sleepy wines—Poppy or
Mandragora and the drowsy syrops of the East.

You are bored? Then I will stop. It is nice to go chattering away, without an interruption, and I have pretended not to notice the yawns which you can't quite disguise. But manners tell me to stop, and you know my manners are indescribably delicate. And now, please, send me a letter full of news: not a little scrap like this, hammered out painfully on a machine (for the benefit of your Eyes), but a mental log and a spiritual chronicle. And tell me that Mrs. Francis is better.

My wife and home-keeping daughter send all due and sincere regards.

Ever

JOHN FREEMAN

ANERLEY
15th. December, 1928

MY DEAR FRANCIS

I was so glad to have your letter. I think of you in Italy, warm and sunny, I suppose, while here we shiver under a Visitation of God. You like this arctic, whistling cold, and sweat in Italy: I hate the frozen time, but must needs endure it. To-day is our coldest day, and gloomiest. The frost has brought fog; while the fog lasts the frost hardens, and the frost can't disappear until the fog goes— a vicious partnership, under which my country shudders. Guess what a comfort it is, then, to re-read in your letter— "The warmth and brightness of the sun are unbelievable"! Plague on it.

I think I told you I was going to Oxford to lecture, and now I can say that the lecture is over and approved by the most stern of youthful critics—Joy. I wanted questions from the audience, but the undergraduate chairman was so nervous—for himself, not for me—that as soon as he invited questions he adjourned the meeting before the questions could determine precedence; and thus the professors who occupied the front seats and wanted to flummox me, were unable to extend their vast reputations.

I have been very busy. We had a meeting at Bournemouth lately, and I went down by car. In a fortnight or so I have another at Truro, and plan to go by car again and spend a day or two with part of the family at Newquay or St. Ives. London is all shops and traffic at present, but next week I shall spend in Manchester so as to prove that even London can be delightful. You, I suppose, will be lying naked under a tree in Central Africa, or bathing in the Mediterranean!

This, therefore, is a Christmas letter. I hope you and Mrs. Francis have a very happy time, and experience a little pang at spending it out of England. Soon I shall hope to see you, for office difficulties may be pressing and I may be begging your help to pluck me from the snares of discontented men.

God keep you.   Ever

JOHN FREEMAN

ANERLEY
Sunday something or other in May
and raining. 1929

DEAR FRANCIS

Your letter was delightful, and I hasten to answer to encourage you, though it means the type-writer, which is supposed rude, but at least is more legible than my indecent hand.

I'm so very sorry about Mrs. Francis—it must be very distressing for you as well as for her. May your hopes of the weather and its benefits be fulfilled, and may you reach England soon with your highest hopes on this point fulfilled or near fulfilment.

I've been very busy, of course, but have snatched a week's holiday. I told you of our plan, and we carried it out broadly but not at all in detail. We lost a week end by waiting for the weather to mend, and started on a Monday morning full of jubilation at seeing the sun. We went by Winchester through

the Forest and spent the night at Ringwood, just near the
cottage where, do you remember? we—you and I—drank
coffee one Sunday morning in February, the Austin pawing
the ground impatiently outside. Then the next day over
Bere Heath to Corfe, Studland and Swanage; the next, over
Purbeck Hills, by a perilous road, to Lulworth, Dorchester,
Beaminster, Cerne Abbas, Bridport (looking again at your
P.O.) and for the night at Lyme Regis. Then on again by
by-paths, picking wild daffodils, to Charminster and other
forgotten places to Wincanton and Shaftesbury, and on the
Friday through Cranbourne Chase to Midhurst, where we
spent the night at the Spread Eagle. We had spent our Easter
there, and it was pleasant to be welcomed again. Catharine
drove the Morris wonderfully, indifferent to the sights of
minster, cathedral and village church, pleased with a succession of hotels, of ascending comfort and deciding our direc-
tion when we couldn't settle without a division. The weather
improved daily, and we found an advantage from the
guidance of a book by John Prioleau, reprinting *Observer*
articles on by-way travels in England. You must see this and
take Mrs. Francis on some of these quiet roads in quiet
counties.

And now to tell you that, on a recent journey for which
I'd reserved it, I read your *Precious Bane* with very great
enjoyment and gratitude. It's the simplest story in the world,
but enriched by character and setting until it gives one the
excitement of the unfamiliar, as well as the satisfaction of
the familiar.

I envy you your northward tour—and yet I don't. Any
beech wood will do for me—"Any little old song will do for
me," says Thomas Hardy, and you should envy me for being
here in Spring. The woods are all a loveliness. This morning
Cathy took me out in her own car, but rain drove us back
soon; yet even so there was a pleasure in the air and in the

sight of new leaves and young crops. We shall have the sight of the Chilterns in their new vigorous verdure next Friday, for we go to Oxford for Joy's majority, dine with her and make merry with her, and return the next day feeling twenty-one years older ourselves.

O, two more things. I went to the Academy the other day, and came out bewildered—pleased with some things and choked with many. There was nothing I sighed after, nothing that gave me intense delight, but of course many pictures can give one moderate pleasure without sending one head over heels. And I've been to see George Moore again, the first time for some months. He was as lively and eager as ever—full of talk, happy to have got over his very serious illness of last year, and now nearing eighty without being at all willing to admit it, nor yet at all afraid of it. He works and talks like a man of—shall I say forty-nine?— only infinitely better.

Now that is all. I turn from this to a letter to Joy, her weekly letter, and then to Notes for a Speech at the Lyceum Club on the Subject of Lord Byron, which I am to deliver, in the briefest possible space, and following Drinkwater, to-morrow night. What the dickens shall I say, what the dickens can *I* say after Drinkwater has said something else? All our regards to Mrs. Francis and yourself.

Yours

JOHN FREEMAN

ANERLEY
14th. August, 1929

DEAR FRANCIS

Your letter reached me at Trunch a week ago just when I needed good news. I was very glad indeed to hear of your cure and to know that it cost you no more than 3d.! But why should these favours follow *you* about so faithfully?

Here am I, on my back again, longing for a 3d. or even a 6d. cure. Cure of what? I wish I could tell you. Weeks ago I came back from a trying Irish journey with a temperature or summat; then I went to Scotland for a fortnight's hard work and came back with a temperature of 104°. Then I started holidays, slowly got better—and then again a temperature and bed. I managed to get home (i.e. bed again) on Saturday. I have been pursued to death by doctors—Parthians and Medes and Elamites and all those other nations that St. Paul names—and to-night doctor and dentist will probably make a joint bloody attack on my indignant helplessness.

—Francis, don't be ill. There's nothing in it. You are not allowed to eat, drink, SMOKE; you cannot walk or ride; you can't laugh (and what is there to laugh at?), you want to talk to people but people don't come, you spend nothing but your money disappears like water. Your only visitors (if you'd admit 'em—I won't) are relations who remind you that they never thought you'd live through 19— and that you're just the age that Uncle was when *he* died.—don't be ill: always keep a threepenny bit in your pocket, to charm away sciatica and everything else.

Forgive this stupid letter—you'll see what part of me is most affected.—I shall be hearing of you from Carter this afternoon, for business is permitted in this room.

My regards to Mrs. Francis and my thanks to her husband.

Yours

JOHN FREEMAN

P.S. If you *see* W. A. H. please give him my love.

WILFRID GIBSON

TO WILFRID GIBSON

DEAR GIBSON

When I saw a poem of yours in the *Chap Book* a month ago, I resolved to write and tell you (risking whether such news had an interest for you) how much I liked it. When I saw another in the *Mercury* a week ago, I remembered that I hadn't written about the first. But I do so now, and in fact will say that the *Chap Book* poem reminded me keenly of a longer one of yours from which I got great pleasure some seven or eight years ago, in just such weather as this—you'll guess I mean *The Hare*, which I've ever since liked more, I think, than anything else you've written.

If this sort of letter really has no interest for you, it none the less seems churlish for a reader never to write it. And in any case you'll understand that it doesn't insist on an answer, especially since it isn't only a month but some years overdue.
Ever sincerely yours

JOHN FREEMAN

ANERLEY
28th. November, 1920

MY DEAR GIBSON

I've uncivilly left your letter unanswered all these weeks, notwithstanding that I was so sorry that your rather hasty departure robbed me of another meeting. I hope the baby is now no longer a worry and that you've an easy mind about all things else in the world, if an easy mind is possible to any civilized being in these days.—I've never yet said a word, beyond immediate thanks, about your book, and I'd like to tell you that I still think that the poem that was in the *Chap Book* (*Nicholas Hall* I think is the title) excellent beyond all but a few of the same kind; in fact I like the first part of the book, the real *Neighbours*, much better than the rest, partly perhaps because I've a faint and stupid prejudice against the sonnet form except for strictly occasional or utterly passionate verse (a pretty wide alternative) and partly because your characteristics seem much more powerfully at work in the economic lyric form than in the apparently but not inevitably severer sonnet form. But I say this with diffidence, the more so that I can't refer my preference to any abstract critical theory, for I haven't one and don't understand metaphysical criticism; but I wonder how far you disagree with me in all this?

I've been working as steadily as I can for some long time past, and have nearly finished (I think) a new narrative poem, the one I mentioned to you. Another long poem (I mean by "long" no more than several hundred lines) is buzzing pretty constantly in my head, but I don't yet know if the buzzing will be persistent enough to force me to write. But I badly want a rest.—I saw Davies two nights ago: he talked and talked in the cheerfullest fashion, full of his plans and luckily full of verse.

I've really not written this to discharge an imagined and irksome duty, and I hope it won't provoke you to reply under that unhealthy constraint.

All my good wishes.   Ever

J. F.

ANERLEY
10th. May, 1922

MY DEAR WILFRID

It was delightful to have your letter, though you tell me little of yourself and nothing of your family—nothing of the beportraited daughter and the sturdy assaulting boy, whose form I remember so vividly. What you do tell me of yourself, that is of your Narrative, is good news, since I believe that you can be trusted with your own work; trusted, I mean, to make good better. And so my hopes of *Krindlesyke* increase, though it seems a pity to have to wait so long for it.

And it was embarrassingly kind of you to tell me of Percy Withers' letter. I knew his name well enough but no more, and wondered many times whether I should—or should not—follow your letter to me with one to him. So all day long the noise of battle rolled—and withdrew when a letter came from Withers himself, to prove that I need not have hesitated. Not that I wasn't still embarrassed, but rather the more; but I was heartily pleased, especially since he had written such things to me as I have sometimes wanted to write to others and have stupidly shrunk from writing. He tells me, too, that Bottomley is with him, and I take that as a sign that G. B. is bettering—a sign I should very much delight in confirming by observation if I have the opportunity in flying to Scotland and back in the summer.— By flying I don't mean aeroplaning: metaphors have to be more carefully watched now that science makes the metaphorical so literal.

Don't laugh at poor Anerley. Anerley had a Fire—in this house, in this room, one evening when my family were basking in an Easter sun at Worthing. I came home to find the maid in tears and smoke, with an account of an exploded heater and visible, smellable evidence to support her. Our spring-cleaning had been finished, the room—for the first time in nine years—had looked quite spick and span; now it was as smutty as a modern novel, and stank like a modern play. We are about to enjoy the throes of renovation again, and you mustn't sneer at Anerley. A presentation copy of

Livelihood might have become briefly incandescent, three little *Fires* incinerated, Georgian poetry might have

> Flamed in the forehead of the Evening sky.

and all because of an American stove, or perhaps a Forest of Dean servant. Well, Whiteleys, who sold the stove, and the maid, who put it out, both behaved moderately well in this emergency, and *Livelihood* still stands erect among my presentation copies.

All which is foolish, but I'm capable of no more. I'm tired, but wanting to talk, and afraid to postpone writing until I'm not tired, for then I might not want to talk but to worry half a dozen projects; and I'm ashamed to delay answering you, especially as I'm keeping Withers' letter unanswered too.

—I told Aiken I'd heard from you, but the remote wild west seems very remote to him. And to me, for the present. I expect to have to spend a night or two, in Cardiff at the end of August, and still wonder if I can get another 150 miles beyond. As for holidays, my family are going to Winchelsea for their summer month, and I join them for a fortnight; and that makes Saundersfoot impossible, alas! But do you mean to let a calendar year pass without seeing Paddington, London Bridge, the Albert Memorial, the Crystal Palace, the Poetry Bookshop (not that I should meet you there, I'm afraid) and the tea-shop where Flower and I daily, and Armstrong and Aiken often, meet to try to eat?

Before I forget: have you seen Blunden's new poems? There are some excellent things, but I don't fancy there are many excellent *new* things, but, rather, pleasant repetitions. I've seen almost no other new verse: Spring has come (and fled again) and nothing seems to have been done by me to make a single moment tarry: every moment has gone like spray from a tree!

Do write again as soon as you can flog your pen. I'm the

worst of answerers, but hunger for letters and mourn every time the postman passes me by.

All kind remembrances to you all

Ever

JOHN

ANERLEY

September 1922

DEAR WILFRID

Your letter met me when I got home from Winchelsea, and cheered a dumb house. It was characteristically warm and welcome! the more so, perhaps, since you're almost if not quite the first to see in that group more than a literary exercise. I'm so glad to have such a scrap from you, though it pricks me with a reproach for not having written during the fortnight I spent at Winchelsea, or last week during long tedious train journeys. But I've never been alone—and you will take that as an adequate excuse, for I can't write even letters when I'm crowded. The thought of your western solitude makes me envious, for it can never be mine. I have to stick to London as faithfully as London adheres to me. Why, do you ask? Because Joy is fourteen and Cathy eleven, and I'm jogging along past forty and must needs save. So I have but the unfevered vain anticipation of what you perpetually enjoy: and I envy you as much as it's wise to permit myself to do. I don't know if you ever tease yourself with thoughts of London and friends here: but for friends London would be intolerable—and so, maybe, would any other place prove. I don't know: I only know that the remotest nook of West Wales is too far and that I wish it were just round the corner, or nestling under the Crystal Palace. The notion that the moon, which shone upon me like a new florin when I went into the kitchen just now to make my nine o'clock tea, may have been shining on Saundersfoot also, gave me no pleasure. Distance, the mere idea of space, is tantalizing and absurd. It is not quite real: for isn't it absurd and incredible that the same moon, the same stupid florin-flower, should be shining at the same moment upon people so far off—here and on my wife at Winchelsea, Joy in Cornwall, you in Wales, Gordon in Silverdale—who might be together and aren't? Write me a metaphysical poem on that, will you? or rather don't, for it couldn't be as good as *The Hare*. It might not be so exciting as *Krindlesyke* either . . . and as to that, I don't mean to speak until I've read it, or parts of it again. I took it away with me, and it was almost the only piece of reading I could give myself. Most of my brief fortnight was spent in idling with Armstrong and Aiken and Flower and writing three short poems (only one of which much pleases me) and a short story. I wish you had been with us—but you've had, I take it, other joys that look down, faintly indulgent in their fine smile, upon these silly joys.

All this is nonsense: I only put it down because it comes idly into my head like a moth, and because I like to get you to speak just as fully of yourself when you write again. I'd meant to start a story on this sheet to-night, but I couldn't let your letter lie here a day and not answer it, for the pleasure of babbling.

My regards to your wife, and an astonished father's love to your children's father. Forgive all nonsense, for the sake of the pea in the bladder: the pea am I and the bladder—all beside.   Ever

JOHN

ANERLEY
4th. November, 1922

DEAR WILFRID

The dozens of letters I've planned haven't reached you, because not one has been written in spite of my intention. But the intention, the plan has occurred when the writing

was impossible or the writer jaded beyond expression; and
I've only known that I wanted to write without finding the
opportunity. I've been away once or twice, on business or
pleasure, since I last wrote to you, and things have piled up
which needed and insisted on doing. Not that there's much
to show as the result of all these exactions: some few verses,
some stories which one or two people like the others won't
print, and an odd review or two. *Krindlesyke* however kept
obstinately away: thanks to the editor's habit of sending all
the verse to a single reviewer—probably a hoar-bearded
antique prosodist in one case, or youthful free-verser full of
theories and clumsy prose. I'm wondering what reviewers
have made of it, for I've seen only the timid *Times* article,
and Binyon's review in the *Observer*; but I can't say that I
waited for reviews to make up my mind. Reading it to
myself the *story* seemed so good, the verse so admirable as a
dramatic medium, that I felt sorry the dramatic intensity of
the situation was diffused instead of being allowed to burn as
it were in the bare brilliance of the conception. In other
words, and put with the utmost brutality, I was often conscious of a dulling or dimming of that brightness by reitera-
tion: the lines folding round and round the flame until
something of its light and heat was lost. I can't think how it
was that when you read it to me just a year ago—I so well
remember it!—I wasn't struck with this repetitive dimming
of the subject, and I can only assume it was because you read
so well. The essentials of the poem remain splendid, the
verse superb in its athletic quality of suppleness and strength;
but I think you faced too boldly or too lightly the task of
rendering loquacity, even rustic loquacity, in English blank
verse. The success you won was too perfect.—I have thought
much of all this before writing it, and only tell you frankly
now because it brings me to another point: that your best
mode, your natural mode, seems to me naked, sharp, spare,

L

muscular verse of *Fires*. There is nothing quite like your *Fires*, nothing like *The Hare*, and if it vexes you to be told so, when that work is so far in the past, I'll only say I'm sorry. A week ago I read some modern poets to a small gathering for a sister of mine, I included *The Hare*: it was the only poem that provoked both applause and a reference in speeches afterwards. Other poems were such as *The Song of Honour* and some of Davies, but *The Hare* struck the hearers in a way the others seemed not to, despite my poor reading. I wished then that I had read the whole volume, and I wondered if that kind of poem wasn't your peculiar virtue.

You'll believe that I feel diffident in saying this, for I should dread to attempt influencing another against his own judgment. I wish we could talk of these things. I only had that one brief evening with you, precisely four months ago, and I wish you could find a regular visit here justifiable from your own point of view. Isolation may be all very well for you, but it doesn't give me a chance when I'm trying to say what I think, for I'm in the dark how far you agree already, or how completely you demur. I don't like the idea of artists living in crowds: the studio notion is abhorrent, for the essential friction of mind then becomes all in all and there's nothing but vain friction; but some exchange of ideas is necessary, for me, and talk is even better than letters. And if you see in this harmless remark a reproach of silence I won't wholly disclaim it: but I reproach myself more. I don't like writing letters with a jaded pen, and simply because I'm too tired to do anything else; but I thirst for letters and bless every postman with the profoundest blessings of Almightiness. Write, then, soon, and tell me how *Krindlesyke* has been received and is selling and how your large family is settling down before Winter's unbarred adamantine doors.

Ever

JOHN

P.S. I had meant to tell you of particular phrases and passages in *K.* that especially pleased me, but after what I've said you would only be amused.

ANERLEY
11th. Feb: 1923

MY DEAR WILFRID

Now I give myself the pleasure of saying that I've read the whole of the new *Daily Bread.* I can't compare it with the original version, for excepting one or two which I've special cause to remember my mind is blank and I haven't the book here to refresh it. It is rather wonderful that you should take so simply and so confidently a mere episode—no story, but simply a stone in the path of a dull narrative—and make your poem of that; and it is quite wonderful that you should so often succeed when, off-hand, one might say that success is impossible. The success, for instance, of *The Garret* (which I fancy I read first in the *English Review* of years ago) is conspicuous: the *tone* is a perfect echo of the sense of the whole unemphatic narrative and thus achieves a still beauty something like that of a morning pale sunbeam lying on the wall of the garret itself. In one like *The Furnace* I don't hear the tone as an echo, but as a stridency, over-emphatic, and I lose rather than gain from the irruption of narrative by lyric verse; for those short-line passages are really lyric. But I mustn't stress this, for if it is a fault (and I'm far from confident that it is) it's only occasional and infrequent; elsewhere, in fact, the narrative simplicity is almost unbroken and there's never a touch of "mere poetry". The book triumphs by its avoidances, though that's a negative tribute and involves of course an admission, viz: that the interest of the stories is necessarily restricted and does not reach intensity except rarely.

This really is the question for the author to answer, or

ignore: I don't mean answer to me but to himself. I can't make up my mind about it so far as your work is concerned. Is the sacrifice of intensity, salience, extravagant beauty, really essential, and is it really so little as to be easily made? These low-toned narratives can be consummate, as Crabbe is often consummate; but are they not sometimes too dull, in their hue and motion, to stir one's heart and mind very sharply? I'm not asking for artificial stimulation, for mere refined sensationalism in verse; but does poetry breathe quite easily and purely in a heavy, damp air, in a dull, damp city? Crabbe avoided dangers by pitching his characters in wild if woeful surroundings; there is a touch of breadth and spaciousness in his East Anglian skies, a touch of the wanton and beautiful in some characters and much verse of *The Borough*. Is it essential that this advantage should be forgone?

Please don't think, Wilfrid, that I'm asking these questions as one whose mind is made up; like Rosa Dartle I'm only wanting to know, but unlike Rosa I'm not hiding things in my heart against your Muse. My question really becomes this—Have you not set yourself an impossible task in writing poetry upon subjects of a sort such as—well, you know: poetry where the point of ultimate interest, pathos, intensity, is so patiently and faithfully subdued? Was it thus that you wrote *Flannan Isle* and *The Hare*?

I've never written such an uncivil letter, I fear, but I'll send it because it expresses the things lurking in my mind.

All my thanks and good wishes.

JOHN

WINCHELSEA
30th. August, 1923

MY DEAR WILFRID

It's a long time since I heard from you and unless my memory is even worse than usual I believe that the silence is

due to you more than to myself: I mean that you've given
me nothing to answer. I feel, in fact, pretty sure of this,
because I've so often definitely expected a letter and have
for so long completely lacked news of you. But don't think
I mean this as a reproach: that would be silly; but I do mean
it to show how much I like your letters and how glad I shall
be to see the next.

You'll see where I am at this moment. I'm having three
weeks here, nearly finished, and I shall leave the town to
my family when I come up next week. I had hopes of doing
some writing, but I have been dry; but I'm cheerful about
this for it simplifies the task of choosing things for my next
book of verse. Articles have occupied me, and these will be
reprinted in a volume to come out next Spring: *English
Portraits and Essays* is the proud title. And I'm half
thinking of a collection of stories when some more have
been published in magazines.—This is my small record of
things done and things proposed.

And you?——

I wish devoutly that I could swoop down on you one
fine sunny morning and find out your doings—Do you
remember reading *Krindlesyke* to me at Malvern, one fine
rainy morning, just before you moved? And do you know
that I've not seen you since 4th. July *last* year? I remember
the date unusually well, for you came to Anerley and we had
a delightful long rambling talk with various people. Pity
that Saundersfoot is a thousand miles away! I so miss opportunities of seeing people I want to see. I meet people constantly and delightfully in London, but not all those I want
to meet. Meeting, in fact, is a necessity as sharp as any of the
unexpressed but perfectly "possessing" necessities of man;
even when there seems little to say on meeting, and both
parties relapse into a brooding silence, the meeting, the mere
contiguity, is a satisfaction: you are all the while dropping

pebbles into one another's deepest, darkest, stillest wells, and hearing the far, quick kiss of the pebbles—one after one. Or if one talks, the most meaningless talk may be the most rich in tone and significance. Well, then, when you are up again we certainly must meet, renew, recover and resavour; and the sooner this is possible the more I shall be pleased; meanwhile the least token of your Livelihood will be heartily welcome.

Ever

J. F.

ANERLEY
12th. April, 1924

DEAR WILFRID

This is not a letter, not meant to say anything, but just *how are you*! Last time you wrote you bragged of your activity: I can brag of my absolute idleness. For months I've written nothing: two poems this year and one (I think one only) short story. Why does vacuity extend thus through all one's being, and leave one as sounding brass or tinkling cymbal? Worries of my daily job perhaps accounts for it, but I hate to think of being so much at the mercy of these externalities.—My *Essays* are supposed to come out immediately, my poems later in the spring or early in the autumn, my stories are still uncertain. This is all my news. I wish we could meet. These four days I've been nursing a cold, with the wildest and worst of winter beating all round; my family go away next week, and I join them for Easter— with misgivings, for I'm tired of this six-months-winter. I've promised to go to Withers soon, but am uncertain when I can: his recent letters give rather melancholy news of himself. If only Saundersfoot weren't so far, if only my time weren't so scant and uncertain, I might tease myself with the thought of a day or two with you. Perhaps you'll be coming up, and coming here, and we can talk.

I hope you are all well. Colds have reigned here, and my elder daughter is having a course of injections against asthma or hay-fever, or whatever it is the specialist has discovered. She's just on sixteen, and intellectually fermenting and expanding at a great heat. I'm a little ahead of you in this excitement: when your eldest is sixteen you will know a little more of the subtle pleasures and subtler perplexities of parenthood.

How are you, again, and good-bye.   Ever

                                                        J. F.

ANERLEY
1924

DEAR WILFRID

It was delightful of you to send me K.E. and I was heartily glad. Never speak deprecatingly: your autographed copies are kept locked up in the bureau, for covetous eyes to stare at through old, fine glass.—And crumbs of encouragement? You did without it for years, you found it afterwards, you have it still in a general, quiet, and slowly-deepening esteem; and no one can tell how deep it is, nor how wide. I don't say this for subtle, indirect "encouragement": one *doesn't* know, and one goes on all the same. One might almost say that it doesn't matter whether one is appreciated or not; but if this is a kind of perfect attitude it is an attitude to be approached more or less nearly by every true writer.—But I preach, as I'm wont to do, and perhaps preach to the half converted.

It is good nevertheless to hear that there's a chance of some of the plays being produced—I shall rejoice: and I shall stay at home. Why? Because (to confess a stupid truth) I'm utterly incapable of enjoying stage plays outside a book. I heartily enjoy reading them, for the dramatic form is an economy, and economy means sharpness and intensity;

but the stage simply bores me, and acting disenchants me, and only the music in between gives me real pleasure. Hence almost the only stage things I care about are operas—my adored Mozart. . . . But you won't agree with me, nobody does, and I'm very glad indeed that your hope of production may be realized soon. Tell me the prospects, as time goes on, and please be a little more generous in your correspondence: I write few letters, but I thirst for them.

Of course you will have *The Grove and Other Poems* when it comes out. Maybe it will be soon, maybe the autumn, and maybe the publisher will flatly decline to risk a penny on it. Nevertheless I shall go on writing till all the seas gang dry, for I don't go dry except as the result of my bread and butter burdens, alack.

All my regards to your wife and the quick growing family.

J. F.

ANERLEY
2nd. July, 1925

MY DEAR WILFRID
I accused you in my mind, though mildly, of a negligence when I found that Withers had heard from you and that you would soon be coming to town with a pack of red Indians, all painted and feathered, and yet hadn't given us word that you might be seen in the flesh. That's to say, I was glad to hear of your intended visit, although so loudly companioned, and hoped you would be sending a card to say that between the Tower and the Zoo you would call in at the Tibbald to lunch. Perhaps the card will come.

And perhaps I've been as careless as you in writing or not writing, although I've heaps of excuses, which I'll keep in the background. All my present tasks are done, but I can neither fly nor run, else I would whisk down to Stammers.

My only visit has been for a couple of nights to Souldern, which I was so glad to see again with its inhabitants, whose friendship I owe to you. *Herman Melville* is done, save the proofs, *Prince Absalom* is done and only waits for September; and now in a blank reaction and sounding emptiness of mind I pause, the more willingly since this house is invaded by relations for a while. What next I shall do I don't know: I'm groping round an idea which will probably be fruitful later on, and so I'm content. I'm supposed to be quiet and self-possessed, as a poet, without the sudden passions of a —well, gipsy; and I'm amused at this and content, especially when the inference is drawn from an alleged technical perfection. God help reviewers who have no logic and no imagination! A poet must needs be contented with his gift, and at *our* age, Wilfrid, I think we are, the only true and honourable anxiety being to keep oneself unspotted from the world—unspotted by vulgar, mercenary, vanity-provoked activities.

Am I preaching? 'Tis to myself, and you'll agree with the sermon, or at least the text; for the text is any one of a hundred phrases of the New Testament which insist that one must care for something more than one's personal gratification. And so, though one may not be contented with the work done, the spirit in which it is attempted may not seem quite shameful to the candid Eye of the Maker above; and that's contentment enough to know. More than this: there's the pleasure of writing—the sense of words oozing from the mind, the sentences taking shape, metaphor giving them light and wings, the perpetual delight, even in small ways, of *making*, whether in verse or prose. So you, who have no other task, need ask no higher happiness than this effort; and I, who have other labours, can have none more blessed than the motion of this pen and this limping brain.

I didn't mean to write all this, but I fancy you sitting in

this room, where you have sat, with your particular stillness and wise silence, and so I wander on.—I hope we shall meet soon and meanwhile all kind thoughts from Anerley to the far West.
                              Ever affly.
                                                    J. F.

Anerley
Monday. 1927

Dear Wilfrid

Your letter has just come, in its fine blue wrapper, and reproaches me for not answering an earlier letter, written in the same heavy and firm hand upon flimsier paper. When was it? I think before I had 'flu or something else—of which I'm long since better. I've often wondered how you stood—whether the family ailments permitted you a quiet mind, and I'm very glad to learn that all's well. But I can't come next week-end for I spend it with my nephew, nor for the next two or three week-ends, for we are a united family (now that Joy is down from Oxford) and I don't want to upset the integrity of this household. But as soon as I may I will send you a line and come for the day. You know how things are with me—so many worlds, so much to do. Yet I've done nothing but a little verse and several articles and reviews—not always of books I specially wanted to write about, and not always articles which people will want to read. But no matter.

We will meet soon. Find me a meadow where there are willows and water, or a hill of beeches. Find me a meadow which will be yellow in May, with hedges washed in haw-thorn blossom—tarnishing, perhaps—and horses nibbling and cows moving as slowly as I do myself and staring no less stupidly. There must be rooks near, and a green-red roof wouldn't be amiss—standing by a muddy weedy pool—and a miraculously white-sailed ship flying over the blue gulf above. And, lastly, two cuckoos, please, and then I'll come.

Meanwhile tell me if you are working and at what. And if you are driven to town—to arrange about court dress* for your knighthood—come to lunch at the Tibbald.

Affly.

J. F.

* You can hire it in Charing Cross Rd., at a Jew's shop.

ANERLEY

20th. Jan: 1928

DEAR WILFRID

I know I'm unpardonable for failing to write, but you have learned to forgive and not forget. I've not forgotten but delayed, being cumbered, like Martha, with much serving. I put off and put off until I can't escape my inner vision of an injured correspondent, blazing forth displeasure and maintaining a look of severe justice that is sharper than physical pain; and then I needs *must* write, so that your Ghost be laid and my evenings grow free of his mute reproach.

I was sorry to hear of your unhappy state but am glad that you are better, as I've heard from Flower and Audrey Withers. I've never thought of you and illness: you seem secure and doubly immortal. You have the frame of an elk, the ease of an ostrich, the toughness of an elephant, the diseternity of a toad—if a toad hath diseternity. Yet you've been ill! You write of tragedies and ills and moving accidents, yet are cheerful and immune: but even you have been ill! My belief in the world staggers, I can't understand, something is amiss in the department of Fate.—But you are better, and my faith is restored. When I hear that you are writing with immense vigour and joy, I shall know that you are thoroughly well and indeed have only shammed before.

For myself: I'm well but not writing. I've been preparing a Selection for Macmillans, which is to come out this spring and prove how elusive is Immortality even when Macmillans publish me; my only chance being the Portrait which Laura Knight will very likely draw for the frontispiece. But I'm not writing. I've written one longish poem lately, but I'm not writing now. January moves on to February, and already the thrush sings me awake at morning, but I'm not writing. A' Sundays and Saturdays I walk and look at trees, but I'm not writing.—While you, in your all but windowless study, immune from the world, write an epic a day to keep the doctor away.

I wish you were coming up again. Don't you know the way to Anerley? I was glad to see Audrey lately, for she's a reminder of you, but it would be better if you reminded me of yourself.

                                    Affly.

                                                   J. F.

                                            ANERLEY
                                        Sunday. 1928

DEAR WILFRID

I touch my hat to you. It is a delightfully full book, for which my heart says *Thanks*. As yet my head can say nothing for I've not had the chance of looking at the contents, though the book has slept on the table by my bed. Visitors, and other oppressions and favours of Fate, have prevented my attention: I am dizzy, like Troilus, with expectation, but must wait until I am permitted a little leisure and a little lucidity of mind. I don't care to give to your poems the odd moments which I can snatch from review-reading and train journeys. I can't read verse at breakfast instead of the paper, I never lunch alone, I have no tea, I dine with the family, I stagger, weary and wrathful, to a bed which only exhaustion persuades me is an easy one. I wake, and drink tea in order to sleep again; I get up, in order to hasten to bed again; I go out merely in order to return once again. Every creak of the treadmill is so familiar as to be dear to me. Turn me into a field and I should neigh until I wore the collar again. My muse is so thankless that I can no longer meditate her, not even with the laxity of free verse, not to speak of the rigidity of what was once mine. But in a few days I shall be able to read, not as you say in small doses but in large alcoholic draughts. Heaven send me the anticipated tipsiness.

Letchworth—where is it? Alas, I vaguely remember: somewhere between Greenland and the distant ice of Labrador. Yet, for love of you, I'll make the venture soon. Not in the car, for we've no expert diver, I mean dRiver, to make the journey across the busy archipelago of London traffic; but one Saturday, by early train, to return by a late one.

Till then again my THANKS.

Affly.

JOHN

ANERLEY

DEAR WILFRID

I've given up writing letters, and only use my pen to reproach those I love for not writing to me. It's notorious that I covet letters: I fawn on the postman, the P.M.G. is my Deity at 7.30 a.m. and 9 p.m., and I ache when nothing comes. *You* don't write, never even send me long excuses for not writing. You write to the *Observer*, in verse, but not to me, in prose. Is prose harder than verse? Have you no senses but ears? Can't you finger your syllables in prose? Providence has given you—for inscrutable reasons—the common senses, and health, leisure, and the country you like; yet you won't write to me who—for equally inscrutable reasons—lack a full measure of these. Give me your quietness and I'll write to you: give me your leisure, your rough and serviceable health, and I'll write letters such as you've never had from anyone; unless pride and idleness, fatal brethren, should deter me.

No, I'll not write more than this reproach, and a plea that if you do relent your obstinate, high-minded silence, you'll tell me something of yourself, your family, your work, the shoes you wear, the thoughts you think, the dreams you cherish, the complaints you smother, whether lyric or narrative usurps all power over you now, and whether you are so busy with success in Wireless Lectures that you've had no thought for people who creep humbly under the Muse's wing and peck at whatever grain falls from stray benefaction.

All my love with this impeachment.

JOHN

ALEXANDER GRAY

TO ALEXANDER GRAY

ANERLEY
13th. March, 1922

MY DEAR GRAY

If your ears twitched and tingled at midnight last Thursday it was because you were talked of here, de la Mare staying after the rest had gone and recalling his meeting with you. It's a pity that six-hundred miles have roared between us, though roaring rather faintly on Thursday: but at any rate I was reminded of a letter which I had meant time after time to answer, and hadn't forgotten to answer, only leaving the writing until I was free from tasks.—The tasks are mostly done—Stevenson, de la Mare, the Moore proofs, sundry reviews, and the latest the texts of an address I'm to deliver at the next meeting of *The Ordinary*, an Oxford gathering of misguided youths who meet to pray and remain to scoff. I elect to talk to them of *The Elements of the Story*, a title which tells you nothing but which may be allowed to indicate my own vague confusions. I hate listening to lectures and wonder why others should endure them; and I'm glad that there are to be so few present on Thursday, a mere thirty or forty, that the term lecture will seem preposterously dignified.

Egotism is the salt of a letter, so I'll continue—I don't think I told you that Christmas Day was vitiated by chicken-pox, which appeared in Joy and, three weeks later, in Catharine. Christmas festivities, which were to be unusually numerous and prolonged, were impossible: we borrowed a gramophone and tried to be happy and the children after all were merry. Since then my wife has had a horrid cold, neuralgia and so on; followed by painters in the house. So there! as these children say. At Easter they will probably go to Worthing—perhaps I shan't, for there's hope of my annual week with Flower, I hope in the car of another bard, V. L. Ellis, Agamemnon's latest translator.

Our company the other night included, besides de la Mare, two American poets, Conrad Aiken and John Gould Fletcher. Aiken I've seen a good deal of ever since he returned to England in the autumn. Perhaps you've seen notices of his last poem—*Punch, the Immortal Liar*, a strange psychological, "new" poem—not in free verse. He's the quietest of men, the acutest of analytical critics: I drink in Freud and Croce (Crock as Moore maliciously calls him) and could talk a new tongue—if only I could understand it. Fletcher I've never met before: he's an old friend of Aiken's, and left off calling him Conrad because (it seems) of his imperfect appreciation of *Jurgen*, a sham romantic-satirico-philosophical American novel—lent to me by someone who bought it in the hope of making money if it should be suppressed. It will suppress itself in six months.—Next day at lunch I collected a puzzle for the children, which will attract your mathematical dispositions: three men present with only two names between them, namely (which is the answer) Martin Armstrong, Martin Freeman, J. F. It was difficult for us to talk to one another except with the extremest particularity.

Let me know how Aberdeen has suited you and all yours this winter. I hope the children haven't been an anxiety. I recalled a dinner I had with you last year, when I saw the announcement of Anderson's new appointment. It might have been you and I could have talked about My Friend the Under-Secretary; and perhaps have waited on you as a Deputation concerning Industrial Insurance, with your old acquaintance Neill still amiably making his not quite innocent suggestions.—I didn't find *Northern Numbers* on the *Mer-*

cury shelves, so I missed you. Are you still immersed in the Science of Sciences? And have you looked it up in Peacock's *Crochet Castle* and the rest?

Do write and forgive my long silence.

Ever

JOHN FREEMAN

ANERLEY
30th. July, 1922

MY DEAR GRAY

I've to thank you for a welcome letter and for a copy of *Gossip*, which I admire. I'm glad it is going in the *Mercury*. Did you see in the July number a very beautiful poem of Blunden's, with a magnificent passage about an arras of yew-boughs, and a rather awkward passage at the end? The *Mercury* poetry has been rather staggering of late— for weakness, I mean.

I'm keeping *Gossip* but returning the *S.W.* letter which reminds me of an editor sending back a sonnet with the sinister suggestion—"Something shorter!" And I like the ineffable assumption underlying the phrase "semi-privacy" of a book: are you not to expect success when you follow up your Heine songs?

I've only just returned from Edinburgh *via* Gordon Bottomley's. Two of his plays are to be produced in London, one at the Old Vic this November and one at St. Martin's early next year . . . poetic drama, you see, is looking up. I've just had a curious correspondence with G. M. An American had charged me with calling a folk-tale in one of his later books *pervertedly erotic*, and G. M. complains that this has done him harm in America. . . . Harm! I hadn't used the phrase and answered in blunt, no, acrimonious terms. Result—another letter saying I hadn't done him any harm in U.S.A., telling me my book was having a great success there, sending me a long long article on it from a N.Y. paper, and asking me to dinner. O Saul and O David!

If letters don't bother you and compel an answer which you're disinclined to give, I'll write again when I've something sensible or insensible to say. All good wishes to your wife and brood.

Ever

J. F.

ANERLEY
17th. September, 1922

MY DEAR GRAY

So many thanks for your *Geophir*, which gave me a very pleasant welcome on my return from Winchelsea the other day. I like the poems, and I like the artist's imagination of your standing in Ludgate Circus and yearning after the purple of your highlands. My daily glimpse of Ludgate Circus gives me a haunted place now. I was talking of the poems to a Museum man who followed you at Edinburgh, and when I spoke of your most delightful stanza he demurred, and wouldn't accept your willow-wren's *vindictive* note as faithful. More interesting was a discussion that followed concerning the Scots tongue: for I've wondered much why it is that the very simplest of phrases, concerning the most primary emotions, wear something of beauty, a touch of romance, when given in your native tongue. And not only that: the neighbourhood of your Scots words lifts our southern commonplace up and up.

"When I look up to Ludgate Hill"

is an impossible phrase for a southerner, but the neighbourhood on the same page, the breath as it were, of romantic dialect (may one call it a dialect without offence?), reflects a beautiful glow, makes a fresh sweetness out of the common words. Down here one could only make:

"When I stepped south from Ludgate Circus
And saw the lights of Lambeth Workhouse,
And heard the clatter of the trams,
And slattern's laughter, driver's damns,
I thought how bright beneath the pines
—Of Guildford gleam the celandines,
And how the crowded cottage sill
—Glows with red geraniums still"—

Tush!

—I don't think it is mere unfamiliarity with the phrases that makes the attraction, for few of the terms are difficult; my disputant thought it was the avoidance of superfluous consonants, making the phrase more musical. I don't know —I wish I had a dialect like that of Barnes, or a "language" like that of Burns. Burns, by the way, I had to defend against Conrad Aiken and Martin Armstrong lately! Nearly all the time I was at Winchelsea they were there too, in a 400 years' old cottage: we talked daily, and especially nightly. I hope your family are very well, and when you write again I'd like to know if Aberdeen suits them. Our small pair—or tall pair—are splendid: at least the one here, Joy having gone from Winchelsea to Cornwall and leaving us to judge of her own health from her lively description of other people.— Do write, please, when the Professor is asleep.

Ever

JOHN FREEMAN

ANERLEY
31st. December, 1922

MY DEAR GRAY

Since New Year's Day means everything to a Scot (as Ash Wednesday to an Englishman) I've meant to send you wishes for a very happy 1923. The wishes embrace your family, but extend no further for I'm half out of humour

with Aberdeen, your only surviving newspaper having—
with forced finger harsh and rude—touched my book on
Moore as though he hated me, or him. . . . Only half out
of humour, I say, because such an attitude is singular and
may be attributed to an imperfectly corrected racial envy.

I ought to have written before, but I've been busy, tired,
idle by turns; but at least I can say I've meant to write. The
family here are well, with fragments of Christmas merriment
surviving in the form of a borrowed gramophone and superfluous chocolates. It's a pity that Scotland is sufficient to
itself in matters (whatever they may be, for I've not the
least idea) pertaining to Political Economy; else you might
find it necessary to seek things out at the British Museum or
Natural History Museum, and then we should see you here.
Science draws stealthily nearer: I'm to meet soon another
John Freeman, a bacteriologist, with whom editors and
authors have been systematically and flatteringly confusing
my astonished self. Don't be surprised, then, if you find me
writing of invisible creeping things and the worm that flies
in darkness.

Pray send me a mackerel for this emaciated sprat, when
you've the leisure and a need of talk.

Ever yours

JOHN FREEMAN

At SOULDERN COURT
BANBURY
22nd. June

MY DEAR GRAY

Your letter was worth waiting for and I was very glad
indeed to have news of you, and especially to read, for the
first time in a long life, a Lecture on the Usefulness of
Political and Other Economy. I knew you could be witty
and amusing and that you would be speaking to Scots, but

I didn't know that your subject was capable of humour, or that even in a lecture humour would out.—It was kind of you to send me a copy.

I came to this place on Tuesday to spend a few days with a friend, "this place" being Souldern, a fraction of a village, eight miles from Banbury and a thousand miles from everywhere else. I don't think you know our poor Oxford and Cotswold villages, all stone and a hundred years old. This house itself has a XIVth-century staircase, tenderly lifted from the old manor house, and gardens of old stone and roses and yew: the roses and yew supporting the stone, the stone seeming to wreathe round the stems and boughs, with gigantic walnut trees towering over all like Ethiopian slaves. For the moment I am the Sultan beneath those gigantic Shades.

I have been hearing much of Bridges and A. E. Housman and Gordon Bottomley who visit here or are visited from here: and I talk of crops and drought and village idiots (the sport of "inbreeding") and watch the mothers of village idiots drawing water from the spring in front of the house, and think how Masefield must admire them and must pray that their fruitfulness fail not; and then I wonder vaguely how lazy I should be if I stayed here always, and why one should not be lazy; and only now remember that this is a stupid question to send to Aberdeen and the expositor of Karl Marx.

But I'm glad that the expositor hasn't strangled the singer, and I'd like very much to see the *Geophir* if you would send me word when your songs are out. I've done but little verse lately—the last is in my pocket and I'll enclose it with this letter, thinking you may like to see it and send it back. If you say it's not like other things I've written, the answer is that I can't help it and indeed hardly "wrote" it at all—the first line waking me out of a kind of dream and the rest flowing from that line when I got up.

I talked Scotch on Saturday with John Allan at the Museum, while he showed me the more rare and precious coins and explained their history to Joy and Cathie:—e.g. the broad-piece which Charles I always carried in his pocket and gave to Bishop Juxon as he passed to the scaffold; a piece that thrilled Joy and will probably appear in the historical novel she has been writing for some time. This novel brings in Milton and Cromwell, and so far as I've been allowed to glance at it, I find much excitement and amusement. Joy's form, you must know, is divided into Stuarts and Regicides and this the most ruthless of Regicides. —From coins we went to M. S. and Robin Flower (whom you may remember) displayed Letters of English Kings and King-Unmaker, and gorgeous illuminated Psalters and the rest, and for three days we lived in a state of historical reverie —and childish nerves.

In a few week's time I shall be within 150 miles of you, but can't threaten to walk over. We have an office Meeting in Edinburgh and I want to spend a night or two with G. Bottomley on my way back and talk of poetry and listen to Mozart and the Russians on the—Gramophone. I hope that all your family will keep well now.

Ever

JOHN FREEMAN

ANERLEY
Sunday. 1925

DEAR GRAY

I honestly think I'm creditor and you debtor in this correspondence which is so lacking in a correspondent element. Like the swallow that doesn't make a summer, or the drops that are wet yet not a shower of true rain, or riches in the experience of the just, or rhyme in modern verse, or likeness in modern painting—like anything you

will that's incontinuous and unordered in your contribution
to my letter-box. I ought not to grumble, perhaps, for my
thirst is to get letters and not to write them. My dipsomania
is cureless and radical: like that of the poor man I heard of
to-night, who can't altogether be denied drink (else he'd
die) nor indulged (else he'd go mad) and so lives meanly
from misery to misery, perforce eager and perforce dis-
mayed. I am that man, and you the worst of nurses.

I'd hoped to see you again during one of your weekly
visits to town, but I suppose you've been busy, or fascinated.
I saw a note lately about a small book of yours but forgot
to take the address and title, and so have neglected to get a
copy. I hope the publication means that you're able to write
poetry as well as economics, and I'd like news of whatever
you're doing. For myself: *Prince Absalom* ought to be out
soon, to the chagrin of your local paper, to be offset perhaps
by the renewed praises of the *Manchester Guardian* and
Christian Science Monitor, which have been particularly kind
to *The Grove*. And I've written the life of *Herman Melville*
(a Scot by descent) for the new E.M.L. series, and this is
expected to appear in the autumn. Other projects loom more
or less mistily ahead, if only I've time to write what I would.
—Last week saw an interruption of everything for on
Tuesday I started with Robin Flower for Ely, Peterboro,
Kings Lynn, Norwich and Bury St. Edmunds: all unfamiliar
and all surprising. I needn't boast about my weather, but I
must about my surprise at what I saw in the Cathedral and
some of the towns. The astonishment of the ecclesiastical
architecture and the delight of the domestic (from cottages
like thimbles to houses like palaces), and the gilded counties
in which the whole scene was set out, were a perfect joy.
Tell me if you can match it anywhere in Scotland. All I
know there is in Glasgow and Edinburgh: and apart from
separate parts and buildings in Edinburgh, and apart from

Holyrood and the high Castle, there's nothing I admire greatly in your cities. I hope you won't think this offensive.

No more, for this is but a kind of flag-signalling meant to provoke artillery. I hope your family still flourishes in their healthy polar neighbourhood: ours contends against the softer wiles of the south, where winter ended on Monday last.

Ever

JOHN FREEMAN

ANERLEY
Sunday. Sept: 1926

MY DEAR GRAY

I don't know whose fault it is that letters between us have dwindled almost to extinction, but I'll try to remedy my own part. And since I can't tell surely whether you are alive or dead, well or ill, I had better do what is easiest, namely, talk of myself. This really is easiest when the talking is done on a typewriter, and if it bores you to read it, it is at least easier to read than my nervous Hand.

Well, the news is marvellously small. All this household is well, but on the point of reduction, for Joy goes to Oxford next month—goes, in our eyes, a child, to finish in her own, a woman. She's keen to be there, but not too confident of doing well; but it's a healthy misgiving. She and her sister are away in Suffolk, for this year our holiday has been split up. I actually went to France, with John Allan who remembers you at Edinburgh though you, I fancy, can't recollect him. I was in Paris a few days, and then went on to Brittany—a small place named Port-Navalo; distinguished only by its insignificance. I liked the coast better than Paris and I liked one or two small towns and villages; but, mainly because it wasn't England perhaps, I was impatient to get home. Yet the coast is beautiful and the unfamiliarity of people and customs was attractive; but I liked nothing so much as the lizards and the lichens on the rocks—the lichens like brighter lizards and hardly stiller—and I know that I needn't go so far as Brittany to see lizards and coloured rocks. I also made some excursions to see cathedrals, churches, dolmen and menhirs (you must let me air my knowledge of the distinction between these—no, never mind), but really enjoyed no sight more than the grime of Victoria Station when I returned. Paris I half liked—that's to say the Louvre, but Versailles and other Vastnesses don't attract me much—I get a little resentful of mere empty size, and don't retain very pleasant memories of it.

And else? Well I've published a book on Melville (you ought to thank me for asserting his Scots blood), and I have a longish narrative poem coming out next month—in all sorts of metre and embodying all sorts of legends and stories of Solomon and the Queen of Sheba. Most of the stories are taken from little known Arabic sources—my scholarship has all been stolen from one or two books which Providence thrust under my nose just at the times I most wanted them.

Well, this is tame enough. Perhaps you will startle me with a more adventurous tale. I think you expected a certain amount of ease in your Professorship by this time, and an answer to this letter will prove that you have reached it. I had hoped to get to Scotland, but have not been near it for two or three years. But if you happen to be called to London by Royal Command or any other, I hope you will give me a chance of meeting you. My office is now removed to a white Palace in Southampton Row, Bloomsbury, and so I am a little nearer the reputable eating houses, and should be very glad to have the chance of a long talk.

There was something else I was going to say, but it has gone clean from "what his lordship is pleased to call his mind". No matter.

I hope your wife and family are thoroughly well and

infinitely better for being out of London—as indeed you once told me they were.

                    Ever yours
                                JOHN FREEMAN

                                          ANERLEY
                                    8th. April [1929?]
MY DEAR GRAY

I was intensely disappointed to find you had called at my office before my return from Dublin, and to reflect that I'd missed the chance of introducing you to the talkative luncheon party of which Robin Flower is the chief brilliance, though not the sole luminary. We could have had such a pleasant time! I wish you were coming down again. So far as I can see I shall be in Edinburgh some time after the end of May, and I always like to turn official trips to a happier account. Last time I stayed with Gordon Bottomley: last week I called on A. E. and saw Susan Mitchell who wrote such an amusing book on George Moore.

Tell me, when you write again, what has happened to your lyrics.

All kind messages to Mrs. Gray and yourself from my wife and

                    Yours ever
                                JOHN FREEMAN

PHILIP GUEDALLA

TO PHILIP GUEDALLA

ANERLEY
Wednesday

DEAR MR. GUEDALLA

Not to bandy compliments, I feel I ought to have said more about your book. It isn't a compliment, though, to say that I've such a stiff mind that my surprise increased my pleasure; but even so I knew I was reading a good book written (forgive me!) by one who can write. That's why I was pleased.   Yours sincerely

JOHN FREEMAN

MRS THOMAS HARDY

N

TO MRS HARDY

ANERLEY
Sept: 1927 [?]

DEAR MRS. HARDY

I hope you will not think me impertinent in troubling you: my visit last Wednesday with Mr. Ingpen has provoked these verses, and I should not like to print them without feeling sure that you—for Mr. Hardy—would not mind.

I don't of course want him to be bothered with the lines, but would you be so very kind as to tell me if you would rather that I refrained from publishing any such allusion to a visit?

And will you please believe how very glad I was that you made the visit possible?

Yours sincerely

JOHN FREEMAN

A Visit to Thomas Hardy

THE Roman road runs by the wall,
And Roman shards and remnants lie
Under the turf where dry leaves fall
  On leaves long dry.
Bracelet and bowl, and naked bones
In Resurrection's sad amaze
Staring amid long-buried stones,
  Take the sun's gaze.
And here, mid talk of times forgot,
The times forgot come back renewed;
Rise Roman shapes above the plot
  Their bones endued.

I shut my lids and straightway hear
A Roman voice—it is my host's;
I look, and from his eyes there peer
    A Roman ghost's;
In his hand clasp a Roman hand,
In his verse hear the ancient tone
Heard once in accents harsh or bland
    By ears now stone.
Time spins back, and a wave of the past
Streams through each idle sense's portal,
And, while long little minutes last,
    I touch the immortal.

ANERLEY
Thursday. [12/1/28]

DEAR MRS. HARDY

Will you let me add one more to the many messages of
sympathy which you must be getting at this sad and proud
moment? As a younger poet who would fain do homage to
a great poet, I was privileged to see him only a few months
ago, when you were kind enough to let me call. He seemed
so full of vitality then!

    Pray believe me
        Very sincerely yours
           JOHN FREEMAN

JOHN HAINES

TO JOHN HAINES

ANERLEY

1st. December, 1917

MY DEAR HAINES

I recognized the poem at once, but I'm glad all the same to be reminded of it. And I'm glad you will look through your letters—and to have your offer of a copy of *The Child in the Orchard*.

As to your questions.

Your surmise is right, Dover's Hill is Campden Hill. It is reached by the road from Weston-sub-Edge, and as you will know was the scene of the Cotswold Games. *Ten o'clock* is the name of a great tree that crowned the easternmost Hill, just above the other road from Weston via Aston-sub-Edge to Chipping Campden. It came down in the gale of nearly two years ago, which destroyed scores of elms around Edward's camp at Romford—elms which I saw when I visited him there soon after. Perhaps the enclosed unpublished poem, *Ten o'clock No More*, will interest you. *Presage of Victory* was written at Weston, and Winchcombe comes into it, as you may have noticed. I fancy there's a good deal of that country lying about, visibly or just below the surface in my verses: especially in an unpublished poem which the faintest encouragement would make me thrust upon you.— Perhaps even these egotistic details may be useful.

Ever yours

JOHN FREEMAN

P.S. All the faint "action" of *Crazy Clay* takes place on Dover's Hill. I ought to say that I'm not a native of that country—unmitigated Cockney, or Cockney overlying

Wiltshire (the very county E. T. knew and loved); but I've often stayed at my Aunt's at Weston of late years.

ANERLEY
13th. February, 1920

DEAR HAINES

 I fancy I told you that when I was ill a fortnight since I had an odd dream which fell very quickly into verse. Here is a rough copy which I'm sending because it is, I fancy, a little unlike the usual—that is, of course, the unusual—poem of its author, and because I'd like to know how it strikes an unprejudiced mind.[1] Let me have it back soon, please, with the other things which I think you've got. What in particular I'd like to know is how the "fantastic" element touches you: it is an almost literal translation of the dream.

 I've just had the final proofs of *Poems New and Old*—302 pages to read through quickly. It's a teasing, discouraging job, but as only sixty pages represent new poems I feel that the mischief's done already and no great harm can result now.

 My Aunt, thinking I'm ill, has asked me to go down to Weston. Perhaps I shall in the Spring and try to meet you; but as I'm immensely better I shan't go before the spring.— I'm horribly busy, with half a dozen things to do and a desire to do only one—and that, verse.

 All our loves to you and yours.

J. F.

ANERLEY
23rd. December, 1920

MY DEAR HAINES

 A thousand thanks—your prompt reply shows that the

----

[1] The poem referred to is *The Wounded Bird*.

lost letter was no loss for me. I hasten to enclose this with Robin's delusive Nest Egg—which is NOT the sort that I covet and can't discover.

I only did the *Housman*: please Heaven it's not one of those you called bad. It's a mere note upon *A Shropshire Lad* which, for all readers I suppose *is* A. E. H.

O I envy you the Forest and the snow and rime. Isn't it my theme? The "Poetry Editor" of the *Spectator* says I'm "such a wonderful hand at trees"! I suggest "Poetry Editress". What you say of host and hostess at the Speech House brings so vividly before me our delicious evening there: the leaping fire and myself on the mantelpiece, you and Flower talking and talking while I looked on or paced the raised floor in the funny bow-window: the host and wenches boarding the char-à-banc and then tramping back a little later; the girls' high, clear voices coming so beautifully out of the cold nimble air, thick with high clear stars. I'll not forget that night, and my heart warms towards you and R. F. when I recall it, as often I do; as also that first night of ours at Marlborough, do you remember, a hundred years ago? after that evening sauntering by those flower'd and sweet-odoured streams. Well, well—my thoughts turn always and infallibly to the past.

O, while I've been writing there have been our nightly "waits"—boys with pure grave voices singing and knocking and singing again their most up-heavenly notes.

Your Forest *would* creep into my Cobbett, which I've just finished for the *Mercury*. In a way it's a new kind of thing, which you may think successful. And you may NOT.

All good and happy wishes to you three.

Ever

J. F.

WINCHELSEA
27th. August, 1922

MY DEAR HAINES

Don't ask for sympathy, or compliments, when you are
well enough to write such delightful letters! Your last came,
with the stories, when Flower was sitting here; for he came
suddenly with a daughter last Monday (and leaves to-morrow
when I do) and has quickened conversation in his familiar
way. Every evening we adjoin to Look Out Cottage and
"sit upon the ground and tell sad stories of the death of
Kings." Of these some have been deposed, Hardy for
instance: some died, Conrad for instance; and we weep over
their corses but pursue our labours with an inflexible
fidelity. . . . "We", you will understand, is C. A., M. A.,
R. F. and J. F., and although one of us usually dissents—it
matters not which, the office of dissenter being transferable
—that does but prick the talk into brightness.

I am very glad to have your opinion about the stories
(thank you for your care in returning them). The others
down here have now read them and urge collection and
publication, since there's almost enough, allowing for one or
two you haven't seen. C. A. suggests *Sleep Pretty Wanton*
as a title, since that's the title of a story that is floating across
the U.S.A. at present. But I must say, speaking impartially,
that it's a decidedly uncheerful collection, if the subjects
alone are considered. . . . I wonder if I should agree with you
if I re-read *The Dynasts* now? You and I are getting terrible
iconoclasts—and you don't admire Henry and George as I
do. C. A. the other day (when we pursued a stupid newspaper correspondence as to best novelists) said that if he had
to decide on five novels for himself, would choose *Karamazov*,
The Idiot, Crime and Punishment, Moby Dick and *The Wings
of a Dove*: a sixth would certainly be *The Brook Kerith*. So
far as novels in English are concerned I should assuredly

choose the last three. By the way I am with you about the Hardy novels—the two most perfect (when few of them are perfect) being *Far from the Madding Crowd* and *The Return of the Native*. Even *Casterbridge* is spoiled by one or two women, and Farfrae; and *The Woodlanders* by the doctor and his Lady. But these two are unspoiled, and together make a perfect harmony—one clear and sunny and one grave and stormy.

I'm sorry for Kerr whom I well remember meeting at your house, briefly, one night.

Well, if your letter gave us great pleasure, as it did, I'm repaying you miserably. Forgive me, and enjoy all your Selves at Tenby; and if you should see W. W. G., give him my love.

Ever

J. F.

ANERLEY
15th. June, 1923

DEAR JACK

When your letter at last came I was minded to fling off a grateful telegram, but remembered in time that I hadn't a shilling in the world. The letter was a delight, and I have half a mind to ignore all decencies and read parts of it at my niece's school next Friday, when I fulfil an old promise to lecture, and have chosen for subject, SOME LETTERS AND LETTER WRITERS—the easiest and, if you like, the most amusing of subjects for young girls. But I won't betray you.

Well, I'm writing at once because I sat this morning at the Handel Festival, all alone, and thought what a happy letter I could send you—if I had the brains. The Crystal Palace seemed crammed. There were four thousand people in the orchestra and choir, the men in black and the women in white. The sight of those impossibly whitened figures rising up as one reminded me of the Judgment Day, and that, I must own, is not a Day I contemplate with equanimity. And I thought too of the smell of all those packed bodies, as they nudged and brushed one another. When the Festival started there was a sparrow flying about, instead of Jove's eagle which Handel would have invited if he could; and every now and then during the performance one sparrow or another would fly across the sky (for it's another sky under that vast roof) and then, oddly, hide for a moment in Handel's wig, which for these occasions is copied on a large scale and hung for ornament in the middle of the auditorium—nave, I should say, seeing that we had parts of the Messiah. One of the soloists was Florence Austral, who robbed a continent of her surname—a very stout, stockish figure, heavy as cheese, with a voice as light as honey. She sang with lovely and easy power—Venus herself might have been singing, if it weren't for the stout figure, the Crystal Palace, and the rest—only Venus would have been as lovely in her—shall I say divestitude? as Miss Florence Austral in her amplitude of flesh and silk. . . . We all raved, and when the chorale was loudest we raved the most. Handel is a great realist. One double chorus rendered, "He spake the word, and there came all manner of flies and lice." Handel speaks the word with singular distinctness—he shouts the word, staccato fashion, and many times; and when he proceeds to flies, he signifies it by a sort of droning and infinite buzzing, and the lice by the infinite repetition of tiny crawling sounds. A blind man who'd never seen flies and lice would know all about their habits from Handel, And he'd know all about the habits of hailstones too, from another chorus, thunder from another— in fact he'd learn as much from Handel's literality of imagination as from any Normal College. But Handel's a great man, and I enjoyed myself—or rather I should have enjoyed myself if it hadn't been mortally cold. Also the company was curious. The place was filled with the aunts of my childhood, each with the score of Handel; sad spinsters, for whom one's foolish sentimental heart insolently bleeds; sitting there in couples, sometimes in worse solitariness, renewing their youth with Handel. . . . He was a great man. It was wonderful to listen to these great tides of sound, the infinite complifications and intertwistifications, sound impeached with sound, melody biffing melody with endless procession, disappearance and resurgence.

Am I disloyal to my admired Beethoven, my adored Mozart, my aweful Bach? Forgive me, ye august Gods—'tis the echo of the opinion of a young woman behind me, who said that Handel was the greatest musician that ever lived, but it *was* a matter of opinion.

> "None else to Handel
> Can hold a candle.
> Wagner's a vandal
> To old Herr Handel.
> Scriabin's a scandal
> Compared with Handel.
> From Rhine to Wandle
> There's but one Handel,
> Nor rhyme left to squandel
> In praise of Handel."

Yesterday Ellis miraculously appeared at the Express, just his old self. I don't know whether this means that he is being rehumanized; I think he has some connection, financial of sorts, with the Adelphi, of which he was talking a good deal. Martin Freeman also turns up frequently at present. Why don't you? Yes, *I* think E. S. is good-looking and I admire her brains and her simplicity of talk. She's a very, very interesting personality.

To-night I was shocked to open a paper at dinner and

read that Hewlett is dead. I liked him—once I spent a week-end with him, all alone, our two solemn selves, at Broad Chalke; we talked and silenced just as we chose. I think more of his verse than you do, and I don't care very much for his novels after the *Queen's Quair*—in fact that's the only one I've a wish to re-read. But I liked *him*. No one could do better than he the *Chronicles* in the *Mercury*. He struck me as rather a lonely man, who'd passed the pinnacle of popularity, but hadn't suffered in honesty. He had a curious mind —very pure, yet (not a word against him) permitting a sort of prurience of imagination. I mean that he slipped his puppets into such queer, unnatural and unhealthy relations— with would and would-notting all through. But I grieve for his death. He was truly a poet in his vision of England; he liked my work and was grateful for what I said in the Q.R., and I admired him.

This typing (I don't know if you really object to it) gives you such good measure that I think I might decently stop now, especially since I have no more to say. I've just written to Percy Withers, telling him I can't go there next week-end because Joy and I contemplate an innocent elopement to some quiet Surrey or Kentish Inn, and how this and that succeeding week-end is more or less pledged. Joy has never stayed at an inn, and she looks forward to it as a great adventure—such as piracy, abduction, bigamy or coming into money—the greatest adventure of all, I suppose. Don't talk to me of books, by the way. I never read now, for I have no time. I review, and think of the books I'd like to read, and wonder if I should read them if I had them, or if I had time. Shall I ever read Gibbon again? Shall I read my Clarendon, or Burnet? Shall I re-read *Clarissa*? There's a translation of Petronius (of whom you boast) just issued; shall I buy it, and shall I have time to read it? When shall I read *The Excursion* again? Pharronida, which I've only dipped in as yet?

and others of your admired Carolingians with the beautiful
names. Bennett has a foolish book about living on twenty-
four hours a day. What's the use of twenty-four hours a day
to me? Can I spend it all at the Express, or reading, or thinking of versing and prosing? Can I spend it all in thinking of
and staring at beautiful English villages? The only time
(almost) that I don't grudge is the time I give to reading
letters. I can never wait for them. Deep depression, rich
anger, seizes me if none comes; I curse the postman, and
attribute it to the discontinuance of Christmas boxes, or the
growth of Socialism, or the mortifying coldness of my
friends. No one writes to say that I'm a fine poet but a bad
prose writer, or a brilliant essayist but a deplorable rhymer.
No one pours out long letters of confidence; no one leaves
his wife in order to tell me all about it; the postman goes by
every morning just as I get up. If I hear his knock I'm teased
with impatience, only allayed as I hear Elsie rushing in
terrified haste to the door, and then taking the whole of the
stairs at one bound. I fling myself on Elsie and the letters in
an indiscriminate embrace, scorning the timid remonstrance
of my wife, and the affrighted eyes of the girl. Many girls
have been embraced for less. So you will guess (yet still
faintly) how gladly your letter was taken, how often it has
been read, with what relish of phrase and voracity of appetite
for every incident. I know you haven't a gramophone, or
many books, and never sit up after ten; I know there's scarce
a word of truth in your letter; and all the more do I admire
the brisk fertility of your invention, the happy simulation of
an interest in a fast vanishing World.

My regards to your long-suffering wife—assuming your
fiction is fact, which it isn't.   Ever

JOHN

ANERLEY
3rd. August, 1923

MY DEAR JACK

Your profession is extraordinary! Don't tell me you're busy, with registrarships, stewardships, chancellories, seneschalleries, butleries galore, when you write such letters. True, as for the matter of them, some of it had better never been written—but I'll deal with that in a moment—oh, easily enough, if mercifully. Yet I'm glad you wrote your last letter, for it restores to me that delicious, that rare, that exalted and exulting touch of superiority which, in a sinful world, the chief of sinners finds it so hard even to remember. And I am glad you say all those things about Thackeray, and am half minded not to answer them but leave them blushing awkwardly on the page—unable to advance, too confused to retire, wishing they'd never been born yet without the least idea how to contrive a suicide. But I'll not exuberate, I'll spare them by sweeping their swollen, goggle-eyed heads off at one stroke. Shall I, though?

Well, let me say that I don't answer for the Georgians of your rubicund sneer: I'll answer for myself. What I dislike in Thackeray, while admitting I don't always dislike it, is his infinite niggling. Had ever anybody a smaller mind or heart than the author of *Vanity Fair*? Don't you see, Jack, his whole art there is in the exact expression in another medium of Frith's *Derby Day*? You almost tempt me to read him again, instead of Dickens, Aksakoff, Rousseau. There may come a time when antimacassars will "bring in" Thackeray again—I smell it coming: but that makes small difference. *Vanity Fair* has ceased to be, because a particular type of small-mindedness, in its particular literary exercise, has passed away. The thing itself can't pass finally away, but its exercise may cease in its old form; and it will remain like a leaf stuck down in Cathy's book. . . . "Here dies, here lies!"—I don't pretend, of course, to take you with complete seriousness: Thackeray, or rather *Vanity Fair* unapproachably the greatest English novel. My dear, *I've* never said anything so harsh of the English novel. Shade of Toots, ghost of the Marchioness. . . . "Janet, Donkeys—a Donkey!"

Forgive me! I've not yet read Bailey's article but want to, for I think him a real critic, a critic who can write. He did an excellent little book on Johnson. I have read the Hewlett article, which seemed not *very* good. I knew how you'd feel, but not how strongly. Do you really take Hodge as a serious personification of the curious creature known as the English peasant? How can you? Isn't he simply a historical generalization? Isn't a King, in our eyes still (certainly in mine) a splendid figure in crimson and gold, with a rather puffy face, with wives and concubines and all the rest that men desire? You can say, if you will, there was only one such King and no such peasant. Well, I know too little of peasants to say. Hewlett, I assume, knew more; you, I'll admit, know yet more—but he only generalizes, dramatises. And what else is a poor author to do? I like the *Plow* as a dramatic chronicle and I refuse to say I'll never write to you again merely because your choice of peasants happens to be more libidinous and "Rabelaisian" (your word, I think?) than Hewlett's.

Don't talk of Cotton: I'd already asked the *Spec*: and your letter throws me into such uneasy expectations that I've also asked the *Bookman*; for I want it but haven't fifteen shillings in the world. My fifteen shillings goes for Catharine's shoes, Joy's ribands, Harvey's sherry, phospherine for Gertrude, fares to Shiplake to-morrow, whither Joy and I go (followed by Gertrude and Cats) to my namesake's, as a prelude to Winchelsea. Cotton for fifteen shillings—why Silk would hardly cost more!

o

O, a story for a story. I think you know Meyerstein—
he's with his people in Edinburgh and I told him of the
bookshops to visit. On his way back with a volume of letters
by Mr. Dryden, Mr. Congreve etc: he saw the *People's
Journal* with full murder reports etc: Excited he took one
and handed over a penny. "Twopence, Jock!" was the cry.
And like a true Scot E. H. W. Meyerstein looked at the
paper, and twopence it was. Now I am haunted by the sight
of his round black head, with its premature tonsure, crowned
by a tam-o'-shanter.

Another story. Conrad was at lunch yesterday and I asked
him about a house on the marsh at Winchelsea, which Cats
and John Aiken had zealously watched the building of last
year and which was putrefied by the painting of curved oak
beams on the stucco'd walls. Conrad said the scandal had
shed its beams—on this wise. An artist lived there and put
his name up—thus, J. M. W. Corot R.I. or some such name.
An evil person came privily by night and added P. to the R.I.
Corot was ashamed, deleted his own name and straightway
had the local jobber in to erase the infamy of the beams.
(N.B. This story isn't true, except in parts.)

Honest Sir, I cannot say more: I am tired and restless.
Gertrude is trying to put a quart of luggage into a pint of
bag. She'll do it easily—but what shall I do when I repack
to come home again! O polygamous felicity of the ancient
World! Conrad goes to America on the first of September—
I don't. And let me tell you while I remember that Joy and
I went down to Davies on Sunday, met his wife, found him
active, heard his gramophone, quailed before his dog, and
heard with sympathy his story of his Anthology. It was
delightful to see him again: *when I see them I can almost forgive the churlishness of friends who live at immeasurable
distance from this small and lovely village of Anerley*. I tell
you, I can't say another word. Add these poems to the batch

you are to return to me as soon as you like. I'll write again before I go to Winchelsea, for it would be cruel to dangle a letter from Winchelsea to Llandudno. I hope your wife keeps well: mine is fagged—so am I, with this letter. Yours ripen and hang their ruddy globes among the heavy tangle of language: mine sicken and rot.

JOHN

Lionel Johnson! Years ago I read his Hardy and didn't like it. Most people like it without reading. The incongruity of his sedate, soliloquiticidinous style, with Hardy's awkwardness, this meeting of Spaniard-like grave scholar and blundering and brilliant rustic was too marked to make a good book. I think it has been kindly and grossly over-valued.

ANERLEY
Dec: 1923

MY DEAR JACK

—Two letters, thanks: but I wish you could have given us better news of Robin and I hope that he's going on well. It's good that he's home for convalescence, so long as your wife does not knock herself up, with no kindly Ambassarder to give her splendid and generous liquers—I can't spell to-night.—I was sorry too for your office loss, especially since (I suppose) it makes you busier and throws you more upon your own fine resources. I never saw your clerk, I fancy, but knew him well from your often speaking of him.

No longer boast of your printed marvels, your Nonesuch Marvels! I have (without purchase) Jeremy Taylor in the Golden Cockerel roost and now—guess what? Well, the other day Martin brought boastingly his review copy of the Nonesuch Donne and flaunted it in my face. He doubted— he candidly doubted his right to it; and truly, I could have written (I thought, while my heart danced and burned within me), a better article upon it than anybody else. I concealed my envy, my anger, my sense of unfriendliness and injustice, and (probably) offered him a cigarette. But I mourned inly. I told Gertrude—once, twice, thrice, of the beautiful book of my admired Donne, and after thrice it seemed clear to her that I really wanted it. . . . Best of women, she proposed that instead of giving me a trouser stretcher, she should give me Donne for Christmas—Donne, or trouser stretcher! Such are the incredible alternatives presented by Fate and Wives. How many men would have chosen trouser stretchers, and gloated over the thought of that earthward pointing crease; but few would dote on the dream of Donne! I, devoted to acute and honourable minorities, flushed at the alternative, dissembled my eagerness, demurred and doubted, and told Martin. He, the betrayer of my innocent peace, provoker of my dark passions, suggested that the amiable impulse of a perfect wife ought not to be discouraged; and straightway I went to Glaisher's —who had just sold the last copy. I sank, I foamed, I gloomed; they smiled, they protested, they all but wept as they promised to try and try.—O age of miracles, O powerful master of the grave's sable eloquence, O happy I; they secured the post-last copy for me, a copy that had been foreordained as mine from the foundations of the world.—And now you can say what you like of this and that, and repeat all those bibulous heresies of the Café Royal: I have my Donne: and the Donor is undone, by her own fine and wise generosity. No matter. True I mustn't look at it until Christmas—but I have it.

Let me decline a little. I've just been re-reading *Far Away and Long Ago*, because of what you said; I like it better, but not enough; it might be finer. It is too objective for an essay in autobiography. My *English Portraits* will come out in February—I saw Adcock about it last Friday and he told me of his Anthology, *The Bookman Anthology of Living Poets*. It has been held up some time, and the living poets have been dying all round him, all except Samuel Waddington, who's eighty-seven and won't die. Adcock was perturbed, and I said cheerfully that sooner or later they'd all be dead and offered to write him an Introduction on that point. I said that I should say that since the Anthology had been prepared So-and-so had died, that the Anthology was killing them off, and that when the children (for whom the school edition was intended) had grown up, it would be an anthology of Dead Poets. Adcock looked amused, looked pained and declined. He felt that something was wrong with himself or his Anthology; for it wasn't as if the *excluded* poets had started dying off!—Do you know we all go to Westonsub-Edge on Saturday week? It will be amazing to be so near and not see you. I suppose it's not possible for you to glide over one day—Sunday or Monday? I'll forgive Robin if you can't.

J. F.

ANERLEY
1st. March, 1924

DEAR JACK

Your letter was a great pleasure: be miserable still, and still write me cheerful letters to give me an impression of your supple resilience. Yours is the precisest converse of taking one's pleasures sadly.

And thanks for your remarks about the two stories. I'm sorry you are so little original and independent, for others, too, have preferred the *Funeral*, and scarcely dissembled a poorer appreciation of *Overheard*. I'm afraid I can't do anything with it now—I don't feel equal to destroying it and making something worse. Robin says there are some beautiful things in it, *but* the characters aren't sufficiently discriminated. Isn't it "Overheard"—the effect of stepping noiselessly on to the fringe of a charmed circle, unnoticed but all-noticing, and listening so intently that you don't describe what you don't see; that circle sitting in dim or newly dark evening, all idle but Sophie—I see her, I saw her first of all, for it was her embroidering of garters that gave me the whole vivid picture as I woke one morning.—Alack, you and the rest tell me I have failed, and you're nevertheless amused at the most trivial of all the stories, one that I wrote drowsily one evening and wondered if it needed typing.

I've no news to repay yours. Martin went to *Methuselah* for the *Spectator*, all the five nights, and has gone now to Winchelsea for a month to recuperate. I met Percy Lubbock at the Williams Ellis's the other night, and found him a pleasant person of my own age—in short, an "individual". He talked of Rome and I talked of staying at home; he talked of Henry James as he knew him, I of Henry as I know him.

I've just been reading some Dryden—the plays. There's a magnificent passage in the *Conquest of Granada*, part two, when the ghost speaks as a ghost should—in couplets:

"I am the ghost of her who gave thee birth;
The airy shadow of her mouldering earth. . . ."

Read the whole passage if you've a Dryden: read it again if you've read it a hundred times before.

Our organ is splendid. Meyerstein was here last week-end and played Bach's fugues on it—Bach's fugues on an organ in one's own house—Bach's fugues! And then Mozart, and *Don Giovanni* on the piano. Tell me not of your gramophone, now, I'm tired of hearing of your gramophone. Our organ is about eighty years old: how old is your gramophone? Our organ has a pretty mahogany gold-impleached face: is your gramophone cloaked in old gold? Our organ shakes the house: your gramophone—? I wish you were here to listen, so that we could, after, listen to you.

I can't make up my mind: shall I send you my two new poems? I want to, but I've bothered you so much of late, and these are my only copies. Shall I? If I do, will you return them at once?

J.

ANERLEY
Good Friday. [1924?]

MY DEAR JACK

Your last letter wasn't one of your best, as you admit, but it was delightful as well as annoying: delightful because it proved that I hadn't overlooked your obituary, and annoying because it reminded me sharply that it is nearly a year since we met! That's never happened before in the last ten years—never let it happen again! Time closes over us, the devil leans from his Cloud and that two-headed Engine— you know the rest. Age makes us bald, dyspeptic and gay— do not let us waste the next half century in these extenuations and demurs. I want badly to come down one week-end and I want to bring Gertrude with me. Domestic snares delay her, the pursuit of duty hinders me, but alone or with her I mean to come soon. I want to see your hills and Severn— I sniff in vain for the sharp damp of your woods and waters —I long for the talk in your rooms: yourself sitting near the tray and glasses, your wife opposite, myself standing at ease and listening hour after hour to the pleasantest nonsense that ever man delivered.

Perhaps you are away now, "picking up" in the best sense. God give you luck, for I'm sorry your energy is so reduced. Your letter doesn't show it but I assume you are speaking truth and so I put you in my Petitions. Do you feel better already? your mind clearer, your temper less prickly, your notions less irrational? Do you already want to withdraw your smutching of Shelley, without diminishing your tribute to *Endymion*? Do you feel you can smoke again and wine again? I have that faith which makes me say *yes*!

I too wanted to be away this Easter, but no: family tyranny forbids. Conrad Aiken's small boy—bag of bones and wisdom is Cathy's name for him—is here, and when he goes Joy's friend comes, and all the time the cares of the world sit heavy on me. I wish you were in London! I've had an urgent letter from W. G., bidding me go there, but as yet I can't. Flower has gone to the Blaskets, blask it! and won't be back for another two or three weeks: he's been queer for some time and has gone, for his recovery, to the most naked of lands.

Did I tell you that I'm a member of the Publications Sub-committee of the English Association? I'm trying to get E. S. to make the principal speech at the Annual Meeting— I've seen her once or twice lately and have found her as simple and downright as her poetry *isn't*. Also I've read *Revolt in the Desert* and insisted on excluding . . . some out of the E. A. prose of today which is being prepared now, and putting in T. E. Lawrence, and only wish I had been on the job in time to restrain them from putting in some others. —You see, Jack, there's so much to talk of! And I've read a modern novel *Jew Suss*, which is Hall Caine plus film technique. Believe me, Jack, reviewers are a cabal of Liars— or of Blind and Deaf.

This book has been praised inordinately, being German and Cinema-like. I shan't soon read another new book that's praised everywhere.

Did you read my article on Churchill as a Prose Writer? Write again, Jack, and say it *is* my prayers.

Affly.

J.

ANERLEY
29th. June, 1924

MY DEAR JACK

I'm writing to you on this machine not merely to respond to your gramophone, but also because my nephew has just cleaned it and so tempted me to do now what I've wanted to do. Also it will make it so easy for you to read, and understand, my letter. I'm glad to know that my prose style, under your provocation, has improved, and I should be glad if I could be sure that your power of appreciating it had likewise grown. But I doubt it. You have no ear for prose. You can appreciate the coarse, casual strokes of a letter, but the fineness of a slightly more careful writing, the effect of meditation, of delicacy, the constant fortunate choice of the best rather than ready content with the second-best, to this you are dense, Jack, dense. You are no artist—nor am I, of course, but at least I have preserved humility. I don't say to you that I'm responsible for the best letters I ever get from anyone, and that but for me you wouldn't write them so well. I don't provoke wit in you, nor send floods in order that you may write to me about them. I don't invent distresses and predicaments for your wife, in order that you may turn them into laughter for me. My claim is modest—I provide you with a reader, until now an unquestioning reader. But all is changed. Not only do I question, now; I violently dissent. Especially when you say that I have regarded coteries, in my prose writing, or suggest that I don't speak out. You're wrong, Jack, as well as dense. What were wits given for? You had them: you have lost them. The art of suggestion, of insinuation, of adroit and damaging comparison, of saying so little in saying so much because of the one thing left unsaid—to these things you are deaf. True you can still hear a big drum, and your soul awakes with reasonable promptitude if, say, Masefield brings out a narrative poem or Noyes an epic. Your ears have become dram-drinkers; you hear but brandy and stout. Is there, then, no sherry, no cold spring water? And plague take you when you suggest that I defer to coteries. I have always avoided them, and pass lightly and unsullied from brief contacts with all. True that I don't willingly vex people, unless they first insufferably vex me; but I approach nearly enough to the limits of the civilized, with only the Hottentot beyond. I have just finished an article on Symons: must I speak violently because there are things I violently dislike? I have distilled a dislike (of his attitude) throughout the article; am I to burn noisome, stinking weeds under his window, to show my dislike? See the difference that civil London makes to mankind.

Not that my prose is unimprovable, nor that you can't improve it; but am I a performing dog? Have you a whip, a hoop, a silver bell and a pocket of candies? Where are your candies? You don't even pay me in honeyed words. It was left for an anonymous critic of the *Yorkshire Post* to say that *English Portraits* showed once again that a great poet can also be a great critic. Did you ever say that? (I wonder what I should have said if you had.) No, Jack. Write again, keep on writing, pray, for I get (I say it again) no such letters from any one else, but don't claim *my* virtues. What should I have left, save the most callous and irresistible industry?

I'm well, we are all well. *I'm* busy on bread-and-buttering, and have done little but write one or two articles, and check the proofs of my poems which will be out, I suppose, after the holidays. I should have liked to have sent you a set of the proofs, but there may be little time; otherwise I should hardly scruple. My aunt is now at Charlton Kings, on the Ciren-cester Road, and as soon as I have time and money I shall go and see her and try to meet you—perhaps when you come over to Robin. You, of course, will never come to town

again, except for Wembley. All my love and write again
soon, flood or no flood. What a chance lost when Noah's
flood came and you unborn!

                                    Ever

                                              J. F.

                                         ANERLEY
                                    3rd. July, 1924

MY DEAR JACK
    It is hard that in order to get a line from you I must
write myself. I never write letters now, or not to the people
I want to hear from, until desperate occasions arise; and here
you've been all these weeks—silent as a worm, glorifying
God only in those adroit legal ways which the worm that
dies not is experted in. Are you ill, or moody, or over busy?
Are you suddenly rich, or suddenly aware that you are rich?
It must be *that*: yet why despise honest poverty? If it is
poverty you despise (I fear it is, yet can't resent it), why
despise the concomitant, the inevitable honesty? Have you
no discrimination, nor manners? It is not recorded even of
the Levite that he spurted the contumely of silence upon the
fallen one's misfortune. He murmured a courtesy, waved a
hand, lifted a gentle lid, moved a deprecating shoulder, that
consoled though without enriching the unhappy certain man,
nameless as I also am.
    I don't write, as yet, to reproach you. The cares of the
world, the deceitfulness of riches have not, as yet, detained
you quite securely: I think you still struggle, though with
diminishing conscience. And if I am right you will send me
a card—or even a wire (since that is shorter)—to say that
you are alive and well. Stay! it is silently suggested to me by
the charity of my own innocent mind that your excellent,
ever-delightful letters have fallen off, in quality as well as
number, ever since your gramophone and your telephone,

your monophone and your saxophone, have quickened the local echoes of Hucclecote. You see I offer you excuses.

I'm well, we are well, they are well. I have relished versing lately, but am dumb again. I'm writing a *Spectator* on Arthur Symons, and find it difficult not to seem cruel: I write of him as he may seem now to others, not as he seemed twenty years ago, and I wonder how cruelly some present bright child will write of me twenty years hence. I've spent a couple of days at Arundel lately—perfectly, perfectly lovely; I had a miraculous walk yesterday and heard *Don Giovanni* last night with E. H. W. M. My wife enjoyed all this as much as I did—not because she was absent but because she was present. Why don't you live in London? Why don't you, one or both, come up for shopping on Friday next, come here to dinner (to meet one or two you know) and go back perfectly happy for Whitsun?—Have you seen Edith Sitwell's *Spectator* poem? I admire it, she admires me, and all's for the best. Robin's been quite queer but is getting better. G. M. is very busy and now gone to rest in France. He's done the Anthology that the *Conversation* referred to—a long *Introduction*, the *Conversation* and the *Anthology* itself all in one volume to be published by Nonesuch! And now good-bye: Levite, I forgive you, from my deep pit, bruised and broken, I forgive you.

Ever

J. F.

ANERLEY
Wednesday, August 1924

DEAR JACK

I have abundant reasons for not writing for so long, but you have only excuses—excuses musical and motionary, may be, but only excuses. My reasons, besides physical weariness and so on, are the absence of time to write about nothing, and the presence of a theme which isn't meant for letters.

Simply, I'm at last writing *Prince Absalom: a Play after the Greek Form.* I've done perhaps half of it, and you'd be amused to see me each evening taking my docile Muse out of her stall, giving her two lumps of sugar, and then climbing stiffly on her back and, looking between her great wagging ears, letting her go whither she will. Sometimes she goes nowhere, but usually she is friendly and serviceable. Sometimes she gives me:

> "Pity hath left the world if justice hides
> And vengeance from some dark hole slides.
> The dancing brain turns lightly into sly
> Practice and subtle treachery,
> And sullen hearts upon faint injuries brood,
> Swelling in monstrous mood,
> Long aching envies and the feverous heat
> Of coveting fingers meet.
> Pity and kindness first are crucified
> When vengeance, with the stol'n sword at his side,
> Slips from the cave of darkness unespied."

Sometimes she plays noughts and crosses with me, or swings her tail idly among the thistles.—I get excited, and then tired. My temper is dreadful, and I sip sherry for soothing. Gertrude has left me, but when *Absalom* is finished I shall, I think, entice her back. At present she is at Lyme Regis with her children, but I shall probably (weak is man!) forgive them all, in fact, I shall go down on Saturday to forgive them and spend about three weeks there, two of which will be spent in talking to Meyerstein and begging Cathy not to tease him. *You* should write a Greek play. You are calm and unexcitable, you don't exhaust a feminine household, you don't feel yourself ill-used if a pin drops or curse the world if your wife's relations call. Happy man, under whose knees no donkey brays!

If you read my article in last Saturday's *Spectator* on A. Symons I'd like to know how my theories struck you. I found it a troublesome article: I took so much pains yet never enough. O that decadent, puzzled, nerveless verse, that verse of moods and limelight notions!

Osbert Sitwell gave me *Triple Fugue*. The two non-satirical stories, *Low Tide* (which alas, I always call low water) and *The Greeting*, are beauties—beauties, Jack. As to the others, I begged him to eschew satire. The answer was an invitation from Edith to stay with her and Osbert for a week-end somewhere in Northampton. I said I couldn't —the rest is silence. She has sent me two more M.S. poems which I admire: we are thick, but as Lauder says I'm the thicker of the two.

Also I've had *Spanish Farm* given to me, and I've written to Alice Warrender to suggest that it should receive the Hawthornden. It's by Allan's brother-in-law (I think), and I believe heartily in "pushing", especially since it's a good book.

Robin is away, Bergen's going to Munich, Armstrong's in the North, Haines (I presume) is dead. How weary, flat, stale and unprofitable! But stay! On the 9th. September (or is it the 10th.?) I shall be in Cheltenham for a day or two, and I shall probably have Gertrude there. Will there be a chance of seeing you on the Thursday or Friday? But no doubt you will be away: nothing falls out as I want.

There are many things I would say, but I've mislaid my head. In truth, I'm not a very good rider and my knees are sore: the donkey is really docile, but her back is sharp-edged; moreover I'm frequently getting stuck in thorn hedges and emerge both dazed and angry. Hence this letter in proof. If, therefore, I don't add anything to-morrow you'll know why. Meanwhile my love to you all. If you answer send to Lyme Regis.

J. F.

MY DEAR JACK

This should be an answer to your last, an answer which I shouldn't have had the trouble of writing if I'd been able to have the pleasure of spending this week-end with you. I had looked forward to it, but I came straight back from the north yesterday and thereby pleased no one, and scarce myself; for I wanted to come—don't brag because, on the verge of senility—as we all are—you've discovered a senile joy in Stendhal. I admired him, that is the *Chartreuse*, years and years ago, when I was but middle-aged; I read it more than once, but perhaps shan't read it again. Looking back, it seems an assured, firm, frigid book; and all the time in reading it you are aware indeed, indeed, of the very pulse of the *machine*. And don't tempt me to demur when you talk of Meredith—I admire the poems immeasurably, but the prose with a very definite and contracted admiration. And you attempt to vindicate him by demeaning those you are pleased to call *stylists*. It's a horrid term, and applied to Meredith's opposites, with Meredith as antithetic exemplar— dear Jack, poor Jack, sweet Jack, Falstaff's diminutive, sad Jack, merry Jack, perverse Jack, Jacket-dusty Jack! I'll say no more, but leave you to the custody of your now-recovered senses.

Style! Style! I can't keep away from the thought of it: its sweetness soothes my breast. I'm still immersed, but not drugged, in Melville and oh, forgive me, most magnanimous and most merciful and most mild Jack, for saying that I've just finished an amazing story of H. M.'s (Herman Melville) called *Benito Cereno*, written somewhere in the fifties, which anticipates precisely and exhaustively the best of Conrad. It's a story of a slave cargo, the successful revolt of the slaves, their schemes and atrocities, the mysterious and cunning concealment of these from the kindly mild eyes of an American captain—beautiful foreshadowing of Conrad's Captain Whalley—the amazing and quickening story of uncertainty and vague horror. Not only the story—the method, the digressions, the slow circling of the mind above the ship, the slow worming of the story all through the timbers of the ship and the bones of the blacks, the telling of the story partly directly and partly by retrospect and documents, the confession of necessity to tell it thus and not otherwise—all completes the anticipation, and with a lovelier and lighter prose:

"Whether the ship had a figure-head, or only a plain beak, was not quite certain, owing to canvas wrapped about that part, either to protect it while undergoing a refurbishing, or else decently to hide its decay. Rudely painted or chalked, as in a sailor freak, along the forward side of a sort of pedestal below the canvas, was the sentence, 'Sequid vuestro jefe' (follow your leader), while upon the tarnished head-boards, near by, appeared, in stately capitals, once gilt, the ship's name, 'SAN DOMINICK', each letter streakingly corroded with tricklings of copper-spike rust; while, like mourning weeds, dark festoons of sea-grass slimily swept to and fro over the name, with every hearse-like roll of the hull."

I'll quote no more—I need quote no more. My hand tires, and this passage is enough to tease your ignorance of H. M.

I know no more than Heaven when —— will be out, and Heaven itself can't procrastinate as much as the publisher does, or his printers happily named —— and ——. The printing was put in hand months and months ago, in early summer, and it is six weeks since it was decided to scrap the vilely printed edition that was thrust upon the publisher. I'll give up writing for sculpture: I'll carve it in ivory or ebony, as Rossetti said.

Write, and again write. Nobody writes to me. I'd like to

see you, I'd like very much to come down one week-end,
but it must be after Christmas. I work like a dog, and you
sneer at *Absalom*. Mad Jack, morose Jack, Monday-minded
Jack, moody Jack, mean-witted Jack, and—most miserable
of all Jacks—modern Jack.

Affly.

J.

ANERLEY
14th. February, 1925

MY DEAR JACK

I ought not to be writing to you, but to Withers, who
is ill. Why should I write to you who never write to me?
You've not written to me once in 1925—a year and no
letter. Years ago, years and years ago, you used to write—
such letters: nobody wrote such letters, and you write no
such letters now. Yet you know how my heart is set on
letters, I mean on getting them, and how nothing gives me
more delight than letters of the dead and living. Which of
these are yours? Must I be content with re-reading? Yet even
so I lose—*I lose the thrill of the postman's knock*, with the
delicious, delirious beating of the heart while the letters—*the
letters!*—are snatched from the box and brought up to my
room. Physically the silence affects me badly, for without
that preparatory quickening of my faulty Organ I am unequal
to the minor strains of the day. True the postman still knocks
occasionally, bringing me this morning, for instance, *The
Best Poems of 1924*: but what is a book without a letter?

Not that I'm reproaching you, but only pointing out that
it's hard for me to write with nothing to answer, for you
know that all my art is artless, a mere faithful answering of
your points, a tossing back (wildly and weakly enough) of
your ball. As it is I'm bound to be as dull and literal as a
newspaper, telling you that we are all pretty well here,
despite a circumambient 'flu, and that Joy is now working

P

hard for her Oxford entrance exam., and that she and I went to Rochester to-day (she talking of Gloster) and saw the Cathedral and Castle and Museum, and the heavenly light on bare fields and rainy trees; and that Ellis has lately resumed (not quite regularly) our luncheon party, and that *The Grove* is out, yet not out, for the second edition like the first has had to be recalled owing to the Printer, and that I've had a busy winter with Melville (now practically done) and contemplate—no more than contemplate—more long poems, and that——

Robin and Allan and Meyerstein and Bergen and I and old Uncle Tom Cobleigh and all went to the Lyceum pantomime on Tuesday, and I'd rather you'd been there too. We lunched together, we dined together, we went to *The Forty Thieves* together, we laughed and drank together, and only sundered afterwards for the sake of our respective wives and families. It was great fun, and happily not ridiculously subtle, nor absurdly refined, nor tediously coarse. There was something of Dickens but nothing of Proust, something of Chesterton but nothing of Noyes, something of clowning but nothing of Freud; there was much of 1850 but nothing of 1890 and nothing at all of 1925. Happy childhood, and happy children we.

Save this I've been nowhere, not even to see Moore; and I've read nothing, not even his *Daphnis and Chloe*, for it costs two guineas and I'm lacking two pence. But this is a familiar story of things undone: nothing becomes me so well as the things I *fail* to do. I've got Tchekov's letters to review because I want to read them: shall I read them before reviewing? It's a bad and expensive habit; far better to gyrate and fantasticate upon a Tchekovian Theme. And I've looked through Turner's *Smaragda's Lover*.

This is all I have to say, dear sir, and it's dull enough. But it's not so dull as I might be, and not so dull as your silence. Can't you write? Is Susan[1] jealous? The crocuses thrust through the grass, and opposite this house the Almond burns in the rain, and yellow tassels shake on the shining saplings. Have you no colour, no tassels, no saplings even? I wish I could write: I wish I could write simple, quick and nervous prose instead of this sad complication of knock-kneed clauses. I wish I could write a long poem in couplets, or a beating passionate tragical lyrical thing in blank verse. But I can't. I can only send my love and benediction to you all.

J.

ANERLEY
24th. Feb: 1925

DEAR JACK

Thank you: not one of your very best, perhaps, but still yours and welcome. Was ever compliment handsomer?

This is not an answer but a suggestion. Get Mrs. Haines to drive you hither next Saturday or the next or the next, and return Monday morning. Won't Robin spare you? Won't your clerks bless you? Won't Susan purr her prettiest and preen herself in sunny light? And Susan can sleep at the bottom of the road—oh, it's quite safe, it's a nunnery—and take us five miles to Hayes Common and then I can shew you the prettiest of bits, and Wickham Court and Church, which are still nearer, and you can walk while Susan ogles all the week-ending cars and all the golf cars of aristocratic clubs. You know our accommodation and you shall see new books and hear Mozart and Beethoven, and perhaps some one else will come in and you shall forget all but pleasure and that one glass of sherry is better than a bottle of claret in the house of the wicked.

[1] John Haines's car.

Why, indeed, didn't you come last Saturday? For on Sunday a smart knocking at the door took me to see—Mrs. Squire and J. C. S. and two small children, all debouching from the most enormous car that filled the road from the Mitre (remember the Mitre?) to the railway. They had run over for cheer and tea and it pleased us well.—Seriously, you'd be very welcome of course, and I'll promise a return before you can say Mrs. Robinson.

Thank you for your note about Joy: she shall go to Oxford.

O but I'm in distress. Did you read my conversation about Steuart's book on R. L. S.? Steuart wrote to Squire appreciating the review, and to me the justest compliments, saying he knew I'd know why he hadn't said all he might about Mrs. S., but that what he'd left out of the life he was putting into a—novel! O Caledonia stern and wild! And now to-day comes the stiffest letter from Colvin, full of categorical imperatives, beginning "Dear Sir" and keeping a sirrish but not dear tone throughout; and then adding to the typed letter a painful scrawl of his own shaking hand, that he felt his letter was too imperative and hoity-toity and saying how much better he could talk the question over if I'd dine with him in his loneliness: this postscript is to "Dear Mr. Freeman". He wants to know if he's one of the "sedulous adulators" and myth-makers, and I can only murmur, Lord deliver me from a merry style, Lord make me dull and literal, Lord make me study safety first.—I fancy even Squire was doubtful, before Colvin wrote: and dare I show him Colvin's letter? And how can I tell Colvin where a myth begins, how can I tell him how I know that legends exist? It's a myth that the sun goes round the earth (or is it the earth round the sun?) and who am I to prove a myth? *I breathe it*, and vomit. Must I vomit on Colvin's tablecloth? I tell you, Jack, there's no distresses like the distresses of honesty—Honesty.

How can I answer him? I've sold the books to buy the
children's shoes, and my sister has the copy of the *Mercury*;
and so I can't for the life of me remember whether here and
there I was using Steuart's phrase or my own (or a cunning
amalgam of the two), unless it's a very good phrase: for I
know then.

But I didn't mean to worry you with my complaints: yet
why not? What's a cough compared with this, or your
body's fatness compared with my wit's meagreness?

Gertrude and Joy send all the kindest messages.

J. F.

ANERLEY
1925

DEAR JACK

Alas, my poor brother, reduced and concentrated poet,
too meticulously jarred! Our trip to Gloster is, not to put
too fine a point upon it, indefinitely postponed and you, like
Life, are indefinitely reprieved. Thanks to Fate, in the
person of our domestic staff, we can't get away for a week-
end, for we can't leave the children to sob their little lives
away. Our domestic staff no longer "sleeps in", so we daren't
sleep out, and the owls of Hucclecote must hoot in vain and
in vain the lambs bleat under the window I like to call mine.
In vain must Susan purr and snort, in vain your pure mantelpiece ache for the friendly friction of my shoulders. Wisest
Fate has said *No!* and we murmur in timid acquiescence,
So be it!

And I have a new suit which I could have worn to Hucclecote. I bought a beautiful new pot of about twelve inches
height, a simple green-gray pot, at Leach's pottery show at
Paterson's Gallery: you know that Bergen is interested in
the English-Japanese pottery at St. Ives. We went, admired,
and bought almost the cheapest of many lovely things for

two pounds ten, our eyes falling upon it with a holy glee
and a wish that we could have got it for less. The suit exactly
matches the pot—a touch of genuine admiration here—and
my only concern is at paying vastly more for the suit than
for the pot. Is it an insult to art? No, not truly. The suit, I
hope, I needs must hope, will last as long as the pot and the
pot endure in its beauty for ever. I couldn't risk bringing the
pot to show you but I could risk the suit; and though it
would seem a little too delicate against the mere harsh early
claret of Susan, it would harmonize the binding of your
Sturge Moore and Yeats and create a rest that peace begets.
Lackaday!

But since we can't come we hereby give you notice that
on Thursday the 25th. June we shall eat in state in this
house, and drink Harvey and cider-punch and talk to a
select talkative company; and if only you were here, if only
you could display a little more *management* of your clients'
business—I presume you have more than a single client—
you would come too. Is it possible that you'll find a pretext
for this idleness?

Thank you for what you say of the orchid. I'll tell Young,
who swore that you'd be sworn not to tell.   Affly.

                                                    J. F.

                                              ANERLEY
                                         Thursday. 1925

HONEST JACK

—Though this, to a lawyer, may be actionable. Read
it tenderly, then.

I'm not answering your letter, your last, your best; I'm
not answering your remarks on Hudson for I've said enough.
I'm sending you this little treasure—this Green Man Orchid
that, when it was growing some four and twenty hours
since, looked in its lower flower just like that portrait of Old

Man Chaucer, with pendent beard and downcast look and hand caught to his breast. For yesterday, O wonderful, Gertrude and I and Andrew Young (a wild flower fanatic like you) went to Colley Hill above Reigate to seek for this orchid, which isn't to be found in Young's Sussex; nor in Shropshire, nor Oxfordshire, nor on Drinkwater's comfort- able Cotswolds, nor in Masefield's daffodil fields, nor by Bridges' silver Thames, nor among your own Noyes's stars. You've never seen it, nor had I until on a mere report Young dashed from Hove to the Tibbald, but it was not there, thence to Wray Hill near Merstham, but it was not there, and still hopeful thence to the Pilgrims' Way, and it was not there; but at last, having faith which might remove mountains but certainly didn't remove Colley Hill or diminish a fraction of its egregious height (alas my puff- ings!), we found it on Colley Hill.

And in return will you tell him, or me, where you found your hundred-flowering Monkey Orchid? If it be at the ends of the earth, thither will he fly and reveal its secret to no other. He's very anxious and he's a friend and loves Doughty and E. T. and admires *Prince Absalom* (in part due to talks with him on the Bible as Quarry) and is only waiting for this chance to admire you. His address is . . . ; mine is—well you know, and I needn't say, and needn't say where my heart is.

I'm not sure which week-end. We have no one to "mind" the house and infants and must arrange with relations. Perhaps the 13th or 20th.—the latter more likely, the former preferred as being nearer.

All my love.

J.

P.S. I'm going to buy the Grierson Milton, "Florence" type! like a dolesman with a cigar. O Jack, give me an extra hour to my days.

Dear Jack

We came here a week ago and your letter came just before Joy and I went off for a day and a night and a day at Chard, Crewkerne, Hinton St. George and Ilminster. We walked, sir, walked, though not all the way, disdaining the saloon cars that flashed vulgarly past us and enjoying the exercise of such limbs as civilization has left active in us. I suppose Hinton St. George is the Hintock (is that it?) of your favourite novelist: the church is littered with dead Poulets, and the live Poulets, when they attend service, are likewise immured within a private chapel, screened off from even the gaze of the sinful or simple, and hung with purple. The Lord Himself must needs be impressed with the super-fineness of this ancient family, and feel rather gratified at their notice.—Else it's a beautiful church in a beautiful village. Crewkerne too is lovely and it pleased us to re-member that Trollope, O.H.M.S., must often have passed through, and perhaps stayed at our Inns and made better use of the stables than people do now.—A day or two before we all went to Dartmoor, and enjoyed it in a continual torrent of rain that failed even to dim the flare of gorse and heather. I hope you will get better weather when you go North on Tuesday and that you have a good time. You certainly haven't been in a writing mood of late, or at least haven't written to me; and I too have been negligent, busy by day and night. Lately I started a long-meditated History in verse —a narrative for Young and Old of fabulous History, and have done perhaps half. I brought it here to work at but am utterly empty and incapable. My hair goes, my genial spirits fail. I read Trollope and Smollett and that new Japanese novel. I've tried Chaucer with Joy, and fall asleep: I read *The Tempest* with her, scene by scene, and again, Who shall deliver me from the body of this death?

Meanwhile I've finished, I think, with Melville and shall send the proofs off finally next week. Never let me touch such things again! The MS. is such an easy thing to begin and end, but then the unending troubles begin. I've been in communication with all sorts of people—H. M.'s granddaughter, his biographer (Weaver), H. S. Salt, John Murray, R. S. Garnett (whom I have to see on Monday), F. V. Morley, and shouldn't wonder if I didn't have to see Horatio Bottomley, General Booth and Vesta Tilley. Nobody knows anything, everybody spreads myths. I rise to every fly, but nothing results. H. M. remains baffling, a mystery, for my baffling and mysterious pen. I shall be glad when it's no longer possible for me to multiply appendices and negative negation.

Why have you bought the Blake? I know it's expensive, but surely that's not your sole reason. I shouldn't want a complete Blake even if I could get it in fortnightly parts. You can't understand the whole of Blake: nobody can. The more you get the less you can understand. All that can be understood and a good deal more is found in the Oxford edition. I'm grateful to Blake, as much as to most English poets, and especially since he's helped me with H. M., but I should assist in a disservice to his memory if I pretended that a good deal of his work is comprehensible or even incoherently intelligible. His stones aren't bread. It's only your Russians who are incoherent but intelligible. And speaking of the Russians, how does your wife like Proust? And speaking of the French man, why can't she say without being pressed? I admire Proust, without such political grudgings as you permit to interfere with your sneaking fondness for Cobbett. It's unfair to say that Cobbett vilified England as if he did nothing else. He was a vulgar man (if you understand the word in any but a vulgar sense) and abused his native land as fondly as a vulgar mother will shout out, *Come here you bloody little bastard—O the darling!* Have you no wits, have you no gumption, have you no compunction, have you no imagination?—When I admit "vulgar" on behalf of Cobbett you'll retort, I know you will, you must!— "Then I prefer a gentleman". I rebuff this with a flourish.— You have Galsworthy, you have Masefield: Galsworthy our sentimental Egoist, Masefield our Egosentimentalist.—It's blood you want in your veins, Jack, when you speak of Cobbett, whereas you've only got Shell in your cylinders. But I'll bear with you still, for the sake of the day when "a short fat man with a botanist's tin can" burst upon my sight at Savernake and began a chatter which, please God, shan't cease for years yet.

I've made a selection of poems for Benn's sixpenny—but I told you this before. I'm apt to repeat all I've said, in this fast-coming dotage. I'll make an end, abruptly, awkwardly, having forgotten all I meant to say. Pity me!

All our loves, in spite of your scurvy ways.

J.

ANERLEY
Sunday. Jan: 1926

DEAR JACK

While Meyerstein is playing Schubert I will write to you—two lines of melancholy. Last Monday I went to Golders Green, thinking it right and feeling it necessary to a sense of debt to be present at Doughty's funeral. It rained furiously all day, and in charitable moments then and since— but such moments have been few—I said it was the rain that kept his contemporaries away. The greatest man, the greatest writer of our time, was to be cremated, and not one of his contemporaries thought it proper to stand or kneel while his coffin passed out of sight. Colonel Lawrence was there (in the dress of a private in the R.A.F.) and D. C. Hogarth: else of men of letters there was not one—except I the least.

I was angry at this indifference, though such a feeling is foolish; but "feelings" are usually foolish. It seemed shameful that Doughty's death should be thus unhonoured and unattended. We do not know whom to praise, to honour, to follow, to mourn. The author of *Arabia* and *Mansoul* and *The Dawn* passed out of sight with less than twenty people to mourn him or realise themselves as impoverished.—Mrs. Doughty, in a letter the other day, told me that he was revising *Mansoul* up to a few weeks ago. "He looked upon his poetry as *his real life's work*." Well, his poetry will be his Monument when all his forgetters are forgotten.

Yesterday Gertrude and I went down to East Grinstead to see Davies. He is well, idle, not too prosperous, anxious to move nearer London, contented with cordial reviews and almost contented with small sales. He had no stories or confidences, but was quite himself. He'd heard that Hodgson wasn't very happy in Japan—and why should he be?

Come up soon: I always say this. Make a fifth at the Pantomime next Friday—Robin, Meyerstein, Allan and I. And do ask your wife to read Meyerstein's *Pleasure Lover*—you don't read novels—and tell me if she likes it. We are all pretty well, but hungry for spring. And I've just had a birthday and realise it's only "fourteen days hard" since the last.

Affly.

J.

ANERLEY
28th. March, 1926

DEAR JACK

I have started versing again, writing three sombre lyrics this week-end which Gertrude detests; perhaps I shall do some more, but summer has been my season of late years. But I write only what comes into my head, or rather what *will* come out of it, satisfied if it is said simply and truly, with some honour to Music. For Music, Jack, is the brother or father (or Oedipus parent) of the Muse—forget music and you forget the obligations as well as the honours of poetry. Let me not preach, Jack, but if I preach it is to myself who perhaps need it little. But few nowadays, it seems, *hear* verse, or care for music if they hear it. It wasn't idly that I named one book *Music*, and when I called another *The Grove* it was because I heard, as well as saw, a Grove full of natural music.—Forgive this egotism, for you won't want me to go on repeating all I've said for years past.

Did I tell you *Melville* comes out on 16th. April? The *Swinburne* of Harold Nicolson is out already and I'm hoping that it isn't one of the "Strachey" books which assume a superiority to their subjects and end by maddening the reader. Swinburne is vulnerable, and every literary prig and snob can tread on his coat; but he's much beyond the prig's reach when all is looked at in the round.

I've no head for a letter, except eyes to read one. I'm vexed at the weather, which is like a curse. No sun to-day but only degrees of gloom, sometimes black and sometimes gray; a cold desolating gloom. Spring hides somewhere, head under wing, disconsolate. I am angry for I feel cheated of time and chances.

We look to see your wife next Sunday. There are frequent trains from Victoria to Crystal Palace, and then a gentle walk or ungentle tram. I hope you enjoy your time in Wild Wales.

Affly.

J.

ANERLEY
23rd. April, 1926

DEAR JACK

Your letter was a pleasure. I meant to write at once and say that you wrote because your wife was at home and I because mine wasn't. But I was tired, and preferred to read myself to sleep, and wake early, and think of all the things I didn't want to think of. Usually I don't mind lying awake —I do it expertly from much practice and explore (too vulgar word nowadays) my own mind much as a squirrel explores its strict cage.

I too am angry, I hate these superior people who are superior to the people they write about. There's only one man who ought to write about Swinburne, and that's myself; and only one whom I'd allow to disagree with me, and that's you—Robin as well, perhaps. Swinburne was *pure* poet. When he wasn't poet, and that of course was often and too often, he was nothing at all, but at least he invented a great phrase, "the noble pleasure of praising", and practised it with a noble zest. What do such fellows as these, crawling over the corpses of poets? There is amazing poetry lying unrecognised in Swinburne—the passage of blank verse which the T.L.S. quoted last week was magnificent—not an unusual word, scarce a word that wasn't a monosyllable, not a single astonishing epithet or simile; the easiest, simplest speech, and yet pure poetry and ineffable Swinburne. You couldn't mistake it—and what magic is it that signs thus plainly as one man's only, that which any man (you'd think, in foolish haste) might have written if he'd the mind? Plague on the Nicolsons and the Gosses of this world.

Did I tell you I was doing Doughty for the L.M.? Squire asked me because he said I was a maniac about the poetry. I didn't want to be asked twice, but I honestly tried to think of a better hand to do it, and I couldn't nor could Squire. I loved him for asking me. I shall go off my head in doing it. The other day I told Meyerstein that he ought to hang up a sign in Gray's Inn—"Odes, Elegies and Addresses at Short Notice. Distance no Object." For you must know that he does things to order quite submissively and deliciously. And then I discovered my own sign—"Home for Lost Cause and Impossible Loyalties"—Impossible, that is, only in the eyes of the children of this world. Melville, Patmore, Doughty—you must forgive me everything, past and to come, for the sake of these honest ardencies.

Irish Plays? Why should I go to a theatre? I can play the fool at home, as well as they abroad. Why should I spend money and energy? Energy is wanting almost as much as money. I tire of work—it becomes harder and harder to live by bread alone, and bread-alone harder and harder to get; or rather the getting becomes more and more exhausting. Write to me then. Restore my zeal, make me live again, bid these dry bones live.

Melville is out, and I wait to see if two continents are aware of his greatness. Or will the brave sprats gore this Whale anew? God forbid that the traducers of Swinburne's genius should perceive Melville's, with their little viper eyes all of rancour and squint.

I shall be in Cheltenham next Friday and Saturday, but doubt if I shall have the luck to see you.   Affly.
                                                                J.

                                                        ANERLEY
                                                        July 1926

DEAR JACK

You've lost your old model-hood as a letter writer. You have abdicated rather meanly, as though to avoid the bowstring, as they do, or did, in certain Kingdoms un-infected with modern ideas. Yet I should not have bow-string'd you, and still pray that you may resume your right mind and your crown and glory.—I've little to tell you myself. *Solomon* is in proof, and is to be out in October or thereabout; and apart from these proofs I've nothing to do:

no epic or lyric or narrative, a mere empty head and slack fingers. The *Doughty* article comes in August. Forgive it, for it will need a blind eye over the latter part which deals with *The Dawn*, and don't blame me harshly for the cruel abridgment. I cut and cut and cut with mighty shears, and nevertheless had to cut again in proof, so that the article should not be longer than the longest on record in the *Mercury*. And it was only the latter part, including *The Dawn*, that could be cut in proof at a moment's notice—literally a moment's notice by 'phone to my office. I'm vexed, because I'd tried to do my best and work up to a grand *Everlasting Yea!* about *The Dawn*; whereas now it is rendered from Handel to—Stainer.

On Thursday I go to Paris—I to Paris!—and thence to Brittany with John Allan, fulfilling an old undertaking. One who never turned his back but marched breast forward has suddenly bolted and flown across a muddy channel, or will be across it soon. I feel guilty of perfidy, and worms are crawling all about me, though not only on this account.

I spent an evening with Conrad lately. I've seen so little of him for the past twelve months (or of you) and haven't kept my promise of going down to Rye. He seemed cheerful nevertheless, and apropos of *The Idylls of the King*, spoke of "the Sword Sexcalibur!"

Do, pray, as I'm doing now—re-reading Fitzgerald's letters. There's only four volumes, but four are sufficient for an affectionate admiration and the loyalty of a lifetime. And *don't* read Garrod on Keats—I've read it for my sins, and Garrod, for his may read his *Mercury*.—But no more. I'll forfeit a whole two virgin pages and not attempt to fill them with O's that mean O. My love to you all.

Yours

JOHN

ANERLEY
October 1926

MY DEAR JACK

You have treated me badly, for I've heard nothing of you since long before your holiday and don't know whether you are well or ill, richer or poorer, in life or in death or in high dudgeon. If I weren't the most placable of men and growing bald atop, I should be angry and write a sonnet upon friendship and the deceitfulness of riches. I choose a nobler part by writing to you out of the fulness of my heart and the barrenness of my mind. The former I can only assert, but the latter I can abundantly prove.

We lose Joy in a week's time. To-morrow a friend motors her and us to Oxford, we put her and her chattels on the pavement at one o'clock, and then burst into tears as the door slams on her pert innocence. Lately she's been the cause of our living in a whirl, though I've been a spectator as much as a victim. On Wednesday I took her to the Sitwells and she saw them all, and was charmed. Edith had been here once, but the others she hadn't seen. Osbert has sent me his book and I'd just read it, Edith is going to send me hers when it appears, and Joy secretly envies me these possessions. Osbert's novel has some very good passages— the more human it becomes, and the less satirical, as the story progresses, the better it is. It's best in the duel, growing in obstinacy and fatality, between the two women, rich woman and companion, and the recurrent picture of the sea hammering the hard Yorkshire coast; the sea reminding me of passages in Swinburne's unpublished *Lesbia Brandon*. I liked the book (loathing the satirical parts) perhaps the more since it is only novel I've read since M. A.'s *Desert*, which I heartily admired. To-day M. A. told me of a short story he's written of another legend of monkery, a beautiful story which makes me itch to use it for verse. With magnanimity and disdain equally serene, he offered it to me for my own: I declined, saying I shouldn't forgive myself if the poem wasn't far better than his prose, and he wouldn't forgive me if it was. I refused—but still itch. What shall I do? Well, I wait for *Solomon and Balkis* to appear. If it weren't my own I should say it was ——: as it is I feel that whatever it is it is my best. Why shouldn't I say so? Last night I had to look up a poem of my own which I'd quite forgotten, and which somebody is singing at a concert. It seemed very unfamiliar even when I found and recalled it, and looking through others some seemed thin enough, and some seemed much better than I'd ever thought them. They were all in *Music* and *Poems New and Old*. My poor memory seemed an advantage: I could read them as not my own but as someone's whom I knew pretty well but not as a poet: and his poetry surprised me. Sheer egotism? A barren mind.

On Monday I lunched with M. A. and Louis Untermeyer, a brisk dapper talkative American Jew of the better sort, who talked so infinitely, though so agreeably, that I don't remember a single thing he said except that Squire had shaved his (Squire's) whiskers off and was heavy in parts, making heavy obvious remarks whereupon it was plain that our sometime slim agile J. C. S. had solidified and would never melt again. O, yes, there was another thing, an amusing account of the opening of the new poetry bookshop, at which H. M. asserted his title to making the speech by asserting his Sacrifices in the Interests of Poetry and Poets. Then H. M. went on to say how pleased they would be to have the formal Address by T. S. Eliot, the finest critic, the most purely originating Intelligence, the most startling poet, that lived now and perhaps ever. After minutes and minutes of this Puff Preliminary he announced that it was a pity, after all, Eliot couldn't turn up and so he would call on a substitute—unpuffed—Sturge Moore! [I didn't hear all this,

but Untermeyer says so and I can believe it. Eddie was there
and told me of an incredible adventure which I'm not free to
repeat, and wrote a sonnet afterwards expressing his disgust
at the whole show.]

I'm chronicling small beer, as you perceive, but it's the
day of small things. You, from your silence, I suppose are
acting great. I'll make an end by saying that Gibson is now
fixed at Letchworth, Fletcher with part of his family is in
America, and so are Conrad Aiken and Bergen. And you are
furthest off of all. Nevertheless I have the honour, Sir, to
remain,
                                    Affly.
                                                        J. F.

                                              ANERLEY
                                     Sunday. Oct: 1926
DEAR JACK
        I was going to type this, since you refused to read my
last; but while I can still read your hand I will hope that you
will use a little industry and decipher mine.

I'm so sorry about Dolly: pray give her our Loves and
send me a card very soon to say she's mending. I do so hope
it's nothing more than a sharp trifle.

I've much to say—to say rather than to write. On Friday
we both went to the E.A. dinner—I'm on the Executive and
Squire is Chairman—to hear Baldwin. I'd never seen him
before. When I got there Mrs. Squire complained to Gertrude that she had no idea where Jack was, and two minutes
later he begged me to find and look after her because he was
spiriting the P.M. out of the room, as the poor man was nigh
fainting with the heat and the crowd; and so, as the P.M.
was to take her into dinner, I found her and shoved after
them with infinite difficulty, and handed her over to Jack
under the eyes of the tired P.M., and thought it too cruel to
bother him with introductions. So we remain strangers, and

as Harry Lauder says, I'm the greater stranger of the two. When he spoke at the dinner he was most excellent——a delightful reminiscent speech, without notes, without formality, without hesitation and with the ease of a man at home with his own thoughts; turning into his own mind for over half an hour and taking out old memories as the child does in *The Toys*, a poem you may faintly remember. Squire spoke and then, when all was over, begged me in agitated tones not to leave; and after a while it appeared he was again wanting his wife, to arrange his own movements and hers; and so ultimately she departed to Chiswick and he home to Anerley, as tired as could be. But we had a very pleasant late, or early talk, and taxied up to town together at noon. I really do wish you had been here on Friday, at midnight, for you would have enjoyed the exhilaration of talk.

E. M. Forster, because of my "profound" Melville, has sent me his new book on *The Novel*. Osbert Sitwell his *England Reclaimed* (I think I said so last week) of which we talked copiously at lunch. He has joined forces (morally or aesthetically) with me! agreeing that insularity is a strength to an English writer, and going beyond my notions in saying that pre-Christian art means nothing to him and as for Egyptian—he detests it: as I do. I think he is taking his gifts a little seriously now, and that the next part of *E. R.* may be better than the first:—he works *slowly*, it seems, and not thoughtlessly.

I've acquired, by one means or another, various books lately: a *Tree Anthology* containing a little copse of my own, and a beautiful frontispiece by John Nash; Martin's *Stepson* (which is an admirable piece, almost perfect in its unassuming mode), his *Lady Hester Stanhope* and *Three Cornered Hat*; I shall build a Martin room and keep him in glass cases. Also Hugh Fausset's book on Tolstoy, of which I must complain a little, for he measures him by the standard of a Girls' High School and finds him wanting—Tolstoy! And I'm hoping to add to the new book of 1928 a new edition of *Poems New and Old*, which Macmillans are very timidly considering—it's not for me to blame their timidity!

I was very glad to read your candid account of the lecture, and admired you enormously when I saw that you had given the lecture in your own village. I have steadily refused to appear within five miles of *this* village: I couldn't bear to speak from a platform one day and meet one of my audience on the station the next day. To me there's something indecent in the bare idea: but you are made of sterner stuff, and are untroubled by this—"complex" should I call it? I think it's my only one, and is harmless: it doesn't lead one to the courts.

I'm not going to write more—I haven't time for one thing, and I've just remembered that my feelings are hurt by your remarks about my writing. Have *you* ever forgotten that you're hurt, and then realized that it is your duty to remember and resent an injury!

Send a card about Dolly, please.

Affly.

J.

ANERLEY
Monday. Nov: 1926

DEAR JACK

My pen has been twitching and so I must write to you.

Two days ago I was as near to you as Souldern and Oxford. I spent two nights with Percy Withers, whom I had promised for eighteen months, and four hours with Joy. She was very well, and soberly happy, finding Oxford mortal cold and herself mortal busy. She has a room in Old Hall, a pleasant-looking red brick edifice of a better time than ours for domestic architecture.—Withers was better than for some time past, thanks to rigid diet and a balance of insulin and exercise, like a mouse in a cage with cheese all round him. He shewed me Wilfrid's collected poems, and had seen Wilfrid at his new Letchworth house. The house is new, the poems are old, but which will last longer the gods only know. Like the house, the poems are "replete" with modern conveniences, the plumbing is excellent (tho' leaving still the smell of scarce-finished b. h. & c.), and I hope that, like the poems, the house is built of decent brick and seasoned timbers. Ten years hence the house and the neighbours may furnish a back addition to the poems. The house has a name on the gate, the poems have a portrait of the house-owner. Macmillan have issued the book in the same style as Tennyson and Arnold and other Great Departed, and Heal's have furnished the house with carpets and curtains like those of *When We were Very Young*.

Turn from things to men! On Saturday I saw the Samuel Palmer exhibition at Kensington—things Blake-like and post-Blake and nearly always lovely and satisfying—and then to E. S.'s to say good-bye to Osbert and talk of S.'s book to its author, and receive *Elegy of Dead Fashion* from herself.

.   .   .   .   .   .

Solomon and Balkis comes on the 16th. I've so far forgotten it that I've started versing again, a few lyrics. Martin has just shewn me his new poem on *Sherry*, a subject he has no right to. I could read him on *Claret* with equanimity, on *Whiskey* with indifference, on *White Wines* with pity; but on *Sherry*, I read him with envy, hate and malice.

Fletcher, with his wife and step-daughter, are in America, Conrad is starting his return hither, and Bergen comes (I expect) at the Year's end. You, I suppose, will never come again: to see you is as great an adventure as India and the

Basilisk was to Alexander. Do you ask who is the Basilisk? I cannot tell, I cannot turn simplicity into a Parable. I only know that you are a very long way off and that unless I come to you one week-end, on the pretext of calling at Oxford, I shall grow old and mossy and a babbler and never hear honest laughter again. God forgive you!

This is a foolish letter, but what would you? Napoleon used to play marbles between his battles. My love to you all.

Affly.

J. F.

ANERLEY
26th. Dec: 1926

DEAR JACK

Thanks for your letter, which was like Manna to Jew. God will bless you for your kindness to the honest poor. Perhaps he has already blessed you with a powerful and seasonable appetite. Just now I got into trouble for telling Gertrude that I'd written to Martin (my only other correspondent at this wan time) saying that we had indulged in the pleasures of the flesh on Christmas Day; the *we* being of course a modest evasion of *I*. So to you I will say that we kept Christmas with decent and sparing appetites, not weighing our portions but pardoning our senses. You, I take it, tippled, O brave spirit.

Joy is at home, tired out but excited. Between whiles I have pursued Aldous Huxley, resolving him into his original elements—a pennoth of Keats, a ton of Wilde, a mountain of Proust, and so on. Luckily he can write, of himself, of his own power, I mean out of his own mind; and this, with a flavouring of scientific words which mean nothing precise to me but make a vague impression, makes him agreeable as a writer of travels. His latest book, *Jesting Pilate*, is very good. I saw Conrad several times last week. There's a danger of his returning to America for a long stay, to take up a job, or to review worthless books in bright and worthless papers. I shall be sorry enough. He's written a novel of which he promised to send me the transcript. No one, as yet, will publish it, because he won't give it away. I believe it's intensely and utterly modern—I'm afraid a little Joyceyfied. I hate Joyce (in Ulysses) and I'm afraid he's a bad influence. Conrad is so easily psychological and does indeed know a good deal of psychology. Why, Martin's letter this morning (he's been Christmasing at Rye) speaks of a fixation—which I take it is a kind of apoplexy, unless it's mere obstinacy of mind. Well, Conrad may go to America and become a fixation there, but I hope still for a certain fluidity in his movements.

I had many things to tell you but have forgotten them all. I ought to stop, then, but a relation has just come in whose conversation I do not delight—one never does delight in the relations of one's wives, which is a powerful argument against polygamy—and so under pretext of writing to you in the utmost urgency ("I'm writing to my solicitor") I can pursue my own thoughts and wear away the time.

I hope I shall see you soon in the New Year, but send me a photograph in case I don't. If you've grown a beard please erase it from the negative so that I may still recognise you, and then send me another with the beard. You see, I'm not sure whether it was your whiskers or your kitchen that was burned out lately. If you were able to claim on your Policy, I hope it was your kitchen, unless you are insured for what is called Personal Accident. I suppose there's no insurance against Universal Accident?

Now we go out to lunch. Good-bye and the happiest of all new years, for you and your wife and Robin and all.

Affly.

F.

ANERLEY
Feb: 1927

MY DEAR JACK

It would be a good deal nicer to listen to you, standing
with your back to the hotel fire, and pouring out nonsensical
opinions over my docile head, but since this can't be I won't
waste time in lamenting, for it is impossible to enjoy your
fire and at the same time this fog. The fog can't have got to
Sidmouth, in fact it can't have left Anerley, though for a few
hours to-day we had sunshine and a soft warmth on the ice
of the garden pond. Sun is better than fog and Devon is
better than Anerley, or at least the Devon villages are better
than the slopes of the Crystal Palace Hill and the only Vale
hereabout, Anerley Vale, which is a slum. But as I was saying
—what was I saying? It was a false start. I think you were
speaking of the weather and ordinarily the weather doesn't
depress me, but the lack of sun starves me and I long for
clear light or light between clouds. And I hate a black February, for it should be a month of promise, the first promise
of the year. A week ago, when I heard the lark above fields
which still sparkled here and there with snow, it seemed that
another Spring had indeed come and I felt a sudden gush of
joy, as though I could kiss someone, or bury my face in the
snowed on dead bracken. But this week has given the lie to
that moment. In Devon you may be luckier, and under the
shelter of deep lanes, where the sun fingers the same spots
morning by morning, you may find heavenly things, un-
dreamed of here.

I am told, and I've told Squire so that he may ask for it
for the *Mercury*, that Bridges has "privately" printed the
first part of a long philosophical poem. I'd like to see it, even
though I may not understand it. Doughty wrote a long
"philosophical" poem in *Mansoul* and gave the last eight
years of his life to the questions he faced there; and what is

the "philosophy"? No more than the simplest dogma, *Thou shalt love the Lord thy God* and so on. If that is Bridges' philosophy I can understand it, and read the poem for its poetry; but if it's more than this it may be less than poetry. Joy says that she was lately arguing—in a paper opposed to her tutor—that the subject of the *Prelude* wasn't a poetic subject, and I tried to shew her she was wrong; surprisingly she agreed with me in the end. The *Prelude* is *essentially* pure poetry, but though philosophical it is not *essentially* pure philosophy—or rather it is pure philosophy and not philosophy sophisticated by philosophers. The philosophy is like our gas poker: you take a heavy gas-pipe, pricked with holes and extended by a flexible tube to the main, thrust it into a black coaly grate, turn the tap, apply a spark, and the gas poker lights up the whole grate until the reluctant coal bursts into its own flame. Philosophy is Derby Brights—and nearly as dear, especially in the Cambridge Press books. Returning to Bridges, then, I hope the philosophy is subdued to the poetry, or rather that the poetry is so quick and energetic that it burns the whole grate.

As a matter of fact, we don't read any poets for their philosophy. Even total abstainers, I suppose, admire Omar Khayyam and even philosophers don't read Browning. *Modern Love* has more admirers than *The Day of the Daughter of Hades* and *Poems and Ballads* than *The Altars of Righteousness*, and *The Scholar Gipsy* than *Oberman*.

Years may bring us indigestion but not the philosophic mind, and we find pleasure in *The Trampwoman's Tragedy* more than in the portentously "thoughtful" poems which commentators love to get their teeth in. But to say this is to talk like Gosse, and I was angry with him this morning when, turning the pages of one of his collections of articles, I saw (what I had mercifully forgotten) that he sneers at *Mansoul*

for its style—its style, Jack, I prayed the Recording Angel
to take a note of this, and reminded him that Gosse was
getting very old and wouldn't be long now. I'd like to see
Gosse trying to talk to Doughty in a better world, trying
to ingratiate himself because he sees at last that they are
making more of Doughty than of almost anybody else.
Gosse will look round for Tennyson and find Doughty
where he thought Tennyson must be: he'll look for Donne
and Gray and everybody else he's edited or written about
so badly, and they'll all cut him—Donne forgetting for the
moment that he was once a Dean and Gray forgetting he was
always an intellectual aristocrat; and Gosse will shiver and
look round for some forgotten Norwegian poet sitting on a
block of ice by the soda fountain.

.   .   .   .   .   .

But there's nothing so incredible as that you have asked
me to come to Sidmouth, and I've stayed away. Send me a
line, nevertheless and say that you're minus influenza and
bronchitis and that your domestic troubles are going like the
fog—but not to return.

Affly.

J. F.

ANERLEY
Spring 1927

DEAR JACK

I'm sorry at your news, sorry first of course for myself,
next that you can't be content with pure 'flu but must needs
follow it with bronchitis, as pain follows sin, and next, again,
that your household is disordered in consequence and your
wife tired out. Look after Mrs. Haines, Jack. Wives are
irreplaceable. Never does convention steal so blessedly upon
the mind, arrayed so fairly, beaming so medicinally, as when
one is ill and fifty. At thirty, and well, nothing seems less

alluring and it's a fine thing to fling a pot of paint at the head of Convention and cry Take that, Madame, and make yourself passable with it: paint, Madame, paint! But at fifty it's another story, for her young rivals are off with somebody else, the scales have fallen from your eyes and you see Convention like a Madonna in the Van Eyck I was looking at to-day—ethereal, flushed and like a throbbing star.

But I'll not preach, I'll only wish you well and that you'll let me come one week-end soon: even that you'll be drawn to town on a scandalous divorce case and tell us all about it.

I've not gone to Wilfrid's. He wired to say that they also had 'flu, and then Joy wrote that L.M.H. is like a fortress holding out against 'flu, noisy with garglings, drenched with antiseptics. They drink chlorodyne, smoke acetylene cigarettes and chew Wrigley's Special Strychnine. So I've stayed at home, looked at the snow, and taken Gertrude up to the Flemish pictures; and now, in the ease of perfect contentment and the steady warmth of the fire, I shut my Trollope and write to you.

I shut my Trollope, I say, having also shut Sadleir's book about him: Jack, never think yourself a prose writer, or if you are tempted, read Sadleir's prose and be saved. If some men talk prose without knowing it, others fail to speak prose without knowing it. He's written a speculative biography with a speculative pen: he wanders among the facts and loses his wits, as he wanders among words and loses his way. Sterne, you remember, wrote the first sentence and trusted to God for the rest; but Sadleir is an atheist. He has dragged together a lot of facts and tried to assemble a body, but he hasn't the ghost of a notion of physiology, and does not know where the head should come, nor where the belly. Happily—and I praise his forbearance—he hasn't concentrated himself upon a single organ of Trollope's person:

there's hardly anything about sex. God be praised! But it's a relief to turn to Trollope himself and re-read *Barchester Towers*, not weighing its defects but rejoicing in its virtues. And Trollope himself, has been a relief from the Labours of Composition, for I've just finished a *Mercury* on *H. M. Tomlinson* and will shortly return all your books safe and sound. I like the Labours of Composition. When I can't write verse it's good to feel I can still write prose, and of course a *Mercury* is practice for a letter to you.

But I didn't mean to write of Literature: I'm not Stevenson. I meant to write gossip: of Meyerstein and a charming sonnet of his in Moult's new Anthology. He has just lost an Aunt, and is half grieved at the loss and half amused at the funeral: happily it has produced a new suit, and he looks distinguished and a little fat. Robin has had 'flu, Armstrong hasn't and Conrad Aiken has gone to America again. Only last night Gertrude was depressing me with a list of friends I never see now—some dead, some parted by wind and wave. I accuse myself of these losses, though perhaps without serious cause—I can't keep people in England when they prefer Japan or Boston. Never go to Japan, Jack: it's only an ugly gimcrack place, all volcanos and bamboo hatstands. I hate bamboo, and Japanese novels, and cunning Japanese faces. Nor Boston, neither: don't go to Boston, U.S.A., where people pour chests of tea into the water, and pretend that the older houses are English houses and the older families are English families.

I must stop. I am asked when I am going to bed. Why don't I answer, Just when I like? I can't say that: I'll end this and post it and go to bed and dream of you and Gloucester, of fire and flood and the seat-flaying geyser, and you in bed reading endlessly Jane Austen.

Send a card to say all is well again.

J. F.

ANERLEY
10th. May, 1927

DEAR JACK

I'm in despair. Gertrude borrowed my fountain pen yesterday to write her letter, and didn't return it, or I didn't pick it up when she said—if she said—"Here it is!" I am like a whale on dry land, puffing and blowing, very irritable, very miserable, and the cause of the misery which is in others. Find it, Jack, for the sake of all I hold dear and send it back. Or 'phone me and I'll send a District Messenger to fetch it, as a thing peculiar and precious.

It is my pen, my friend, my ass, my meat and drink, my charm against poverty, death and disgrace. Lacking it I can use no other: I cannot write, I cannot spell, appetite fails me. Other pen I have none and to beg I am ashamed. I cannot borrow, I will not. Borrow! I abhor promiscuity, and of all things promiscuous I abhor the pen.—My pen! It has written *Solomon* and *Absalom* and a hundred lyrics: it is more *me* than I am, and without it I am not myself. It is a noble, sable, elegiac pen: an English pen, never descending to use foreign phrases, never permitting me to fall into the clichés (plague on *that* word—you see what the absence of my pen has done) of my contemporaries. A noble, a magical pen. Hold it in your hand, remove the cap—the crown I should say— place it at your ear and listen!

"And it remembers its august abode",

murmuring of rhyme and verse and woods and hills, and above all the beating of the kindly heart which it protects even while it interprets. Its echoes are august or intimately tender, or spare and thin—but always mine. It has written cheques, letters, lies, flatteries, truths, loves, regrets—these galore: it is not an apologetic pen nor a mean pen, nor a powerful pen, nor a boastful pen. *You* know what sort of pen it is surely. Doesn't your hand quiver strangely as you near it? Thou shalt not covet thy guest's pen. That pen is the only black thing about me: it is the "point of rest" in my art.

Send it back even for Gertrude's sake. She feels humiliated —she's never failed me so before. If it comes at once I can forgive her. For a day and a night I can endure my penlessness and she can sustain my reproaches; but longer—who knows the limits of endurance. I feel pensive at best, dependent at worst; soon desperation and pengrance will follow— see the corruption of an innocent heart already: that I, the most austere, should be reduced to this villainous penning.

Pity me—and Gertrude.

J.

ANERLEY
25th. October, 1927

DEAR JACK

You are a dear to give me two letters for my one or none, and in them the story of Washburnia. I should have liked to have been with you, in your startled approach to this fulfilment of legend. Truly did the prophet say that the old men shall dream dreams, but to *see* them in realization is given to few besides prophets.

I can give you no news to equal yours. Our house is gradually assuming a civil aspect, to be undisturbed for three years or the duration, and gradually, too, our minds are moving about in worlds once realized and long confused. The change in my fortunes (I forgot this was "news") duly occurred and is now of infinite distance and as yet imperceptible benefit: twelve months hence I shall have an egg to my breakfast at least twice a week and never have my hats cleaned more than once. I don't like being rash but I've already disposed of some very old clothes, while yesterday, in a frenzy of extravagance, we went to the "pictures" a-purpose to see a film which had moved Eddie—*Metropolis*.

I'm glad we went, for we are cured of extravagance.—Not that it was very expensive, but the change of fortune isn't so marked that we can disregard sixpences, as yet.—I've bought Norman Ault's exhaustive Anthology of lyrical poetry to the 16th century, but as yet haven't read it through as I like to.

And I've acquired also, by the author's gift, O. Sitwell's *England Reclaimed* a series of truly delicious Eclogues. I'm lunching with him to-morrow and shall talk of Eclogues and bucolic matters and a yoke of bullocks and so on. But to-day was *the* day, for early this morning I went up to our nearest hills, through woodlands of wet fire, and saw and heard autumnal miracles; and these I have enshrined in verse which, if I have time to make a copy, I will send you with this. And this is a reminder that you shewed me some verse of my own which I've not printed, beginning "How are those berries lovely in" I forget the rest and I will say *Thanks!* if you'll send me a copy of the twelve lines. I think they were mine, and very pleasant.

> They might be done by Donne—
>   Can they be mine?
> Or Alfred Tennyson:
>   Yet are they fine.
> Keats might—and might not—
>   Have written as well then,
> And Shelley now write not
>   Songs to excel them;
> Even august Landor
>   Be proud to own them,
> Though his sly candour
>   Has ne'er yet shown them.
> Let mystery end now
>   At my petition:
> The verses send now
>   For the new Edition. . . .

I mean for the new edition which my agent is asking Macmillan to endure; to contain *Poems New and Old* and all my short poems *since The Grove*.

I have it on my conscience to do a *Mercury* on A. But mum's the word—I would, and would not, being perplexed, after many years, by a strangely feminine quality of mind which appears in some of his work. *Must* one tell the truth, or keep silence altogether? I thought I had mastered every evasion, tangled every question, confused every quality, in these articles, to my own satisfaction and the readers' astonishment: but what am I to do about a touch of the feminine in one I'm so fond of? Assist me, oh professional prevaricator: assist me so subtly that I shan't even know that I'm prevaricating and Satan himself shall stand confounded at the legal serpentining.

Ever

J.

ANERLEY
13th. Nov: 1927

DEAR JACK

Thank you for the copy of my verses: I want to include them if the new edition can be done. It is on the knees of Macmillans: I picture them, solemn and gray-headed, sitting in a row with my *Poems New, Newer and Old* on their vast aguish knees, like a row of Ebrew prophets but kinder. As a very young man, very young indeed, I had a similar notion of Ibid as a prophet, Ibid of mysterious footnotes, as solemn as Macmillan but white-bearded not gray: infinitely wise, infinitely dull.

And I return your own poem with thanks. I like it, and wish you had troubled—a little trouble would have been enough—to make it better.

About the E. T. letters. I have a number of them, 1914–1917, hardly any earlier than 1914. I doubt if they are of general interest; they are mainly upon purely literary subjects, including my own poetry, and I don't think they are particularly good or self-expressive. And where they are self-expressive they are inevitably melancholy. But I would not therefore refrain from publishing them, but I should rather like to make it a condition—if you would agree—that *you* should be sole or at least joint editor. . . .

Injudiciously chosen, the letters might only give the impression of a melancholy and thwarted aesthete, or a man humiliated by failure. If his entire available letters are to be published, they can, and must, make their own impression; but if they are to be selected, I fancy some care is needed to choose fairly. Your collection of E. T. letters, I imagine, would be among the best: my collection of *your* letters will be superb, and so I hope you will live to 90 and that I shall publish them all as soon as you are a corpse.—But let me know what you think about editing E. T.'s, for that is a real problem. Would you object to my proposed condition?

I was in Oxford on Thursday, with Gertrude, and saw Joy, who insisted on lunching again where you had taken her. She is infatuated with Gordon's lectures, and still perplexed with her own essays. Her tutor still insists upon her producing a really good essay, and still insists that she hasn't done so; and the poor infant is in despair, tinged with mirth.

I wish you were coming up: I'd like to have you here a night or two. How can I write when I want to talk?

All my love.

J.

ANERLEY
Sunday. January, 1928

DEAR JACK

A happy new year to you, of course. *Did* I thank you for Harvey's poems? I've written so many letters that I'm sure I must have written to you, and yet I'm sure I shouldn't

R

write to you in the midst of mere "thank you's". I am glad
to have the book, but wish Harvey didn't write jocose
poems. There are some "light" poems which I enjoy, but
jocosity vexes me. I'm in the mood to be vexed, and a letter
is my escape. At lunch to-day Gertrude asked me, "Will
you have gooseberry fool or marmalade tart?" knowing that
I love marmalade tart. I said, "Marmalade tart of course!"
but she answered, "You must have gooseberry fool!" and so
saying served me so. It wasn't so much the loss of the tart,
or even the personal indignity, though I know you have
sympathy in both; it was the deadly reminder of the ways
of Fate, that's always tempting you to choose but giving
you no choice. Most of us choose, and most of us know that
we haven't a choice but think we choose what we have; only
the sadly elect, you and I, are aware that we are mocked and
forbear to acknowledge it or give Fate the pleasure of seeing us
wince. Only, on Sunday, at lunch, with family peace around
and a turkey within, so sharp a reminder—'tis too much.

Enough of lamentations!—last week-end we all spent at
Brighton, but I was lamed with a bad foot and teased with
fomentations, as well as bothered with a cough and kept
awake at night by a wind which made me frightened. But
I'm better of one complaint, if complaint is the word for my
seraphic temper, but still frightened at the weather: indeed,
on my way home I was thinking of floods, and Dorothy's
predicament two years ago, and wondering how she and you
were braving the waters now.

On Friday I'm going to Liverpool University to lecture
on the Difference between Prose and Poetry: I wish I could
see you on my way back, but Fate again forbids. A week
later I take the chair for Edith Sitwell at an English Association meeting, where she will be "defending" modernist
poets: as chairman, I suppose, I shall be unassailable. And
lastly, Macmillans will bring out *Selected Poems* in the late

spring. J. C. S. has made the choice with me, and I'm trying to get a drawing by Laura Knight.

And that's all my news. I'm ashamed to condescend to "news" in a letter to you, but since I'm condescending I may as well tell you that my last news of de la Mare was that he was better and had dismissed the nurse; also, Abercrombie has been (may be still is) in a nursing home and is getting better.

I wish you were coming here, even for a single night, but I've wished it so often that it's become a kind of dull, habitual prayer which one says over as a rite, in childish fashion. It would be strange if the prayer were answered, and you found yourself unreasonably and protestingly drawn hither by a compulsion you could neither understand nor resist.

All my Love.
                          Affly.
                                              J.

                                         ANERLEY
                                  Sunday. June 1928

DEAR JACK

The Sabbath, seven o'clock, a brief interval between talk and listening: Hucclecote, a brief interval, a sleep and a vision between a drink and a drink. Dolly has gone to Cheltenham for Robin, you wait, glass at side, looking at the last poems you've bought and thinking of me. It's only three weeks since I left you, and I've been to Scotland, and half through England again; and now, returned and satiate, my first thought is not of wife and children but of you.

When I came back on Friday almost my first duty was to take Robin—not your Robin, my Robin—to the annual dinner of the English Association. It was a good dinner, as big dinners go, only marred by the fact that Robin had turned teetotaler, or queasy in his stomach, and couldn't *clever*

drink. He remained sober while Newbolt delivered sober, polished sentences about the guests, and his contemporaries at Oxford, and the mission of English; he was still sober when Lord Sumner, avowing his ignorance of all tongues but his own, avowed also its supremacy, I madly cheering him from my table and Mr. and Mrs. G. S. looking on superciliously, as who should say, What about the poets of Czecho-Slovakia? But Robin was roused to a fury past that of alcohol when B. rolled in his seat, rose, and praised Sir Henry Newbolt, for whose sake, it seemed, and for whose sole use the English language had been perfected. He declared that the Lyric was the greatest achievement of our race, and I preened my feathers and began to listen; and Robin also purred. But when he said that Newbolt was the greatest living master of lyric, and quoted phrases to prove it, we gasped, fidgetted, scowled, puffed, and then sat in the silence of extreme dejection. I'd never seen or heard B. before, and couldn't be pleased at this heavy rolling figure rolling out his solemn extravagances in a way which the author of certain essays and epitaphs should never, never simulate.—Don't go to dinners, Jack, unless you are a speaker yourself; and if you are a speaker, let your extravagances be plausible, not impossible. And use not vain repetition as the heathen do, nor confuse your mind and your hearers with things incredible; but let your yea be indeed yea and your nay be not neigh; and bray not against the truth because you were at Oxford with Sir Claude Chump, but rather keep silence about his chumpiness, or if silence be difficult, smile at him so that he may not see the smile and yet no one else beside shall miss it. There is kindness as well as truth in the right smile, and an ironic dissimulation is pleasing in the sight of the Angels. Do not say, By God, ladies and gentlemen, Sir Claude Chump is the finest living poet; for all the rest of the poets will treat you opprobriously for that. But say, with happy ambiguity, No one present to-night will question the place of Sir Claude etc. etc. And having said it you may, during ironic applause, drink yourself into a nicer subtlety when you speak of the Chump influence on English poetry.

I've been away so much that I've no news for you. I've been invited to contribute to an American anthology of Revolutionary poetry, and to the funds of the "Rebels"—the name is their own choice—whose triumph is, it seems, delayed only by want of pence. I am contributing nothing. And I've had a letter from Will Monroe, ex-professor of psychology, concerning Hewlett and Melville and American poetry. He lives at *Couching Lion Farm*, and sends me a photograph of himself, the farm, and his dog Scottie. I am going to send him a photograph of Drinkwater (as *me*), this house and the two cats. He denounces the Oxford book of American verse, which I think I saw on your shelves, and left there.

Dear Jack, I meant to write a long letter, but I doubt if you'd read it. I'm sleepy, warm, lazy—it is late, so I'll close this unfinished Letter with love.   Yours

                                                                  J. F.

                                                      ANERLEY
                                                      Oct: 1928

DEAR JACK

Since your letter came a fortnight or so ago I have seen Frost often, and on Tuesday he and Mrs. Frost spent the night here, meeting Robin and the Ingpens and charming them all. Mrs. Frost isn't too well, but yesterday she was able to go down in the car and see Davies. Frost found him delightful, ready to take up the conversation just as it had been dropped in 1915, to present him with a new book, duly signed and beamed over, and then to remark that he didn't know if Frost cared for poetry. He's lunching with me and Squire to-morrow. Also, he's met Ellis again, and Ellis, admitting that he wasn't greatly attracted years ago, now says that he is. He took Frost round to his new flat in Charlotte Street, not emphasising the obvious rhyme to the Street, and showed him the kingdoms of the World in all their glory. ITEM: a high secondhand desk, at which Ellis can stand and write his name immortal, if he wants to. ITEM: a large Gong, nearly filling one room in the flat, so that he may summon himself to breakfast. (I couldn't summon myself *from* it, for Ellis's present diet is mainly onions, of a peculiarly affectionate and lingering attachment). ITEM: a set of fire-arms, tongs and the like, also secondhand, made out of swords. Ellis is amusing and happy, I think, but gets bored with M. because he will only talk of himself; while M. gets impatient with Ellis because he is so lazy, and so contemptuous of his Native Land—like every frequenter of the Latin Quarter.

Did I tell you a story? On our way back from Lyme Regis, of blessed memory, Gertrude was taking her way from an hotel at Romsey, with Cathy and a neice who was driving the car. (How do you spell neice? I like my way, but think it is probably wrong; but happily, in Heaven there shall be neither marrying nor giving in marriage, and thereby nor nephews nor neices). She fell and she cut her face and mouth and hand and knees so badly on the loose gravel that a doctor had to wrap her in sticking plaster and baste her with ill-smelling unguents. A week later my sister and her husband, a parson, called on Sunday, not knowing of her state. Before they entered I warned them to take no notice of the horrid Object: she was patched: we had a difference—and she would not like any reference to be made, and so on.

THEY TOOK NO NOTICE. Gertrude was surprised, but *she* took no notice, and they took a hasty leave. And now

Gertrude is annoyed because (a) they believe me, (b) they must have seen I wasn't hurt at all and (c) therefore must have assumed that she wasn't a match for me.

I will never joke again.

There's no more news. I can't write, I can hardly read. I've to give an address at the Elian on Goldsmith, and have nothing to say. I am one who never turned his back—hence, Pity me.

Affly.

JOHN

ENGLAND
Fine Sunday in October
[October 16, 1928]

DEAR JACK

I'm sorry you have bronchitis. I never knew a man so prone to the superfluous. While it is still summertime for me and my Aunts, you lie tumbling in the sheets. A rook squawks as you bark; your uneasy motion is overmatched by the starlings round your Cathedral and over Trafalgar Square. While you cursed the world this morning after breakfast, we were on Hayes Common, there to praise God from Whom all blessings flow. The sun was out and all the colours of the Orient and Occident; the air was cool and sweet, the berries brighter than wine. The car was drawn up by the road as Gertrude and I sauntered over the turf, and seemed the only unreal thing in a world all real, as we sauntered reluctantly back to it. Cathy had gone out before breakfast, and we didn't meet her as we did last week. Stay— did I tell you that Cathy had a baby—Austin? I hope you didn't misunderstand me. She isn't modern and England isn't America. She has a little brisk, bouncing, bumble-bee-sounding saloon of her own, second-hand but first class. She uses it to drive to her coach of afternoons, and indeed it is needed to drive her to her coach. She drives excellently,

Gertrude safely but less dashingly, I not at all. This afternoon Cathy will meet Blunden at the station and bring him
here for the evening. I had a pleasant time listening to him
on Tuesday, after he had listened or tried not to listen to me
on Goldsmith at the Elian. Last Sunday the Frosts were
here and Kerr came too. He was extravagantly talkative,
and, seeing him off at the gate for the last train, Frost went
to some pains to reassure him that there was "no offence".
Next morning Frost regretted that he'd argued with Kerr;
he avoids arguing and felt that the austerity of his pure self-
possession had suffered. They didn't hit it off too well,
especially when the Papist Kerr (why must he call himself a
Papist?) averred that the Anglo-Catholic Eliot was too great
a poet to be questioned: you must accept him humbly,
reverentially, in the same way, apparently, as Kerr himself
accepts Dante. He drew the usual parallel between Eliot and
Coleridge, to prove that the Waste Lands is as great as The
Ancient Mariner. How? Why, Coleridge was laughed at in
his own day (universally? Ah, never mind that), and Eliot
is laughed at now; hence—! You know, Jack, I have no
logic, but I suspect that there is a little flaw in the deduction.

Nevertheless, we had a delightful afternoon, with many
people, and a heated evening with these few.

Sassoon? I've not read his new verses, because I've never
cared much for the old. But I'm reading his Fox Hunting
prose book, with pleasure. Strange that Proust should ride
to hounds. I know the comparison with Proust is now—
what do you call it, otiose; but it is unavoidable, as it was
with S. Sitwell's recollections. S. told me, when I said this,
that he'd not looked at Proust for years, and of course I
accepted this as final: no one would dream that Proust's
manner could retain its influence more than six months. In
Sassoon's book it isn't so conspicuous, but it can be smelt.
There is some nice writing, and an air of pleasant modesty;

but is this nice writing?—"Aquamarine and celestial were the shoals of sunset as I hacked pensively home from Dumbridge." And the next paragraph begins with the same sort of phrasing: "Absolved and acquiescent was the twilight". What is the meaning of an absolved twilight, and in what is that kind of twilight acquiescent? Don't let me quibble, Jack, but show me that I'm wrong.

There's no more to say. I've bought Hardy's last poems, but hardly looked at them as yet. I've got Wilfrid's two books to review. I ought to have written before but I was away when your poor letter came. I was in Nottingham, and Gertrude met me with it at Oxford, whither she had taken Joy for the sad beginning of her last year. I typewrite this so that you may read it easily. I can write it just as easily as with a fountain pen. . . . If you like I can write it JUST AS EASILY IN CAPITALS, THOUGH YOU MAY THINK THIS BOASTFUL. $948;\frac{1}{4}8\frac{1}{2}743\pounds,2\frac{3}{4}8?\frac{3}{4}$ $28=?345@8:=6$ $\frac{1}{2}8'3$ 697 @ : 3 $94''85@:5$:9589: of my cleverness. But enough. I wish you well, and that you will write to me again to say that you're well.

Affly.

J.

ANERLEY
Cold Monday in December

MY DEAR, MY VERY DEAR JACK

—Pig that I am and unworthy of uttering endearments, for I've not written to you for ages and ages uncounted. Nor to any, dear or less dear. Had I the habit of speculation, I might have written to tempt a letter from you, but I know that your letters are as sudden and capricious as the seasons; and so I only write when I cannot *but* write and am not too tired to hold a pen towards Gloster. I have been tired, tired though well: my brain is dried and—like my best shoes (now at the cobbler's)—has a hole in the centre; I am so full of infirmities, in mind, body and estate, that I should be an object of respect and pity: no, reverence and pity, such as was bestowed upon the mediaeval idiot. By day I suffer a lethargy, by night hallucinations beset me; the waters go over my head but can never put out the fire that gnaws my bowels. My eyes squint, my mood unsettles, my ears are heavy, I reel to and fro like a drunken man but am not drunk. I cannot think, I cannot talk; music makes me weep, laughter makes me mad. And I can't write.

But I won't ask for sympathy. You, surrounded by your wife, over-arched by Robin, enclouded by the fumes of claret and tobacco, are impervious to pity and have no scales for my tears. Yet I may be mistaken: misfortunes may be yours. I fancy you in the recurrent pangs of an indigestion, and lying down with an insomnia. Your doctor, yes your own cunning brother, has forbidden you liquor and ordered you to walk daily to Gloster and back. You are dieted, and now smoke is bringing on your bronchitis and so you may not smoke. But Dolly smokes under your nose and all over you, like Belial, and drinks your large whiskey at night under your enraged eyes. You see visions, but not of pleasantness. You give to Missions, but find no ease; you have been to church but come away uncomforted. You hear of men who have suffered like you for years, and no relief. Your office worries you, clients come not, marry not, die not. Once the death of others was in truth meat and drink to you; now the deaths that might have gladdened your professional eye make the eye of a rival happy. Your silk hat accumulates dust, your tails deepen their summer creases; the income tax authorities become more authoritative, and will not believe your returns.—I pity you, though you have no feeling for me!

But let us not recriminate. In a few years Mussolini and Alfred Noyes will be dead, Masefield forgotten, and I only left. You will begin to grow bald, I to grow staid. You will fatten, I shall stoop. Vice and prosperity will abound in you, misfortunes will strike me in vain, yet still strike. Christmases will come and go, the waits will huddle round your door, the postman will bring you letters and you will say, I *must* write to John! and still you will be round and happy, quite as round and nearly as happy as I wish you. And for the sake of the humble wishes forgive the nonsense, remembering that while many a true word may be spoken in jest it needs the very deuce to smell out true from false.

All my love to you all.

JOHN

TRUNCH, NORFOLK
Sunday night awaiting another storm
July 21st, 1929

MY DEAR JACK

From the best you've turned the worst of correspondents, bar one, and if I've been more remiss I will tell you why.—I've been away so much this summer on tedious business, the last time being for a fortnight in Scotland. Cathy drove us all up to Edinburgh, and then I left the others and was taken round the uttermost parts of the North, into every place where people have had the habit of birth and death. I ate at Taymouth Castle (now sunken to this poor service), I mourned over the sad lonely stones of Culloden, infinitely reproachful, I slept in the sound of Scots rivers, came back to Glasgow and home to London—with 'flu! 'Flu's a beastly thing in summer, Jack. I seldom get a temperature, but I showed a temperature this time of about 2000; with my usual alacrity, I shed the fever at once, but who can shed the weakness of 'flu at a word? Virtue has gone out of me, gloom has come in. I have powers of locomotion, but they are poor; in this strong eastern air I sleep, but never enough and hardly better, perhaps than at home.—

You've had 'flu, but for heaven's sake don't get it in the summer; get it in the winter, when you can't stay out, not in this tropic weather when you can't stay in.

Well, we came here last Monday for a month, and the Ingpens join us to-morrow. It's a sad village. Decay has touched it incessantly for generations, and this comely farmhouse has not been spared. The melancholy of deciduous houses, shedding their strength year after year, tries one's nerves. Fine old cottages are vacant and rotting, and jerry has put up others. There's a drought, and the landlord won't spend a penny to repair a pump in a cottage a little way off. The flower-garden here is delightful, the fruit-garden is a disgrace, perfectly neglected. One is tempted to judge the people hastily and say they are dull and indifferent: all their energies went in building a considerable church centuries ago, and sustaining two large pubs ever since.—While I am here I may try to see Mottram, and we shall all re-visit the Broads, several miles away. I've not heard from Armstrong lately but am "expecting". Robin was asked, and declined, to apply for the Welsh National Librarianship at Aberystwyth—a good but too official job. He will, I believe, become Deputy Keeper of the Dept. of MSS. shortly. Meyerstein is back from another sojourn in the slums of Redcliffe, and still moans over his Chatterton—and fate, poor fellow! And Joy has just had her result from Oxford—which doesn't excite anyone with special gratification.

I've been reading the new Lady Byron book. I think I'm glad to have read it, but it leaves a nasty taste in the mouth, and after this close contact with one of the Byrons, you want an emetic.—Nothing struck me as so caddish—though it was legal—as when he retained the money (£20,000 I think) which came to him under the marriage settlement after the separation—it was when Lady Milbank died. Isn't it incredibly shabby?

I don't know when I shall see you, unless you are coming up to town, when you will be joyfully received. But write to me as soon as you find time and a mind to write. I've missed your letters. I don't know, but they might have averted this 'flu; and even now, a post-card might diminish the twinges across my shoulders, a letter even the stiffness of my calves, and a joke would explode the ambient flatulence and enable me to see things simply and happily.

My love to your wife and Robin.

Affly.

JOHN

ANERLEY
10th. August, 1929

DEAR JACK

You are a Saint and not a Sadducee, a Brick as well as a Botanist. A month ago I asked you to write to me at Trunch, for to cure my Ailment; you wrote, angelically as Goldsmith, and a week later my Ailment vanished. But last week, at midnight, it returned, and a Doctor from Cromer discovered it was a germ (name and lineage unknown) creating a new temperature. I managed to get home last evening, but Jack, I've never been so remorselessly examined, there and here, in all my life of examinations. A man's vitality is low at 2.30 A.M.—that's when I was most rigorously peered at, sounded, tapped, pressed, scratched, tickled and dazzled. I came out of it all myself, with the secret germ unidentified, and my organs warranted "as before". I'm afraid to boast, but I feel the Recording Angel will have a smaller terror for me now.

Well, I'm here for another week, and if my dentist can be got at he will take up the task before I resume perpendicularity. But I'm really very well, thank you, and when I say you I mean——

That when I got home yesterday I found a bundle of

letters that had been sent to Inverness, missed me there, had lain untouched a month, and then coolly handed over to the G.P.O. for return. And this in spite of the fact that the base swine had my address on their Register! Now one of the letters was yours, one of your best, telling me of Martin and H. M. (what the deuce has *he* got to do with people's affairs!) and Davies. And oddly, another was from Martin, which likewise removes a fear and a fret.

I don't see why you should despise Blackpool, but I do see why you should hate it. You won't be able to walk, because it's all sand, you won't be able to ride, except in your car, you won't be able to stop drinking (it really is a beastly place for drinking) and you won't be able to stop eating if you are as lucky in your hotel as I was on two brief visits in 1927. I think I stayed at the Imperial Hydro (Hydro only means that there's running water in each room) and was very well and expensively fed in a Louis XVI room. The air will blow you off your feet, and I'm only wondering —not what you will do but what Mrs. Haines will do amid the seductions of cockles and whelks.

I won't write more. I hate writing in bed. Thousands, more fortunate, are rolling home in motor-coaches from Brighton, Margate, Southend: but I lie here. I can also smell their happy inebriation, but me may nothing inebriate. Others, fewer perhaps, are preparing for church, but I am compelled to lie here unhoused etc. Others are going court-ing and to be courted, but I, who have (like you) the common capacities, lie vexed and alone in this large bed. And why? Merely because a man I've known a quarter of a century and who has various letters after his name, says he is studying his conscience this time, and not mine, in keeping me abed.

Pity me, Jack,—but don't tell me so. One day I'd love to come and see you—and I will.

Affly.

J. F.

SIDNEY HODGSON

TO SIDNEY HODGSON

DEAR HODGSON

Thanks so much for your letter and your kindness in trying to get the Hazlitt at a price becoming Honest Poverty.

May Quarritch quake and quack in Quell and his last breath be quenched in Quire.

Do turn up again at lunch, but not on the same terms as before.   Ever sincerely

JOHN FREEMAN

ANERLEY
2nd. January [1928?]

DEAR HODGSON

So many thanks for this copy of the G. M. letters, which I read with the greatest pleasure. He was the same G. M. in the 80's and 90's as at the end of 1926, when he wrote to me saying that his aestheticism is more to him than his friend— the Incorruptible old man.

May you and your family have the happiest of New Years!   Ever yours

JOHN FREEMAN

EDWARD MARSH

TO EDWARD MARSH

DEAR MR. MARSH

Thank you for your letter. I shall be very glad to see the poems you mention in the next Georgian book. There will be no need for you to trouble about writing to the publisher (though I've told him) as the books are wholly my own. If I might make a suggestion, it would be that you should look at one or two of the poems which have appeared lately in the *Statesman* as I have the fancy that you might prefer them to some you've named. If you like I can show you those I mean—leaving the choice still wholly to your own judgment.

And do you mind my asking if you've thought of including poems by Edward Thomas ("Edward Eastaway")? It isn't modesty which says they're finer than mine. If you should take to the idea, from what you (probably) already know of them, I could mention the matter to his widow this weekend and then to his publisher.—I hope you won't think the suggestion officious.

Yours sincerely

JOHN FREEMAN

DEAR MR. MARSH

I am sending you some of the *New Statesman* poems, and one or two which Squire has in hand for his paper:—of course I'm anxious that you should have the opportunity of taking whatever would be best for the anthology.

I quite understand now the difficulty with regard to Edward Thomas's work. I didn't know before the principle which restricted your choice—perhaps it's unfortunate that fine work should be permanently excluded from representation. I've had the privilege of seeing probably the whole of his verse—both that which is about to come out this autumn, and that which hasn't yet been arranged for; and I only made the suggestion because so far as my own opinion might stretch or be worth anything, it would be splendid if the next Georgian book included any other new poetry of comparable individuality and power.

It will be very kind if you will return these cuttings etc. when you have looked at them.

Yours sincerely

JOHN FREEMAN

ANERLEY
1 August [1918?]

MY DEAR MARSH

Your letter was very welcome: some day we must talk over these things—say, when I've given you evidence that to throw over the brief lyric isn't suicide. Rather is it a withering than a rejection: leaves falling before the fruit comes. It seems to me that modern poetry must, if it live an hour, express personality and a view of the whole that's outside personality and time: must express them both and cannot indeed express them independently or singly; and so inevitably one tends to the longer (not always the very long) poem—the lyric prolonged into steady reflectiveness, the brook becoming a lake fed with unnoticed springs and holding at least the image of unsurveyed hills and moving clouds.—That isn't clear: one wants verse even for definition, but I won't bother you any more.

Here's a copy of the *Fortnightly* poem. Don't trouble to

write to Selwyn and Blount: I will see to them. And if I can better that flaw in *The Body* I will let you know at once.

It was nice of you to write such a long letter in answer to my restive one.

Ever

JOHN FREEMAN

ANERLEY
9th. Sept: 1918

DEAR MR. MARSH

—But I must thank you for your own liking of *The Body* and for sending on Abercrombie's card. It's praise indeed that has followed that little poem, but it makes one, oddly, the reverse of proud.

Sincerely yours

JOHN FREEMAN

ANERLEY
5th. July

MY DEAR MARSH

I don't intend to go on boring you with letters and extracting such kind compliments, but I want to say

1. That I was never farther than now from throwing over form, and please God never shall dream of doing so: that would be suicide indeed. Things I am doing now will show you that it is at least as great an urgency of form as of content that drives me to . . . well, longer *lyrics*. Content is the root—not fixed in a pretty crystal bowl but growing in the earth and sending up at length some flower which is neither form alone nor subject alone, but truly the *flower*—the poem.

2. I don't except even Donne from the obligation of form: nor does his work ask it.

3. I can't apologise for not agreeing with you about the two lines in *The Visit*. True the second line you quote may run into a different metrical shape, but I find it fits into a

shape which sixteen preceding lines have already clearly determined; and I fancy it has some value too—as sound supporting sense, by reason of a fractional retardation and then prolonging of the "knock".—I'm fairly certain about my rhythms, yet grateful for such close "sounding" of them.

Ever

JOHN FREEMAN

WILFRID MEYNELL
and
ALICE MEYNELL

TO MRS MEYNELL

ANERLEY
1908

MY DEAR MRS. MEYNELL

I read the other day your beautiful article in the 'Chronicle' upon the Brontë book, and was very glad indeed that you should have emphasized so justly the excellence of Charlotte Brontë's prose. It is such a rare excellence, and is, moreover, so seldom recognized, that an article such as yours, speaking with authority and enthusiasm, is as necessary as it is welcome.

What you say of her score of pages of noble prose prompts me to suggest that you should give us a little volume of English prose—something after the style of the "Flower of the Mind". I don't know a single satisfactory book of the sort, and it seems to me that the only way to make a good selection is to work solely on the austere "principle of beauty"—disregarding every lesser consideration. (The twenty pages of Charlotte Brontë's would themselves form the key-note)—But who else could do it?

Pray do not think this impertinent: no doubt you yourself have at some time or other had the same idea in mind. I am sure a companion volume to your verse anthology would be generally welcome.

I hope you and Mr. Meynell are quite well. In a week or two I expect to be able to send you (greatly bold) a little book of my own verse, if you will be so kind as to accept it.

Please give my kindest regards to your daughters and all I have met at Granville Place; and believe me, my dear Mrs. Meynell,   Yours very sincerely

JOHN FREEMAN

261

ANERLEY
19th. September, 1911

MY DEAR MRS. MEYNELL

I had thought of calling with this book, but I have had such sharp misgivings on its account that I decided to defer my visit until the little volume was in your hands. I remember that Francis Thompson's superb poems were dedicated to you, and I have—for more than one reason—a disturbing sense of presumption in doing the same. But since you have been so kind as to allow it, I dare not apologize for the book's small value. I only wish the poems were infinitely better, and so wishing, nevertheless beg you to accept them.

I was very glad to hear from Mr. Meynell last week that you were all well. If I might come and see you all I should be very pleased. May I come on Sunday evening?

My wife sends sincere good wishes to all of you. I need not say that mine go with them flock by flock.

Believe me, my dear Mrs. Meynell
Ever sincerely yours
JOHN FREEMAN

TO WILFRID MEYNELL

ANERLEY
30th. June, 1916

MY DEAR MR. MEYNELL

I telephoned to you one day this week but heard you were all out of town and no one knew when you would be back. Hence my writing now to give you my small piece of gossip which, after the pleasure of seeing you all, my visit was meant to convey. It is merely that I am soon bringing out a book of essays to be called *The Moderns*, including such clamorous people as Shaw and Wells and diverse

writers as Henry James, Hardy, Thompson and Patmore—
and so on. I preferred you should get this morsel of fact
direct from me—the more because of your unique interest
in two of the "subjects". My fear is—and it is truly no
merely conventional one—that your interest will not be
easily reconciled to my clumsy attempts at critical work upon
Thompson and Patmore; but I hope when you see the book
you will succeed in forgiving me. I will tell you more of it
when we meet, and if when you are in town and a little free
you would just ring up and let me know when I might call,
I should be immensely pleased. After next week I shall be a
fortnight away, and again from the end of August.

Will you give my very sincerest wishes to Mrs. Meynell,
whom I count on seeing when I call. These small verses
from a small child of eight may amuse her as well as you.

My wife joins in all my wishes.

Ever yours

JOHN FREEMAN

E. H. W. MEYERSTEIN

TO E. H. W. MEYERSTEIN

DEAR EDWARD

Forgive my delay: I should have written before, I know, if only to say how welcome your letter was, except when you talk of retrenching and hiding in Kent when you might shine in town. Don't retrench, neither in expense nor affection, neither in labours nor animosities. Abhor that vacuum to which retrenchment leads, covet that wealth which prodigality enlarges. Shall a man who writes or will write eighty stories in six months mew up his brightness and retrench his exuberance!

I'm glad you went to Felpham. I know that cottage, that oft-repaired thatch. I know those ladies—who knows them if not I?—I know hundreds of them, Jane Austen knew them, and E. H. W. M. knows them now. But I've only your version: what did they say of you? Did they detect in you the grand detector, the inquisitor, prying into their minds as the doctor stares at their tongues? *Short one*: He seems a nice young man. *Old one*: H'm. *Short one*: It's a pity I didn't go back. I was taken with that young man. *Old one*: Oh Emily, how can you. It's all very well to talk of Blake's house, but it might have been the spoons. *Short one*: No, no, I'm quite sure the spoons are all right. It wasn't the spoons. It really was the poet he meant. *Old one*: Maybe, but I'm sick of Blake;—and so on. Forgive this trifling. I can't write, I can't work, I can't think. I want to write, a kind of simple, ever so simple play on faint Greekish lines, with Chorus and Messenger, and for subject?—*Absalom*, who's always fascinated me. Pray for me, Edward, that grace be given.

Don't retrench: don't lop off weeks and days, don't snap a finger, don't pare a finger nail, even. Come up and squander yourself.

Ever

J. F.

ANERLEY
30th. December, 1925

DEAR EDDIE

Forgive this spotted card: I don't know what spots these are. They may be a disease, they may be a meal. I ought to have sent you a salutation before, but I counted on seeing you at lunch yesterday. To-day I've spent mainly in bed, utterly fatigued by a cold, and a sleepless night. I've wondered about your experiences, but must now be patient, supposing that you stay on at Morants until the New Year. A happy New Year and may your rabbits never die!

> "Let others pine for princely gem,
> Poisonous crown, snake-diadem:
> I pine for none nor plot with them,
> But press my anxious footsteps after
> The Shade of E. H. W. M.
>
> Poor fools, whose happiness needs be
> Confused with sensuality!
> Who mask with mirth wan Misery!
> More welcome far the honest laughter
> Flung backward by M. W. H. E."

Ever

J. F.

To E. H. W. M.

On his giving me the Author's copy of *The Angel in the House*
with the Poet's Revisions.

You would, would not, and at last fain must give,
For 'tis Possession's dear prerogative
To yield what most is yearned for, never weighing
Gift and receiver but, with fond delaying,

Coying, denying and willing and retracting
Till mere despair compels at last to acting.
So may in nightlong sudden blind embrace
An unwist visitant be held—her face
Part a delight and part a dumb rebuke
That eyes unsainted should in her eyes look.

And I, receiving, how shall I receive
A gift you had the heartless heart to give?
Harder my heart! Love scorns a love so tender:
I take the gift—but never to surrender.

J. F.

4-4-1927

ANERLEY
22nd. October, 1927

DEAR EDDIE

I'm so sorry, but the "misunderstanding" is all yours
and not a bit "polite". I've so much anxiety that all you
write shall be your best, so far as I can judge, that I can't
pretend merely to assent when I think that a particular
phrase is misplaced. "Honest" admiration seemed to do you
less than justice and suggest doubts that ought not to exist:
how could I *not* say so? If I can't speak simply to you, of
your own work, to whom can I speak?

Pray believe that I'll never speak to express offence, and
that what might seem at first sight a quibble isn't meant so.
Let us not stand upon finer points or I shall do a Gotcherie:

Strange DEATHS of Two poets	Double SUICIDE Of Notorious AUTHORS	Gassers GASSED

Enough of this foolery: remove these baubles.

Here is R. C.'s poem. The more I read it the more I like it, but I confess the latter part seems a weakness. The reference to himself is too diffused: there's no rock-like condensation there but only the fluid lava of verse. Wouldn't it gain greatly if the rather fine egotism were concentrated into a stern, savage stanza?—Yet the poem is fine and compels quick admiration. True there are flaws, e.g. in stanza five and the assonance of its last three lines; and "fruitlessly as I with nets of rhyme" seems almost a conceit compared with

"The years are undulations in your flight"—

which is a great line. But small flaws matter little.

But for prognosis—I don't dare. It seems to me that with a right subject he might make a great poem: God grant he may.   AFFECTIONATELY

J. F.

I shan't be able to turn up on Monday, but if this letter satisfies you send me a single line on a card signed as above.

LYME REGIS
August 13th, 1928

DEAR EDDIE

I hasten to tell you of an adventure: the moving accident is now my trade.

This morning we all—numbering eight—took our way to the beach where we picnic: ourselves and the Ingpens and Bergen and Uncle Tom Cobleigh and all. Light showers interspersed our talk and Bergen's doze, but we ate and sauntered, and then moved because of the tide and ate tea and prepared to drink it. But a heavier shower came on as we drank, and as it increased we saw that the beach had emptied save of ourselves and Fate. The rain became still heavier and as we crouched under our waterproofs the tide advanced—wild and white. Nothing remarkable in this? True; but you remember the steep path from the beach, a path rather difficult when the mud is dry, and imposssible when it is wet. The heavy rain had made it greasy—the eye itself could not climb the steep path but fell back bewildered and bruised. What should we do? Bergen, the quiet hero, addressed his Debbish (?) figure to the task, but fell back, muddy and defeated, into my arms. The rain still poured, the tide still advanced. Then we remembered that two daring lads had left the beach by another cliff, rising above a concrete embankment that was meant to hold back the tide— ominous thought!—and support the sliding earth. The two youths appeared and we decided to thrust Rosalind up to them so that one at least might be saved. Poor Rosalind was frightened to stay, frightened to leave, and her mother was visibly and audibly agitated. So Rosalind, brave and shaking; was hauled up the cliff, but with such difficulty that no one else would follow her. We shouted to her helpers for a boat to be sent, but doubted if a boat could live in such a sea; while the rain still poured and the tide still neared. And Cathy felt that she at any rate could not endure a small boat in such a wild sea: *Leviathan* herself would have been unsafe to her. Mrs. Ingpen's distress increased, "Can't we do *something*?" she cried. I looked cool and wise, speculated, reassured her, and did nothing. Her distress wasn't for herself, nor all for Rosalind, nor Ingpen: it was for Shelley! Who would honour Shelley now? She turned to Bergen but even Bergen was helpless. Afterwards, however, he said to me that he could have climbed the cliff at the expense of his clothes; but what could he do then? Save himself and leave us to perish? Consider his dilemma! He is meditating a masterly study of Ethics:—could he save himself and then give his life to Ethics? or could he die with us and leave his Ethics unwritten? No one would listen to him if he left us to die so that Ethics might survive; no one could write his Ethics if he did not live. Crueller difficulty has seldom faced a mortal:—and this, and this alone, kept him silent and inactive.

But Fate, who kept us all for mysterious and distant purposes, ended all difficulties. St. Peter or St. Christopher, in the form of a fisherman, appeared on the heights with a rope and dragged us all to safety. It will always be my proudest boast that I was the last and the wettest; but of myself I will not speak. Yet I owe it to Posterity, to say that, faced thus with Elemental Death, I was not alarmed for myself or for poetry. I hadn't a thought in my head nor a tremor in my heart: rhymes did not haunt me, nor the torment of unfinished masterpieces. Believe me, Eddie, there's nothing so steady as an empty head and a groggy heart. What the rest thought and felt I don't know, but they certainly joined me in thanks to the fisherman who saved us and Roger joined me in hot whisky. Other accounts of this adventure may reach you from others, but this is the first, the true and the only reliable story of Literature on the Rocks.

Accept this as a poor return for your letter which I was so glad to have. A still poorer return is the news that Squire, while liking your Sonnets, about which I spoke to him, has returned them saying that he's too full for anything at present. The only consolation is that I know he's returned some poems by Young which are nearly as good—perhaps very nearly, in their different way—as your Sonnets. I'll let you have them back when I return home.

Thank you for *Vanity Fair*. I've started it, and may finish it, but Ingpen tries to put me off by saying that the style is so slack, incorrect and what not. What can I do between your fire and his ice? You know I've never an opinion of my own.

No more: forgive me for turning you off with a mere literal story of a few minutes, when you embroider so beautifully: but what would you? Truth, alas, is invincible. We all send love.   Affly.

                                        JOHN

WILLIAM MONROE

TO WILLIAM MONROE, U.S.A.[1]

ANERLEY
20th. March

Dear Mr. Monroe

Please forgive once again a very erratic correspondent. I've letters and papers to thank you for, and the book on Whittier has also come. As to the latter, I don't imagine that Squire had the faintest responsibility: I think he is only dealing with entirely new *Lives* and such a "sinker" (I like your term) as you speak of couldn't possibly have passed his guard.—*Whitman* is another matter. Bailey's book seemed to this Englishman surprisingly good and liberal, for you must know that Whitman isn't an English god. There are no English gods now, since Hardy died and Doughty died. All our Bright Young People write Bright Young Novels of sex and cynicism, and there are few poets to write anything at all. This is of course a crude statement of the facts, and you will find many exceptions: I simply state the broad tendency, which means that the best work is as quiet and secret as ever it was. Imaginative work is like a bulb, that needs darkness for its roots and light for its head; and roots and green shoot are alike unnoticed by the side of red cabbage and hydrangeas and rhododendrons. And so please don't be surprised if I know almost *only* my friend's work: among novelists, Martin Armstrong, R. H. Mottram and E. H. W. Meyerstein. As to our poets, you probably know as much of them as I do, and I won't presume to teach you their names; but I am trying to get some of the little-known and admirable ones into a new Anthology of English, American and Colonial

[1] John Freeman never met William Monroe, an American admirer of his work, but they corresponded.

poets, which the *English Association* are bringing out on both sides of the Atlantic.

Pray forgive my not writing before, and think how busy I must be, in earning a living *not* from literature, to neglect so long to answer a letter so welcome as yours. Please write again.

Ever yours

JOHN FREEMAN

P.S. Whitman—there's an excellent new American book full of new matter, edited by C. J. Furness—*W. W.'s Workshop.*

TRURO

27th. August, 1928

DEAR MR. MONROE

I must thank you for sundry reviews and articles which you sent me lately: I must thank you even more for those which refer to yourself and Scotty than for the one or two which refer to me. I feel like writing to a hero of the past or a figure of the distant (to a Roland of the Horn) or Huckleberry Finn or Amundsen (if he is not dead), for I live and move and have and get my being in town, and nightly dream of the country; while you, no doubt, because you live at so splendidly-named a place as Crouching Lion Farm, dream of Broadway and Fifth Avenue, or Piccadilly and Westminster.

Please don't think that I've moved to Truro, which is in Cornwall and possesses a new Cathedral and a cracked bell. I still live in the smallest of London's suburbs. But some weeks ago I came with my family to Lyme Regis, in Dorset, where we often spend our holidays, and to-night I came over here. Lyme Regis is very ancient and irregular. Mediaeval remains are seen here and there and hidden (I suspect) everywhere. It was the scene of a siege in Stuart times, and of one of Jane Austen's novels. It is very small, very much in need of town-planning and (thank God!) very much averse from it. The streets are like ladders: the river floods it, the sea eats huge mouthfuls of its cliffs which crumble like green cheese. You can't walk, you dare hardly motor. But there are inns, and lanes, and field paths for scrambling through, and cliffs to fall down, and wild flowers as common grass, and a wild sea seething hither straight from Cape Cod.

And having told you all this, I will end by repeating my gratitude.

Yours very sincerely

JOHN FREEMAN

P.S. I open this to say I'm wrong. It's not the Cathedral bell but the Town Hall bell, right under, over and all around my window. It rings quarters very slowly, pauses for an irregular period, then rings the hours. Some time after, the Cathedral clock does the same, again at irregular periods, and so stretches every hour into something Unknown, Unmeasured, Incomprehensible. There's so much time that you never know the Time: half past five by the Cathedral is at once followed by a quarter to seven by the Town Hall. There's no constancy, no normality. Einstein came here to test his theory of the Relativity of Time and was rather vexed to find that it was confirmed; for when a theory is confirmed it must needs be discarded and a new theory invented. And now I go to Breakfast by the Cathedral Clock (by which I bath'd) but they will probably give me *luncheon*, by the Town Hall Clock.

ANERLEY

18th. November, 1928

DEAR MR. MONROE

I'm not sure (it's so long ago) whether my last letter thanked you for the papers you sent me, or whether manners and memory failed me once again. The papers didn't interest me so much this time, for they were concerned mainly with persons who wanted to be—or *not* to be, I forget which—President of the U.S.A., and who are to me as mythical if not as mysterious as Gog and Magog. But it was kind of you to send them.—I'm glad you already see some of our English papers: now that you are adding the *London Mercury* to your list you will have as much of me as you can want in prose, and a deal in verse besides. And as to verse, I shall be frankly interested in hearing what you make of the unfamiliar pieces in the *Collected Poems*, and ought to explain that (against my will) the title is ambiguous: the Poems are collected, it is true, but the collection is selective and not comprehensive.

You speak of your stars among American writers being included in our E.M.L. series. Poe (by E. Shanks) is supposed to come out next Spring, Whitman (by John Bailey, a very good book) no doubt you have already seen; Hawthorne I'd like to do but James has done him already. Mark Twain ought to be done, certainly, and I admire so much some of his work (to-day I've finished re-reading *Huckleberry Finn*) and his letters, that I'd like to do him. Thoreau I'm not sure of, but Emerson (whom you don't name) surely ought to be done first. He's a prose master. But I don't know if the Editor of the series will include any more Americans yet awhile: I must press him. I can't succeed in getting Chatterton included, though the best writer on Chatterton (a friend of mine) is anxious to have a chance for his subject; and I've vainly asked for Patmore and Doughty, equal Singularities and equal Geniuses.

You know, I suppose, that Frost has been here: it was pleasant to renew old friendship in person. If you see him he will be able to give you news of many people here, and in return I will only ask for any news you can give me of Conrad Aiken and Arlington Robinson.

Yours ever

JOHN FREEMAN

DE V. PAYEN-PAYNE

TO DE V. PAYEN-PAYNE

DEAR MR. PAYEN-PAYNE

Now that I *have* looked at your little family booklet I can thank you for it more sincerely than I did on Sunday. It was very kind of you to add this to my prized collection of signed copies. Do you remember that years and years ago you gave me, through Ingpen, a copy of Swinburne's *French Lyrics* signed in your impeccable hand?

I'm greatly fond of these pleasant tokens—the man that gives me something of his own, signed with his name and mine, gives me something of himself and makes me a friend to the scaffold and beyond.

Ever yours and gratefully yours
JOHN FREEMAN

ANERLEY
1927

DEAR MR. PAYEN-PAYNE

Your little books have come and are very much appreciated, especially one of them can now take its place next to the other Swinburne item which you gave me some years ago. Please believe that I am very thankful.—We ought to have talked more of Swinburne: fools think him a small poet, or a merely extravagant figure, without sense or meaning, not having in themselves the wit to understand the "masculine persuasive force" beneath the fluency of movement. It's always a pleasure to talk of one's admiration, but a mere duty to talk of one's dislikes; and alas! one indulges the sense of duty rather than satisfies the need of pleasure.

Yours sincerely
JOHN FREEMAN

283

U

SIR MICHAEL SADLER

TO SIR MICHAEL SADLER

DEAR SIR MICHAEL

I should be proud to be your guest and dine in the temple of the *Martlets* on the twelfth, but it looks at the moment as if no one will be able to dine anywhere a week hence, alas! But if all's well (it could hardly be iller) I can catch a train from Paddington which, at 7.14, will give me just time to slip into Decency. I should have to hasten back next morning.—The pleasure of remembrance will be mine, and I'll willingly read some verses.

I know I've to thank you for all the kindness of this invitation. I hope I'm right in supposing that Lady Sadler is better.

Yours sincerely

JOHN FREEMAN

ANERLEY
25th. May, 1926

DEAR SIR MICHAEL

Your last letter with its superabundant message makes it hard for me to write at all, even a letter which ought to be addressed to Lady Sadler. I hope all the pleasure wasn't mine, but I think the best of it was. However, I won't refuse, and all I want to add now is that I've asked Squire to try to collect the four numbers of his strike-time *Guildford Gazette* etc. and send you a set. I delayed writing in the hope of being able to send a set myself, and if you don't get it in the course of a week pray tell me and I'll try again.—Meanwhile I must have the last word in thanks to you and Lady Sadler.

Sincerely yours

JOHN FREEMAN

ANERLEY
15th. November, 1927

DEAR SIR MICHAEL

It was kind of you to write so, in the midst of so much business as you must have. I was sorry to miss you, but glad to hear that you were well again. I had heard from Squire that when he was in Oxford a fortnight ago you hadn't been accessible: hence my resolve to take my chance in calling. It was at the dinner of the English Association that he told me this: we had been listening to the P.M.[1] on his early Loves among books, and if you admire his character as I do —I hope so—you would have been delighted to listen to his fragment of autobiography.

Please give my remembrances to Lady Sadler.

Yours sincerely

JOHN FREEMAN

[1] The Rt. Hon. Stanley Baldwin.

MARJORY SAMPSON

TO MARJORY SAMPSON

ANERLEY
1st. January, 1918

DEAR MARJORY

I start this note at lunch, so as to have at any rate the virtue of starting, to my small credit. I was glad to hear your voice so shiningly cheerful, when I wished you something or other this morning, and I shall be gladder when I hear it a little nearer than by telephone. But that no doubt will be many years hence. Meanwhile I'll tell you that in the American anthology which reached me this morning there were some amusing biographical notes of which the most amusing for me was one giving a wholly fictitious account of a scarifier with whom, for better or worse, I've the closest familiarity. It amused me to read of his bacteriological work in Russia during the war, the more so since I'd been laughing about new "stunts" in verse—threatening a physiological stunt and then an insect one. Indeed there were certain verses lately deliberately suggesting the Human Heart as being aired by something or other, as the earth by worms. For science, Marjory, science is all the go, as I was reminded when I read lately some sonnets by Masefield. I think that much might be done with (or without) slugs, tadpoles, lice, spiders (see Fabre), bees (don't see Maeterlinck) and conger eels. Do you know anything about conger eels? "Love Songs of the Lower Creation" is a title I've got in reserve; for I don't see why one should sing the lark and not the lamprey—logically I don't. It's only the imagination that fails, and imagination can be supplanted by a text book. I once studied earth-worms for the sake of a metaphor— rare conscientiousness. The result wasn't a good poem, though; which proves the natural antagonism of art and morality.

But if you had come this week we wouldn't have talked of anything so dull. These sedacities could have been achieved—and at any rate you could have joined in the singing of *There is a Tavern in the Town* (a great song, Marjory) and *The Wearing of the Green*. We've had times of singing with piano and fiddle, it seemed there was never anything nicer than our voices, or happier than those happy or mournful airs.—True we also played games with the children, but felt ourselves a little too old to enjoy them as much as the children did. It suits us now to sit quietly, enjoying dullness, talking easily and slowly, letting the talk fall and then picking it up again casually, and looking at the fire when there was nothing else to say. These are the extenuating pleasures of the forties, to which the blithest come.

                                                                Later

Had you not come on Thursday this letter might have been protracted indefinitely; but I've been "dished" by your coming. I wish you were coming again to-night for then we could talk of Karamazovs. I thrust the subject under Gertrude's nose a few minutes ago but she scarcely sniffed at it; and now she's gone early and tired to bed. I wish you would talk about the Karamazovs: you told me that you had read it, once, I think. I've got at my third reading of the wonderful book, and I'm more impressed now than ever. When I say impressed I mean astonished, overwhelmed. There was never a simpler writer—never a writer to whom things were simpler—motives, ideas, passions, hopes, betrayals. It doesn't mean that he simplifies them: he didn't, for they are already simple to him and he knows that many things cannot be simplified and remain what they were in truth. The immense confusion of the Karamazovs isn't really confusion of perception; it means that the confusion of conflict has been seen clearly, simply, sensitively and rendered into human language. Dostoevsky was capable of living the lives of other men; that is what it is to be an imaginative writer. The lyrical poet is capable of raising his own life intensely —or of being raised to intensity. The psychological novelist is capable of living other men's lives as they live them, inwardly and outwardly, visibly and invisibly. None was greater in this than Dostoevsky. He was simple because he was not confused. He did not have to invent because he imagined; and the difference between imagination and invention is, I suppose, the difference between men and marionettes, Shakespeare and Dumas.—These were the things I should have liked to say, and provoked your protest; but since it seems you're not coming—though it's not yet ten o'clock, I'll stop.

And I'll wish you good-bye and the time to write me a letter, and the kindness not to write it merely as an answer to this, for the garrulousness of which I should blush if blushes were still part of my accomplishments.

Ever affly.

JOHN

ANERLEY
14th. November, 1926

DEAR MARJORY

Please don't be disappointed at having a letter from me instead of Gertrude. She's ill, but is getting better and I think you need have no anxiety at all.

On Tuesday she went to the Lord Mayor's Show, which seems to have been very much more interesting than most— as you will have gathered from the papers. She seemed all right until Wednesday evening. She ate nothing and had rather a restless night. On Thursday she did not get up and when the doctor came he suggested appendicitis. . . .

By eleven on Friday morning she was taken to the Cottage Hospital, and soon the surgeon came and told me that the operation must be made at once. By half past one he was able to tell me that it was quite successful, and that it had proved to be very urgent indeed. . . .

This morning the 'phone message was that she was going on as well as could be expected—a familiar formula but satisfactory—I will drop you a line in the middle of the week.

Gertrude has not been particularly well lately, but I thought it was because of the sudden and severe cold and her bustling about with Joy; but Dr. Phillips now thinks it must have been pending (pardon, I didn't mean a pun, though I feel thoroughly pun-inclined) for some time, though it would have been impossible to determine anything a fraction sooner. So all's well.

I think I have told you everything I can, and with all circumstance. I promised her last night that I would send the weekly letter to-day, but you may be sure I should have done so without promising.

But I can't write her letter for you. I can't write letters like hers. I can't write letters full of facts. I have a difficulty in confining my pen to literality, and always want to tell lies. I've given you a page of solid facts, and now feel an imp of mischief at my elbow, and I can't answer for what may follow. Only last week I sent my Sunday letter to Joy, full of extravagant inventions—I mean lies, saving your presence —and she believed every word of it till near the end, though I hadn't meant to deceive the poor innocent. It's a dreadful propensity, which I've given up resisting. Freudians would say that I have suppressed love of Truth, hence the escape of lies. But I don't believe them. It's only fun, that doesn't beseem my years but which you must put up with as I do.

You, it seems, have had intense sun; we have had perpetual

rain. Everything is flooded, and yesterday was one prolonged deluge, concentrating the rains of October to
February. To-day is sunny and the leaves come goldenly
down with any breath of wind, spinning in the clear air like
dragon flies grown suddenly dizzy. You can't believe how
lovely the trees look, as I sit typing this and looking out
over the garden. There's an unending succession of pale and
bright colours, and quick motion everywhere. But I won't
go on like this—Joy, pert minx, calls it A.C., that's to say,
Aesthetic Cant, and I tell her it's envy on her part, arising
from her inability to distinguish oak from ash and elephant
from flea.

I hope all goes well with you. Read, if you can get it,
Sacheverell Sitwell's *All in a Summer Day*—a kind of
autobiography, which is very good indeed. I was looking
forward to seeing a "Russian" Ballet which he has written,
with music by Lord Berners, but doubt now if I shall go.
Instead I shall stay at home and write an *Ode on Recovery
from Sickness, with Appendices*. Excuse this nonsense, and

Believe me

Madam

With profound respect

Your humble Servant

ANERLEY

P.S. I forgot to say (in explanation of the signature, which
may surprise you) that I have provisionally patented the
title of Anerley, Baron Anerley, against the time when I
accept a Peerage. The reason of this seeming haste is that
the next Labour Government will be making a large number
of Peers, to carry their legislation, which by the way I am
credibly informed will include the *abolition of the whole Army*
(there's for you), and so I don't want anybody else to bag
such a nice-sounding name. But please don't say a word—
just address me as hitherto, without even a casual my Lord,

307

or your Ludship. Between old friends such formalities may be dropped without offence.

ANERLEY
18th. January, 1927

DEAR MARJORY

I called for you this morning at 9.35, but you had gone to Egypt. I was vexed rather than disappointed, for I suspected a trick, and it meant I had to go to Hayes all by myself. But when I got there I was compensated for I had the whole common to myself and the hills towards Surrey. There was not a walker, not a car, not a 'plane; there was only Kent and myself. I didn't miss you until I saw the gorse and picked this for you, saying *Look, Marjory!* but when I turned round you were in Egypt, wherever that may be. You were lying idly by the Congo, watching Nubian babies playing with Gold Dust, while I walked over the silent and wet earth, looking for gorse, until I came to Coney Hill. You don't know Coney Hill? then I can't tell you about it, only that there are oaks as old as your Pyramids, a pool as still as your Sphinx, and beeches green and bronze like the image of your Pharaoh. It was all quiet and ancient, with a pale blue sky above, dark woods beyond, and below a stretch of coloured meadows, rising and dipping and dimming into the far-off. And so home, with this Gorse to tell you of what you have scorned and lost. May it tease you to tears and excite you to delirium and may you catch the next boat home.

Ever

J. F.

ANERLEY
1929

DEAR MARJORY

Ulysses? I think you can get it still, but only in Paris or some other licentious city. But you needn't read it— many people talk of it without having read it. It's a fatiguing book—very long, often very dull. You would have to hide it under your pillow, or pretend your mother had sent it or the chaplain's widow had found it among her husband's books and lent it to you. It would be quite profitable to get L.'s copy or buy one through a friend and lend it to the wives of the British Army. Old ladies would love it—especially the . . . scene, and the dialogue between Bloom and I forget the name, when they meet for . . . And the passage about . . . *You* know! Colonels' wives would make a great fuss of you if you gave them a chance of reading it.—For an alternative, one's own dreams in a disturbed night could be retold to all and sundry and the same delicious effect achieved.

But I haven't a copy: and I regard myself as a model of industry for having read it right through.

J.

P.S. You had better burn this letter for your own sake, if not for mine.

ANERLEY
July 1929

DEAR MARJORY

Your letter is delightful and so welcome. I like having your reminiscence of Highland scenes, but I only saw them as it were in a film, rapidly. I went in one day, all sun and wind, from Glasgow to Inverness, not by the most direct route, it is true, but still rather too quickly; although, perhaps, in the vaster spaces of the north, speed does not rob one of the relations of one part to another in looking at the scene, for it unfolds but slowly even if one is going steadily at 40-50 miles an hour, and one can dream, or drone, upon the almost lazy and reluctant succession of mountains and moors.—I remember we lunched at Taymouth Castle, now sunken into an hotel and bar, and walked through the park to the river and loitered by the shallow noisy waters—the same as I had seen in snow at Birnam, under trees more huge. I should have liked to have stayed in the park, and slept elsewhere than in the enormous, fantastic "hotel"—but my destination was Inverness. I *did* go to Strathpeffer and the near Falls, and saw the head of the Canal, but no more; and I *did* see (and was sadly impressed) Culloden and its sad accusing stones. But after that I went away from your parts, though I cast eyes at the Firth, and sped on to Elgin and then the east coast towns, only leaving them for Perth and Glasgow again. So I'm conscious of disappointing you, since I can only welcome your rhapsodies over the past, and not all my enjoyment of things more recent. But really, you are to be envied for that happy, ineffaceable background of memory: nothing can do away with that, nothing can make it less precious. I wonder you don't pack up at once and fly off there, with Dennis and Bracken, and not come back until cold and autumn drive you. But perhaps, at heart, you are an universalist, and Surrey scrub and Sussex down and Felixstowe beach mean as much to you, *being present*, as Scotland absent. Do you really know what you most love—can any one know? I think, for me, at this moment it is a daisy in grass, or thyme: something small and undying—or always dying and renewing.

Don't sneer at the car! It is Cathy's pet and I'm clay in her hands. I ought not to afford it, I don't know if I can afford it, but it pleases her so enormously that I also am pleased. Besides, you must remember that it is very useful to me, and on this plea I justify anything I like.

Please write again soon. Nobody writes to me, except income-tax collectors, and they make me ill: indeed, after a fortnight in Scotland, I got back to town to find two "demand notes" (polite phrase!) awaiting my return. I *was* ill, came home to bed and am just getting up again.

Ever

J.

LILIAN AND MARGUERITE SMALLEY

TO LILIAN SMALLEY

ANERLEY
9th. March, 1906

DEAR MISS SMALLEY

It had been my intention to write you fully and tediously about the Concert of Saturday last; but time and affairs intervening have spoiled the impressions. I feel as if I had fallen in the mud.—At the time of hearing, I could hardly forgive your absence, plausible though your excuse was. Had the excuse been less plausible I should have been angry at your deprivation.

All I could say of it now would be mere verbal extravagances. The sounds rose up often in violent waves and then, instead of smiting, simply dulled one as might waves of a faintly lethal atmosphere. You feel at one time all nerves and then all veins, receiving and quivering with a thousand momentary impressions. You feel, feel, feel—are gulfed in wanton abysses of sensation, and are conscious (though this may be personal only) of a curious absence of stomach. It is strange to listen to fine music merely with the senses, to let the rhythm govern one's pulses, to breathe the sounds sensuously, and feel them dancing in some odd corner of the brain, to feel them as drops of rain steady, distinct, soaking: to feel them falling on one's heart-skin taut over a small space, falling as drum-sticks on a drum; to feel that the waves that rise and recede and swell again so obediently at the motion of the white hands of the conductor are softly washing round and over one; to feel the infinite languor of sleep yet not to sleep for sheer delight; and to feel the same delight tease you with its melancholy fullness.

It is easy to exaggerate one's feelings, and I don't pretend that I felt all this at one recital. But in looking back all these memories rise as out of one pool, flown thither from many nests. Frankly, fine music makes me sometimes sleepy and sometimes discontented and often disagreeable.

I have many things to say, on this and many subjects, but am infinitely tired and dull-witted and could not entertain you (which is my only justification for writing to you) and could not annoy you (which is my only pleasure in writing to you) and my head is like a dusty cog-wheel and jolts like a —— who is not —— enough to feel happy.

I could send you some dainty new verses that I like better than I'll admit: but come and hear them. They are called *Violets in December*: and it took many weeks to get beyond the first line.

Yours abruptly

JOHN FREEMAN

P.S. Not so abruptly yours as not to be able to hope you are now very well and happy.

ANERLEY
22nd. October, 1906

DEAR MISS SMALLEY

As you will be anxious to know how my days and nights have been spent, I take that as an excuse for idling. The days are nothing: 'tis the nights only that count, and I have been happy several nights last week.

By the way, Monday evening was very pleasant even without you, but it is irritating to think how much pleasanter it had been with you. And do you know that Marguerite herself didn't come? Politeness forbids any comment, but she says she did not get our message.—Women! Women!

Thursday night Gertrude and I were in town—not for public pleasure but family communion. So about midnight we walked jubilant through jubilant streets, as much a part of them as the lamps that lit them. There was softness in the air, sense of the happiness of night and its abandonment.

You became a poet walking there, full of superfluous lyrics; lights flickered and gleamed, and there was shining of a thousand eyes! And amid the ring of hooves and bells and the clangour of motors and their sad, long drone was heard chiefly the cheerful babble of human tongues, native and foreign, with no distinction of wise and foolish.

Friday again I loitered, where the Empire and Alhambra flung out their living streams—so bright, so contented, so careless, so jubilant—two thousand poets pouring from each shining palace. Eyes of cabs peered incessant, large and mild and golden; bells and whistles were busy; and casual raindrops dispersed the merging crowds in bright alarm. A night for wakeful dreams!

And I had immersed myself in the great tide after hearing Beethoven! There had been music rising from the purest of wells—a horn and strings piece, and violin concerto. And then the great fountains were broken up and the flood of the ninth symphony came. You of course know it by heart, and to you so well-experienced it comes not with the repeating wonder that it has for me always. The adorable soul of the man who had command of such adorable music in him! the sweetness of that music, rising out of how great strength! beauty infinite.

Then with a brief interval came Sullivan's "In Memoriam". I had never heard it at Queen's Hall before: please God I shall never hear it there again. After an easy melancholy opening you get a debauch of noise, utterly un-memorial and im-memorable, till at the end there was but a violent orchestra spurting and sputtering huge gouts and clots of red sound, and an organ thundering out its iron-tongued supremacy. Immense was the applause! Asses near me brayed and grinned, and I cursed. . . .

So I came down Regent Street, through Leicester Square, through the ouching streets and by the Park heavy with green glooms. For years I have wanted to write some worthy verses of nightly London—and am utterly incapable; I shall die with them unwritten.

Well, there is nothing more to say, but that I had giblets for dinner to-day, deliciously sunken in creamy potatoes, and drank coffee over the fluttering pages of *Romany Rye*. Yesterday morning I cut myself a little in shaving—but am now whole. Had you seen me yesterday you would have noticed that I wore a green suit with a white and green waistcoat, brown shoes and brown and fawn socks; green shirt and tie of darker green, and brown hat. I mention this because it will of course interest you, and these facts are not without importance. Green has a somewhat quietening effect on the mind of the wearer—and I had not worn the suit to a music-hall for a week. So yesterday my native restlessness was a little subdued: I stayed home in the evening, read a little and talked much to Gertrude.

Pf! you perceive the vanity of Montaigneizing! *He* has made grave trifling for ever impossible to poor limping men who follow him. You may love Montaigne; you cannot follow him in his self-revelation. His mere garrulity is wisdom; his chatter has the authority of inspiration: and we are fools who read him so unworthily that we think we can copy him!

You must be very unhappy! Are you, just now, darling or nurse? I am amazed at your obstinate, contumacious humility, and am almost driven to think it is the mask of extreme arrogance. Well, I have an immense favour to ask. Do you remember that you have some unfinished verses of mine about women? I fancy you said you had them with you, among other superfluous nonsense. Will you be so condescending as to send them to me? I have no other copy, and want to include them in a small selection I have been planning of trifles heavy as lead.

... In exchange, I send some new ones. The Picture is of a low hill, mist-veiled but just perceptible. Dead men are lying wherever you may look, and the earth seems to breathe release and the trees to rustle relief. There are stars and moon; and the whole picture seems sentient. Do you know it?

I can't tell you who the artist is, or where the picture is now. I only remember *it*.

Just now I saw a most noble and wondrous sunset. Rose-leaves rained softly down the west, as delicate and evanescent as wishes, pink and amber, and pure as a child's thoughts.

> "Rose-leaves falling slowly
> Far down an amber phantom West—
> Leaving the phantom earth how lovely and lowly!
> A rose-leaf fluttering down a wilder West."

O pardon me! I forgot you hated verse.

Yours, I know not how or why

JOHN FREEMAN

ANERLEY
11th. January, 1907

DEAR MISS SMALLEY

I write to you now, not for your instruction or entertainment, but simply to defer pressing and unwelcome tasks which the Devil has prepared for me here in Purgatory. Figures I hate, and I am figure-ridden as by a strong-kneed night-hag.

Ruskin, whom you admire so much, and reverence so truly, and trust so amply, and read so seldom, is just now telling me the story of his early life. There is a curious half-interested aloofness in his regard for the solemn child that was Master Ruskin. Too serious and pondering, lacking fun, lightness, bravado, the formal, rigorous, yet tender training of his childish years may yet have been the best training possible for him. One wonders what would have happened to him in the strenuous tumble of a public school in the early nineteenth century. Surely he would have grown less dogmatic and more tolerant, and withal the less and more, less inherently powerful and noble. Yet one would like to see him at a modern picture gallery exhibition of some little esoteric society: or at a modern music-hall. Wordsworth was drunk once, and is not the less Wordsworth for that. Indeed, you may say that every poet should be drunk once in his life. . . . Depend upon it, 'twas not for nothing that blind Homer was reputed vagabond: the taverns of Chios knew him, I wot!

And so Ruskin tipsy—once!—in Piccadilly, addressing to unresponsive lamp-post or policeman one of his glorious dithyrambs upon modernity, were a sight to comfort our uneasy hearts. His virtue may distress us, his utter stainlessness be an ungentlemanly reproach: such solitary red light would have brought him to us—how humanly!

Ruskin's virtue was always a little severe: we never feel so warmly to him as when he reveals an unsuspected fault or folly, flaws that help us to forgive his austere excellencies.

Would it not be easy to draw a hateful portrait of Ruskin, merely by selecting maliciously from the man's unimpeachable qualities, characteristics, actions. Let it not be known that he was irritable, violent, stiff in opinion, powerfully-prejudiced, abusive. . . . How unpleasant, indeed, he would have been to us now, but for his inveterate habit of self-portraiture. His egotism has saved him, for us.

How few men have written an entertaining autobiography! I think of Swift, and wonder what sort of "Praeterita" he would have left us—with breaking fire of indignation, wrath and dusky passion, sudden flame of tenderness; sadness over all.—No! when he came to the age when men, looking back, find it good to make record of the elusive past, Swift surely must have found the past only too intolerably poignant for speech.

And what sort of thing would Byron have made of it? Would he have dared ever to be simply affectionate, regretful?—alack, he would have had to write, I suppose, what no man, or none but men could read! Burns would have made it an inestimable book; but only Rousseau *has* done it before Ruskin, and with him one swings from admiration to contempt, and rests finally in pity.

In *Praeterita* Ruskin has given one of the few things we could not well spare.—If this, the byplay of his tired mind and recreation of his soul, should prove more permanent than all his artistic-architectural-industrial lava of fiery words!

I do not know why this was not sent you some days ago: indeed I do not know why it should be sent at all, but to give you the trouble of reading bad writing unprofitably. However, I will tell you of *Antony and Cleopatra*, which I saw last night from a luxurious shelf in His Majesty's. Doubtless you, omniscient, have heard the "production" termed "lavish", "splendid", etc. etc. through all the perished vocabulary of journalism. Well, it is all this. The music and scenery are very good, particularly the latter: though I must confess not astonishing to a lover of the ballet. Indeed I do not know that in this respect His Majesty's far surpasses the Alhambra or Empire.

But there were grievous cuts, and audacious interpolations; and it misdoubts me if the latter, albeit splendid, can excuse the former. One whole scene, with Shakespeare's magnificent contrasting of triumph and lovely shame made manifest thereby, was simply dropped unworded. And strange—or is it strange!—the thing that gained heartiest acclamations was the interpolated tableau! Methought I could distinguish the soft hands of you clapping it.

As for the acting, distinct from the impeccable setting, it was pretty good: one manages to forget Tree himself; and Cleopatra is so diabolically handsome and sinuous that one *ought* to forget her. For the play, staged as I saw it, is plainly immoral. "All for love and the world well lost" is the motive and glory of it. For you feel that the real conqueror is not Caesar, not Death, but an unsanctified passion. Antony, and Cleopatra's, is the triumph; and the world well lost indeed that buys such triumph. And that is not the morality of the Church or indeed of the world: too unrestrained for the Church and unhallowed, too audacious for the comprehension of the world. To forget this is to confuse our common standards of right and wrong.

And Shakespeare, like every artist, can put such witchery into our hearts that we look with admiration on scenes which must needs fret and irk the serene eternity of saints. In this play, it is not, of course, that the trammels of conventional morality are broken and contemned: that were a slight thing, almost inapt of due "artistic" treatment. The rectitude, or otherwise, of Antony's passion is not in the question at all; but the sanity, the absolute legitimacy of such destroying passion—for us, reading it merely, like man acold hearing of a fire, so splendidly blind and mad and irretrievable.

At His Majesty's the play lost nothing of its prideful sensuousness and deliriousness, nothing of its ultimate immorality. Indeed the players were visibly innocent of any such meaning lying asleep within the subtle words. Tree himself takes it as "educative"! and the black-robed bepetted brethren were there, innocent too.

Essentials apart, I had one keen disappointment. These following great lines were spoken not as they should be, being Shakespeare's verse, but as an actress might speak them:—

"O withered is the garland of the war,
  The soldier's pole is fall'n; young boys and girls
  Are level now with men; the odds is gone,
  And there is nothing left remarkable
  Beneath the visiting moon!"

Enough of this! I'll swear that you've never read the play at all.

You're both coming on Saturday?—after tea, if you please to defer your blessing of us? but this is insolent.

To-night I meditate on your joint virtues—marvelling.

About six Saturday? bounty-bestowing women—so prodigal of your presence—I grow lyrical bethinking me of you.

J.

ANERLEY
31st. December, 1915

MY DEAR LILIAN

I see you've forgotten our number—we were sure you'd forgotten the road and neighbourhood too, even our actual existence. I thought that only as a shadowy ineffectual ghost could you remember me, after so many months and over so many miles.

This is not an answer to your letter, which came this morning. I write at once in order that I may just squeeze into the gasping year its single act of virtue; but really I had intended often to write, and even promised myself that I would surely write on Christmas Day. But I've had many disappointments—and this one from myself, for I find—not without surprise—that I didn't write on Christmas Day.— Well!

It is nice of you to send me even a few lines. What you are doing at Darjeeling only the wise Saints know:—do you mean that you took an uncomfortable journey merely for the sake of jeering at me from Kinchingjunga? What is that but a molehill a pin's head higher than another molehill, and a few hasty centuries older, and by so many nearer to its doom? Don't you know that the mountains will be the first to go—just cracking and collapsing like a pie crust? A thing like Kinch—and the rest of the jingling name serves only as a sharp reminder of mortality. Its snows will melt, its central heats die, and a water cover all that was there; and what you've been staring, staring at with your huge gray eyes is but a frame of old bones and dust.

Do you want to know anything of us? There's nothing to tell, except the usual story of small things, and one day as like another as your mountain is like any other mountain. We spent Christmas quite alone, the first spent "to ourselves" since we've kept it at all as a family. The children were very happy—especially at being surprised at six o'clock with a private banquet under coloured candles; and happier still at not being compelled to eat turkey (which they loathe). Then we music'd with all English airs.—And that's the story of six months.

No; I was thinking if I should fill this page, but I won't. Let all that might be added be left to your imagination, if it can sink to such tiny things, except that I am,

Yours affly.

J. F.

P.S. The New Year will have quite a rough chin when you get this, but I hope he'll bring you more mountains to look at, or whatever else you desire.

TO MARGUERITE SMALLEY

ANERLEY
31st. May, 1905

DEAR MISS SMALLEY

Gertrude has confessed to handing you some papers of mine to read, which I don't want you to read. You are hereby charged to return them, or burn them, unread, instead of wasting your time over them. Know that Gertrude's punishment for her humiliating (to me) indiscretion will be meted by the speed or tardiness of your response.

Do you know that your sister is getting superlatively priggish? Writing me about the Academy show, she avers quite indignantly that she went simply for the pictures, and indignantly repudiates my suggestion that a pure and exalted devotion to art (I mean Art) was not the sole reason of her visit. Of course I don't believe her, but it's annoying to have my intelligence rated so low as her repudiation implies. Such a loftiness of aim is not to be tolerated: you, now, are under no delusions. You are not to be deceived: you have almost masculine insight, and more than masculine malice. (I should have said on Sunday that, until twenty-three, girls deceive only themselves: after twenty-three women deceive others, sometimes only, sometimes also. Deceit always. This of course is hardly more than a theory, as yet.)

Theories, by the way, are delightfully provocative of laughter. A man is seldom ridiculous by his actions, or by them only: his notions mark him for crazy. Pope surely was a long way off when he spoke of great wit being allied to madness: he should have said, the little humours. Somehow great powers or great hearts transfer madness to circumstances: you sooner think the world tipsy than wrong. But the crotchets and whimsies and peacock introspections of lesser men are eternally funny: what right have we to think, save the right of folly, or to speculate, save the right of blindness, or to condemn, save the right of guilt? littleness alack! is seldom laughable in the pigmy: only provoking. The mirror exasperates.

So we know what we do when we acclaim the praise (Dryden's or Jonson's, I think, but I can't be pothered with looking) of Shakespeare, that he held the mirror up to nature? Did he?—no, or I'm sure we should hate him. Or it was one of those fat distorting mirrors, broadening into nothingness all the ugly angularities. Be sure that Shakespeare knew the intolerance of pigmies.

Ibsen, I fancy, holds the mirror up to nature but his is the lugubriously-lengthening sort: an inverted humour controls him. Is it wise to shew anger to pigmies? . . . 'tmay be the exasperation of the mirror.

A fool and his theories are soon parted: a puff of clean wind and they are gone. But he spins them again, and sometimes, by who knows what impossible chance! he snares some sentient atom of fact or truth. Do you notice that great writers or painters don't speculate? they affirm, sometimes so boldly that you fancy they will break the bones of the universe of sensible things, of experience, and burn them into a brief white light, to illuminate their one or two unfamiliar assertions.

The chief benefit of a fact is that you can theorize about it. See how busy the speculative spiders have been casting threads between Shakespeare and Bacon, for instance. 'Tis a proof of our indifference to most great writers that we chatter about them so incessantly: ours is not the indifference of silence but of incessant and irrelevant gossip. Now and then we are enslaved beyond redemption: Shakespeare or Homer imposes a strait bondage upon us; we are dominated by him, cradled and nursed in him. We are taught to reverence him whether we know him or not, to praise him whether we understand him or not, to quote him whether we love him or not. We can never have another Shakespeare because we are overwhelmed by the first. Nine-tenths of us hate him but are afraid to say so. We don't find his women our women: his men are many of them tedious creatures. It is but the unfailing flame of pure poetry that keeps the love of the few, and the reverberation of great praise which claims the homage of the many.

So Hamlet is a tissue of theories and baseless fancies and idly ingenious affirmations and timidly audacious questionings; and the Prince of Denmark is long forgotten; and the very mime on the stage must incarnate a theory, and lecture o' Sunday evenings about it. We are all enveloped in a vast devilishly malignant web of Shakespeare and Shakespeariana, in the company of theorists of every imaginable kind, from metaphysician to brain specialist. Inappeasably voracious is the man of this brazen idol: irreflectively servile the mass of worshippers. Very humourless is Shakespearean criticism. Do you care to know how many of his lines are "end-stopped"? what proportion there is of feminine endings? or a score other trivialities? Men have given their lives to these things and after many years produce—a theory!

Savourless nothings are their words. But such a man as Coleridge—is he not born to spin dreams, to pass his life not in reasoning but in divining? Half his reported table talk is about Shakespeare and his contemporaries: but he would talk insuppressibly of anything you might choose. And his Lectures on Shakespeare are but expanded talk—lacking, sometimes happily, the casual checks of conversation. His criticism, I think, is alone and apart because of the brilliance and infinite variety of his speculation. He is the only one of modern critics who dares to stand up to Shakespeare, to measure him by his own mind. He did what it is said an actor must do: he made himself a projection of the character he considered. Criticism became self-divination. And it is supremely good when a man speculates aloud about himself, and unconsciously. No marvel that the stream of his talk was inexhaustible: the well was deep, and Shakespeare was bucket and chain.

Coleridges are rare, but surely it is not impossible to learn that the one eternal subject is the personal, the one inexhaustible well is self, no matter what the bucket. And there can be but one authentic discovery: but one needs to be schooled in this by Sir Thomas Browne and Montaigne (Te Deum Laudamus). There are remote isles and untravelled nooks of experience of which we need never tire to talk, or to hear. When we know this we can begin speculating. Coleridge wrote a Theory of Life.

I owe thanks to your uncle for sending me to a book of Kipling's—*The Day's Work*. He spoke particularly of the opening story *The Bridge Builders*, which is uniquely fine. Several of the stories in the book deal with not exactly new themes in an entirely new way. Mr. Kipling returns to the inspired method of the nursery, and through the eyes of childish wonder interprets the voice of machinery, horses, wild monsters, and railway engines. They all talk. There is a naïve childishness in this: a casting back to the time when nought that moved was flat, and five years of unconsciousness could put voices into the dead as no poet could.

Needeth not to say how amazingly clear they are, in the best sense of a shallow word: so skilful and so easy-accomplished that one might almost think there is nothing but the novelist's easy skill. As when a fiddler fellow astonishes us with a surpassing cunning we say it is mere technique and straightway dub him virtuoso; so because Kipling's stories in this book are so wondrously worked we may toss it off easily with the same clod-witted dictum.

Let me tell you one illuminating Shakespearean theory, which I have just happed on.—That Hamlet was a woman in love with Horatio. That way verily lies madness, for Hamlet and his commentators alike.

Yours ever

JOHN FREEMAN

"O to be free of the travail and questing,
O to be free of the fool-thickened war,

Free of the palpitant trouble unresting
  Unceasing of sadness and madness ajar.
O to be free with the joy-winged swallow,
  Free with the wild rose, free with the lark;
Free with the weed in the roadside hollow,
  Free with the last bird lost in the dark."

TO LILIAN AND MARGUERITE SMALLEY

BABBACOMBE
4th. July, 1904

DEAR AND HONOURED LADIES

You will observe that I am endeavouring to obey your injunction to write more plainly and more largely.

Let me admit, in the first place, that I was sadly disappointed when I opened the welcome fat envelope this evening. A little tired with much walking and the heat of the sea, tired with many delights, I came upon your budget with enraptured expectancy.

Lack-a-day! Do you not know that she *only* gives who gives more than is expected or justified? You are churlish in enforcing me to such privation of wisdom. How can I learn except *I* have a teacher? how can I write, except to reply? or lament, save to duly responsive souls? or praise, except I have somewhat to praise?

Little enough occasion can I find in you for praise.

Last night heavy clouds were driven over a blue heavy sky—quite suddenly enveloping all save the extreme west.

While we watched, the gold became fire. Sank the sun behind the tall trees, the purple cloud remaining a perfectly straight and immovable rampart above him. Behind the heavy branches he glowed—a cherub in hell: a ring of flame for a fire-proof clown to jump through: a frying pan in the

Y

making: a Christmas tree toy: an immense orange:—and whatever else stupidity may be suggested by the weary wit of fools—all these was the setting sun.

I have never known Nature to be so original and daring. For Nature really is lame and undevising. Patience has ruined her, as the same false virtue has ruined many men. We are continually having to assist her: and she takes our assistance and all advice something stubbornly. Her paths are so circuitous, her tricks so stale, her invention so sterile. A million years ago she made man; and has never sufficiently got over that poor triumph to be able to improve on him. I fancy the horny-handed Nurse turning the noisy brat round with all the amazement of ignorant vanity—pulling his hair out to see if it has really grown from within: wrenching his arm to find the joint: and adding in various imbecile ways to the unhappy youngster's inevitable perplexity and rage. He has already done something with that same intractable-idiot Nurse, and given a few million years he will infallibly turn her out. For it is astonishing how much he has done for himself. Nature has bound him down to three-score years and ten: yet he has immortalized himself. He has reared himself and clothed himself, doctored and buried himself what time Nature stands apart, back bent, clothed in knitted jersey and the red petticoat of the very aged, and rubs palsied fingers, saying "Dear me, dear me". And she, who does not die, depends on men who die daily for understanding and immortality. And he understands her, probes her,—child as he is, flouts her!

Withal he has infinite pity for the poor bungler. She has bound him by laws which restrain nothing of his soul. He even wonders if she herself be not far more straitly bound by what far darker compulsion! And, anyhow, he is undaunted. Powerful and blind as she is, equally, she goes flinging diseases and deaths, agonies and perplexities and disabilities, wantonly at him: nothing that he does but is done in sorrow; nothing he achieves but it brings regret because the achievement is imperfect: every strength of his is flawed, every beauty violable, every joy dashed with bitterness. Yet man, who endures all this and understands something of it, is greater than she who merely inflicts it ignorantly.

She, the gap-toothed fumbler, has lost what sense of plan she may have once had, and now moves half in ignorance, half in wantonness.

Nevertheless, it is wonderful what she has done. She has made just here a green shady space on the breast of a great cliff, and strewn it with ivy and fern and tall trees: at evening there is a violet shadow over the whole space. Just now bright golden columns are revealed between the yielding leaves, and I am altogether content in the umbrageous quiet. A thousand miles below waves are breaking a restful rhythm. Noontide rest is rarest and surely the most welcome.

So Nature, to give her due credit, has done wonders. But man has helped her.   Yours reverently

J. F. F.

O this is all too cold to suggest the keen intensity of my worshipful regard. Reverent? I am on the extreme verge of reverence—so reverent as almost to topple into the chuckling abyss of derisiveness. REVERENT!!!

ANERLEY
12th. April, 1905

MY DEAR LADIES

One of you is a shameful vulgarian:—you "feast your eyes on" the shifting colours, indeed! Truly an exquisite pleasure that must needs be so described. And surely it was not your eyes only that feasted; surely not on colour alone that you feasted—oh gross indignity! 'Sdeath—has there been no cake?

And the other is shockingly mistaken. . . . Dost think that

Montaigne is no more than a shadow of Emerson? I conceded the suggestion to your indolence, and straightway you conceive Montaigne's merit to be that he is Emersonian, forsooth. Pray is it Shakespeare's chief excellence, that in one or two lines he is Tennysonian? or that Webster, when he writes

"O that 'twere possible that we
Might hold some two days' conference with the dead!"

is *honoured* to suggest to the same immortal singer his lovely stanza

"O that 'twere possible
After long grief and pain,
To find the arms of my true love
Round me once again."

And, prithee, let me assure you that Emerson was a tireless pilferer: every essayist is. But only Montaigne confesses it.

Give you good day: I forgive you both.

I think I have the advantage of you even now. . . . Every morning I am assailed by sharp scents of hyacinth and daffodil, and heavy odours of wallflower—a tangle of scarce distinguishable fragrance. And keener and welcomer than all is the thrill of the smell of new cut grass. . . . Tell me, have you any pleasure more stirring?

"The hyacinths fane filled with incense,
The daffodils memoried bells,
These waken a sense hid within sense,
A yearning that kindles and swells;
And wall-flowers fervid and sunny,
Ranked tulips' bright burdening wealth—
Each blossom o'er-heavy with honey
And faint with the burden of wealth."

'Twas but yesterday morning I had a letter from Dr. Mansie, in praise of Balzac's *Eugenie Grandet*. His praise and pleasure are as decided as yours. Miss Smalley's (minor) pleasure is quite a negation of her usual ostentatiously negative attitude. You have feasted, no doubt (literary cannibal), on Balzac's portrayal of character.—Prithee, believe without questioning that some of Balzac's are *not* suited to your taste. When you are emancipated from Methodism and all negativeness (by the way, how could you —a mere bundle of negatives—feast—on anything but cake?), it may be different. But even Balzac is unequal, and would disturb your general indifference. (I am enraged at your unrepented insolence—I could repay you with good wholesome abuse, ripe archaic English. But I won't: it is dangerous to teach a good pupil.) But there are many of his novels written at the same white heat, transfused with passion, heightened and deepened with an almost incredible sincerity. Here is a man, one might say, who takes the whole of modern life for his province, reading it all as a mania, or wizard phantasmagoria—moving and coloured, sometimes flaming feverishly. The mania of wealth, of ambition, of science, of lust, of art—he broods over them all; and one fancies him asking, Life itself—is it not a mania?

"O life too harsh,
O lips that will not ever cease from sighing!
    O tardy Death,
Too late to heal, and late to stay the crying!

    O love too fierce,
And cruel lusts all gracious thoughts upsealing!
    What will you leave
For death to heal, who comes too late for healing?

    Too late, too late!
And vain is all remembrance and all weeping.
    Too tardy, Death,
To grant us aught save the last quiet sleeping."

I am minded to write you something of Johnson: I am still reading of him and he has been much in my mind lately. One of you (I hope not both) is too deeply immersed in a comfortable feline dilettantism to attempt eight volumes: *Daily Mail* snippets would possibly be sufficient. But the broader interests and more erect dignity of the other of you will be fascinated by the masculine greatness of Johnson. Do you know that he was so poor as to learn the art of living from beggars almost, yet so proud as to reject scornfully the proffered help of friends? that himself irritable and at times intolerant, his house became a home for some whose affairs had made them unhappy and peevish, and he bore with them as well as a man may? that he carried home a poor homeless wretch whom he found fainting in the streets—carried him home on his own broad back? that years and years after the offence, he did penance in the market place of Uttoxeter for a proud fault of his youth? that the sight of him in pain and gloom, nigh death, brought tears (I think) to good John Wesley's eyes, who wrote—how could he write it without grieving?—when he "spent two hours with that good man Dr. Johnson, who was very ill"? and that by many his charities were better known than his writings?

But what care you for these things? It is time now for you to be feasting your eyes on the last flickerings of light from the west. Have you missed your beef (ugh! boiled beef) and jam? . . . Meanwhile the light fades, leaving you, I am to suppose, replete.

There is a bird and a star hanging there perhaps, clear in the strangely luminous distance.

> " A bird, a star,
> In the sunset singing,
>   One near, one far;
> But each in my heart is singing."

Sometimes, just now, the west does indeed seem the soft bier of a perfect day; and one hour upgathers all the lost hours of the light as cast blossoms. The recalled moments, not long to be kept, are for a space rich and fragrant with associations: and then it is hard to speak but in metaphors. The closing flowers speak freely as they shut; their fragrance wanders in strange capricious currents. It is caught, lost, recaptured, and lost again, as suddenly as a pure thought. Says Matthew Arnold—

> "Come airs and floating odours, to convey
> A melancholy unto all our day."

At evening the melancholy is softened and sweetened with a delicate sense of rest.

Later, only the star sings.

Good wishes and thanks.

Yours

JOHN FREEMAN

ANERLEY
22nd. February, 1906

LADIES

You are obtuse, impenitent, and amazingly impudent.

Certes, I expected a letter—but not a squib: an apology—but not a defiance: a plea—not a gibe.

And this from those who have eaten my jam, my apple jam, my marmalade golden as my weekly half-sovereign, my cake: who have devoured ravenously my cream, my pudding: who have stolen my golliwogs and confounded my temper. Fire and fury!

Injurious women! I could invoke plagues on you; but then you would have a morbid satisfaction in your own punishment. I would teach you better manners, but that you would at once estimate the moral value of them. People like you are so absurdly occupied with your moral "progression", forsooth, that you have no time or interest for anything but to flout those who don't care tuppence (do you blush at the word?) for moral anything.

You betray me into bad verse and worse temper.

No, like Bernard Shaw, I am a fluent "liar". I read your seven pages of ill-concealed annoyance gladly—impervious to your shots.

For know, O most graceless among women, that I came home happy last night by my favourite train, and not ingratitude, nor spite, nor envy, could dim or defeat my satisfaction.

For I came from a music hall through Piccadilly homeward. True, I could not get into the Oxford under five shillings; true, in a sudden freak of folly I turned away and contented myself with the "Palace"; true that I had to forgo my usual call at—where you get glorious coffee and sixteen different kinds of sandwiches. But—I had been to a music hall!

Do you understand that even your letters were impotent —then?

One of you calls me ferocious: the other fool. One uses American slang: the other Methodist cant. Am I a dog? I feel these things now as I could not feel them last night.

And I raise my voice in lament—

O my marmalade and my cream; my books and my jam; my "poems" and my pudding; my cake! all unworthily were ye bestowed on gross Philistine women. And O my talk, my reading, and my letters, my elephantine epigrams and laborious elucidations of the obvious! Ye have been wasted on middle-class minds.

Will H. M. S. be concerned to know that I am not used to receiving letters with such a "profusion" (it is her word) of indecent words such as c——s? Doubtless, Mrs. Smalley

would be astonished and pained to know of it: but fear not!
I will persist in magnanimous revenges, albeit the magnanimity is unappreciated.

But "ferocious" and "foolhardy"! Manners, manners! I
am driven to the gasping staccato of extreme surprise.

I will *not* re-read the vile, broken-kneed, spur-galled
cacophony which you call verses. You will ask me to read
Marie Corelli next, or Silas Hocking; or to listen to Coleridge
Taylor (there!); or to look at Academy pictures. The *form* of
the verse is vile and vicious, with the vileness and viciousness
of an idle and anti-intellectual middle-class.

"Foolhardy and ferocious!" . . . fire and fury.

Ah me! and—O saddest of all reflections—I have taken
you to ballets.

I repent me of all the good I have done and of all the evil
I have not done. I repent me of cake and cream and jam: of
pudding: of all the "delicious confections" that have been
offered all unworthily. I repent me of—and of—I repent me
of ballets.

Henceforth you shall go to conventions, cat-gatherings,
"mutual improvement" societies, for all I care. By heaven,
you shall go to class and not a word of far-sighted friendly
protest will I utter.

Yours sorrowfully

JOHN FREEMAN

After a Music Hall

"As I came through St. James's Park
   The mists drew like the skirts of a ghost.
The toll of twelve upon the dark
   Fell, and——"

No, I won't, though. Finish it for yourself.

EXETER
June, 1907

MY DEAR PUPILS

When I stirred from a brief drowsiness and looked through the window I saw wonders. We were passing great dim trees and miles of hedges as dim. The sky looked blue but there was no light—only a sense of relief of the heavy darkness that weighed down on the quiet fields. There was a singular beauty in this vision, and as I watched I saw the beauty deepen as the night began to withdraw. I saw that there were mists and vast vapours spread over valleys and hidden hills. Here the mist would lift and shew solemn trees against the soft sky: there it would fall to hide them. They seemed to step appealingly from the darkness, then remain a moment unstirring and grand, until caught by the loose skirts of the mist they trembled back into vagueness.

There was real, tender light. And then could be seen separate little currents of cloud that curled and eddied around: delicate ends, spirals and whorls; and great flowings to and fro—making the early morning mysterious. They moved low over the waters of a broad river and its tributaries, which shone at whiles with a faint radiance. Near at hand some poor ruinous buildings would be made fantastic by the partial vesture of vapour, standing dim and uncertain; while much farther off—clear of so marvellous an encumbrance —things stood in the sharp radiance of the first sweet light.

You might call it the shyness of virginal morning—the delicate withholding of own intimate beauty. Soon enough the sun will come, soon the noise and sight of men bringing the daily profanation: there will be shameless rending and unholy nakedness of the land. But just now, for a few long moments, our sweet young earth, our holy and happy earth, is casting her vesture from her and catching it back to cast it around her again.

Walking through the clean silent streets before sunrise, smelling eagerly the clean thrilling air with its opulent odour of pine trees wet with rain, and then seeing from high ground the long frayed lines of colour which seemed to rise from the East so long before the sun—and so long after ourselves— all this was wine in the blood of us unclogged by heavy dwarfish slumber. We breathed—and it was happiness enough merely to breathe, and we were so happy that we did not talk about happiness but looked and spoke contentedly of such trifles as we saw. It was happiness enough to breathe—I had not been so happy for several hours:— indeed since that pleasant late hour in your garden on Thursday (do you remember, and re-feel, the grave untroubled quietness, the intimate colours?).

Happiness depends, of course, on such simple small things and carries with it the sense of such simple great things. Here on the high cliffs of Budleigh Salterton one has sight of wild flowers all but washed by the patient sea. For the sea is patient and quiet. Here and there she has broken off odd lumps of red earth, and you come across strange ends and threads of paths abrupt and alluring. She has eaten so little in all these sad years of warfare, and the violent waves have not been very violent here. Nevertheless bit by bit the land is taken with its wild treasure of flowers and grass and bushes, to feed the wilder treasure of sea forestry shining in the "deep divine dark dayshine of the sea".

Patient and laborious sea! Gulls are flying over the violet waters, swaying high and white above her, and showing the delicatest transparence of pink in their easy and unecstatic flight. My swallows, whose flight is sudden and ardent and ecstatic, are nowhere here. It is enough to see the silent gulls white and pink above the violet sea.

Walking from Budleigh to Exmouth one feels the delight of great winds, the delight of sharp woodland smells, the delight of sharp sea-savours, the delight of birds flying, the delight of heavy mass flowers, the delight of climbing and striking feet, the delight of the goal. These are the seven delights of the cliff-side walk.

These quiet cool leisurely towns—these dignified home-towns! I am sitting here in a restaurant every door of which is painted pure white—and this in London, I said derisively! The streets are clean: one could lick the stone and brick walls.—Angels of cleanliness have wept tears of joy over this sea-sweetened place and made it spotless.

Then there is the joy of eating large ripe strawberries mashed in thick soft cream; indeed two or three of me are enjoying ourselves utterly. There is, of course, nothing for the local preacher, little for the critic, little for the rhymester, and nothing at all for the amateur of pleasure. Still, the rest of us are doing very well.

But O London!

> "Ah London! London! our delight,
>   Great flower that opens but by night."

Stands Piccadilly where it did? Has the Empire fallen? Is Victoria Monks still at the Tivoli? What—what is the Alhambra orchestra playing this week? Can the moon rise over St. James's Park while I am so far? Alack your lonely pavements and untrodden-by-me streets! The very stars look down on Leicester Square in vain for men.

> "While I am far, while I am here,
>   While I am longing for the nights
>   Hung with the silvern and golden lights."

O to be in—now that Lauder's there! But tell me, you un-worshipped gods, where *is* Lauder?

Traitor that I am! It is more than two weeks since I saw ballet and drank claret beneath the silken roof (old yellow silk miraculously pleated) of the enquiry room of the Alhambra. Where be my dancers, my singers, my wearers of purple and gold and every proud and perfect colour? my luxurious cigarettes? my contented saunterings at midnight?

O London, London is my delight.

Monday evening

We have just returned, and find your letters. Did you feel a throb these two hundred miles away? "O you adorable women!" I cried, and for the moment I forgave you much, "You blessed powers of the air, so busy on your bountiful bestowings! I charge you forget not the Daughters of Smalley. Nay, rather leave your petty ministrations of the poor and stupidly unfortunate, your superfluous visitations of the wretched, and make the plenty of these my friends more plentiful, satisfaction more satisfied! and if there be just now any feeling (oh! how natural) of loneliness, any sense of the alienation of two hundred miles, any sorrowfulness—console them with words of equal comfort and wisdom."

I tell you, Marguerite, it was to no friendly spirit that I devoted you five minutes later. Adorable woman? Zounds!

Oh and I had thought you a deserving case! I had had kind thoughts of you and when I watched the waves and wrote to you of their beauty, I thought of your solitary watchings of them at Bournemouth and almost wished you here.

It is not here I wish you now!

At Exmouth we saw marvellous flowers:—huge snowy bushes of White Marguerites, houses half covered with the flowers of glorious climbing geraniums. I spoke of you and said—enough. I will not repeat it.

Far differently do I speak of you now.

And when I think of what letters you *have* written—the subtle reflection, the profound philosophical considerations, these lightened by wit and readiness and humanized by sympathy, the poetic phrases, the correct spelling—when I think of all this my anger is redoubled.

Lilian has written better—but how little she has written!

Tush! I contemn you both. Strawberries and cream, strawberries and cream. Adorable women, forsooth!!

By the way if you call at home for roses and whatsoever other flowers may bloom just now, you will see on the table a book which de la Mare sent me (together with one of Benson's which I have here)—entitled *The Cloak of Friendship* by Laurence Housman, a very considerable poet. You may take it and read it, gratefully, for I believe it is a well-written and, what is more, well-spelt book.

Am I to think of you both looking up at the abominable roof of the Crystal Palace what time you listen to the *Messiah* to-day? You are atrociously lucky.

Ah yesterday, I mind me now, we clambered over a stile and stepped into the rich depths of a little solemn gorge filled with rare ferns and liberal flowers. The warm wet odours of rich earth washed round us, satiating us as with wine. Divinely dim!

Well, well, I will not finish now but simply stop. *We* have been to the Cathedral (how much better than the Crystal Palace) listening to a Festival—poor thing that it was.

Yours humbly

JOHN F.

J. E. SPINGARN

TO J. E. SPINGARN

DEAR MR. SPINGARN

Your name is known in England, but I did not know you had written verse as well as editing our critical writers. It is very kind of you to send me a copy of your *Poems*, and though I haven't yet read the book quite through—tasting it slowly now and then, as one may do with lyrics—I have read enough to find its quality. If you will guess what I do like from what I don't, you may turn to the "Caroline Ditties"—especially the second of them. A true Cavalier would not, perhaps, be quite so cavalier-like: the subject calls more for the playful touch than for that warm sensuousness of—wasn't it Carew, who treated it in a poem called *The Rapture?* My memory is poor, for it is years since I read that poem.—One might well envy your freedom of form and luck in rhyme, and wonder whether this can be a first book.

With many thanks, and good wishes from this small spot of suburban England to your vast U.S.A.

Sincerely yours

JOHN FREEMAN

P.S. I have stupidly missed the "jacket" of your book, and only now notice that it is *not* the first. Please forgive my speculation.

J. C. SQUIRE

TO J. C. SQUIRE

2nd. May, 1915

DEAR SQUIRE

I shan't be the only one to speak of your article on Rupert Brooke, but I'd like to be one of the first. I didn't know him, but admired him and was shocked at the news. I heard it in Gloucester in the loveliest spring week I'd ever known: and that made it all the sadder. And I was glad to see what you said, and to see what you hadn't said: most of all at that touch at the end which told so much of Brooke, and you.

I hope you're all well.

Ever yours

JOHN FREEMAN

Thursday

DEAR SQUIRE

With characteristic and precipitate honesty I returned your *Gosse's Poems* when I sent the article in. Would you mind bringing the book up again and I will send round for it.

I'm still bewildered at being asked to make an article longer: broader, lighter, looser, obscener, I can understand. But longer!

Ever

JOHN FREEMAN

P.S. The stone which the builders rejected. . . . *The Dial* begins to print the stories you despised—one at any rate.

[1917 ?]

MY DEAR SQUIRE

This is a Note of Sympathy. The *Times* man says that *A House* is all about nothing, and that houses don't face

335

tempests, and so on. The Ass! And then he coolly takes over
your metaphor and says your superstructure has "passages"
of ugliness. The Ass! And best of all he corrects you with
Drinkwater's *Reciprocity*—the dear, naïve, affectionate old
Ass! I hope he is not a friend of yours, or if he is, that you
won't mind my calling him *ASS*.

It's the same old syndicated ASS that says that I'm afraid
of the commonplace, when the Lord in Heaven knows it's
the only thing I'm not afraid of and feel at home in. What is
"excessive choiceness"?

Well, we're "a little taller than the general"—General
Who?
                        Yours
                                    JOHN FREEMAN

                                    16th. July, 1917
DEAR SQUIRE
    Ever so many thanks for the two books, the inscrip-
tions and the annotations. There's a great leap upward to
the *Three Hills*, and from that to *Twelve Poems* and *The
Lily* a huge leap. I could have understood your going from
Baudelaire to *The Lily*, but I couldn't have imagined your
going from Baudelaire to *A House* or *The March*, I don't
like translations from the French: if they're good they're
polished: if bad they're varnished. But these other things of
yours have simply captured me—steadily but no doubt the
more surely for that. They're so firm and hard but *not*
polished. It's absurd to say such obvious things, but until
The Lily is sold out the obvious things need saying—and
then never again. That's all I'm doing for Jackson's paper—
a stupid article saying with stupid emphasis, I like this, and
that and the other—book! And that's the best thing a critic
(no critic, I) can ever say, after all: anything else he'll only
say from the egotism of ideas, hatred, envy. Envy, perhaps,
has crept into my notes, but may not be detected; only if

you see them and find them too objectionable, you needn't put it down to pure envy.

Is it in the faintest degree significant that I love best those where the form is most regular? *A House* even more than *Acacia Tree* or *The Stronghold*?

Thanks again.

Ever yours

JOHN FREEMAN

8th. August, 1917

DEAR SQUIRE

Well, I *was* glad to read *August Moon*—twice aloud, and so reading it didn't miss so acutely the *form* which I did miss on reading it to myself.

There seems nearly always something of evasion or indolence in irregular verse, unless the passion behind the poem is felt in it, making its own strong native rhythm; and only very seldom is anything won which would compensate for the loss of form. I don't know if one can argue from the fact that the lines which are most delightful are usually those most definitely "lines"; for it can be retorted that they seem delightful only because they are definite. But I do think that emotion seeks for and hungers after and wholly needs form, and needs it not only for resistance, as a swimmer needs water, but for the very means of life. So far as the free versers are dispensing with form, and not seeking or making a new form, they are fundamentally, metaphysically and even demonstrably wrong—and nothing could be wronger. I suppose in the abstract the ideal would be for every poem a new and different form, the expression of every lyric utterly completing and enfolding—simply *embodying*—the individual impulse; but since the mind hardens and grows firm, and character comes more and more surely into the work—half blessedly and half not—the form tends to repetition, embodying over and over again the same passion in nearly the same shape—and this, not always because inspiration has failed but because it hasn't, the passion becoming a ruling passion, the idea pure Idea, seeking satisfaction in repetition merely because it is incapable of satisfaction.

Does this seem nonsense? I haven't the ghost of an "idea" about poetry, and no "Theory" of verse. "One's Mind's made *so*"—and the difference between maturity and immaturity, between man and man, is only that some know at last, more than half unconsciously, how their mind's made and let it move where it will. Which is the elementary, forgotten wisdom of the world.

I'll get the astonished publishers to send you *Twenty Poems*: it was (I think) 1909 and (heaven be praised!) a lot happens in 8 years. But I'm not deploring the *Twenty*, for it was written when I had but lately, belatedly, begun to write anything at all fit for the severe eye of myself and another. And I'll send with this letter, or afterwards, two or three poems you've not seen, the longest of which Jackson is apparently very nervous of accepting.

Ever yours

JOHN FREEMAN

ANERLEY
8/10/17

DEAR SQUIRE

Do you know, I've been wondering and wondering why you print those things of Yeats? Others might well wonder why you print other poems and it doesn't become me to guess—I know it's an editorial weakness. But what *is* Yeats doing?—With his balloon of the mind and his spiral(?) of No Go, and his batch of detestably decadent verses a few weeks ago. What has he to do with rouged women lying abed in silk trousers and nasty fat furtive cardinals, and the rest of the cheap Pierrotism? What has he sold himself to? I can't help bursting out when I see a man like Yeats doing things that simply aren't worth anyone's doing; and if you see things in this sort of verse which I don't see, then I'm utterly wrong and humbled.—But here's an odd thing! Because these seemed so nauseous I turned to the 1895 *Poems*, with all those early lyrics; and the later work had so poisoned the earlier in my own mind, that all the old pleasure was gone and I could see only a kind of Frenchification, an easy Symonsification.—"Only" isn't quite correct: there were exceptions, e.g. the poem with the refrain "Come away, oh human child", a lovely Allingham-like poem. But in others there were only the early leaves of decay, as in these later poems I can see and hear only the late decaying leaves. I think it grievous to see such a decline—and then to suspect that it's no decline. And I can't help thinking.—If such a man as Yeats falls to such a coarse temptation—for it surely is a coarse temptation—what hope is there for X, Y and myself? What worm has got into his heart?

Ever

J. F.

4th. August

Dear Squire

I have just been reading your characteristically generous paragraph in the *Outlook* about the poems. The critic in me whispers a hundred misgivings; all the rest of me breathes clear a thousand thanks.

And still my huge debt to you mounts up.

Ever

John Freeman

12th. March, 1919

Dear Squire

This is the poem I spoke about when last we met. It may induce you to wish unsaid half the things you've said

in your *Statesman* review, for which I am your somewhat
bewildered debtor. In spite of all you say about *Memories*,
this is as simple as *Robinson Crusoe*. And I've had such a
satisfaction in writing it, and the gift of a subject is always
a divine good fortune (never so much as with this) that I'm
overpaid already and can stand any amount of criticism—
except the criticism, which I may have yet, that I've dis-
honoured the great subject.   Ever

JOHN FREEMAN

5th. August, 1919

DEAR SQUIRE

So many thanks for this, your latest book and gift.
When I turned from *A Far Place* (which I'd seen before) to
a newspaper I found myself reading your beautiful rhythm
into that poor prose. Perhaps that is the most exquisite poem
in the book and in any of your books: I think it gives me the
readiest pleasure. But I'm most attracted to a less perfect
thing—the third of the "processes". I don't know whether
the form is quite adequate, but the poem exists for me almost
independently of its form, and astonishes me by its psychological revelation. It *is* creation. It is exact and excitingly
true, even truer than the "first process"; and it pleases me
the more because it proves over again for me the plain fact
that it is only by imagery—by poetry—that the mind, its
"processes of thought" and its emotional process, can be
expressed. It excites me on its own account as a poem, and
because it's the *kind* of poetry that remains to be written.
All that living pool of dark deep water remains unnoticed,
and it's the essential poetry which isn't of our time or past
time but of all time and no time.

Thanks again.

We've intestinal poisoning in the family. What have you?

JOHN FREEMAN

Wednesday

DEAR SQUIRE

Your letter followed me from here. If a fortnight's time will suit you I will call and show you or send what I've got— but you know I've not been doing lyrics lately. Or you might use one you've had for the *N.S.* e.g. *The Evening Sky*, which I think one of my best. And I'd be proud etc. to be named as one of your Contributors, though I don't know what you will get except psychological narratives, in verse. I'm glad you are going to do a literary monthly, until I reflect that it may stop or hamper your own verse; and then all your innumerable editorships appear swindles, for which prosecution is already overdue.

Ever

JOHN FREEMAN

Thursday

DEAR J. C. S.

While the Crystal Palace fireworks have been going off to-night I have been looking through *Poems: First & Second Series* again with a professional eye and purpose; and it struck me that I had never seen them so vividly before. I was quickened with admiration and envy as I re-read some familiar poems—*Rivers* (the end of it), *A House*, *Winter Nightfall* and several others. I blamed myself for not reading them again and again lately (though indeed I read nothing), and it seemed at last merely lazy and mean to let the last post go out to-night without telling their Author how they excited me with their beauty of visible and invisible.

Nothing more sure and touching, nothing more beautiful, has been done in our time, I said to myself, than some of the poems in the two series. And I repeated it aloud to my wife, and she merely said, "Well, I always told you so".

Did you know it?

Yours

J. F.

ANERLEY, S.E.20
23rd. September

My dear Squire

When I got home at the end of a week's delicious walk I found your book and your own hand in it. You'll believe I was delighted. And then I was amazed and annoyed to think that I hadn't seen a single notice of the book any-where:—not a word in *The Times*, although they have a column or so, this week, of petty little notes of petty little books of verse! It may be your comfort that so was Shelley treated.

I'm sending you (not in return) my narrative piping hot: I think I told you that it's a true story[1]—my psychology being truer still. I don't know what to do with it, but I'd like the copy back when you've read it.

I hope your enlarged family is prospering. Oh, you remember giving me Hewlett's new poem? I was so taken with it that I couldn't help writing to tell him so, and received the nicest of welcome answers—full of talk of his own aims and pleasures in poetry. I was glad I'd written.

Ever

J. F.

Monday. 1925

Dear Squire

I'm sending a set of the *Melville* proofs: can I have them back? I've not read them thoroughly yet—there are p's and q's to be disentangled here, interworded there, and nicer harmonies—or nicer elements in that Other Harmony —to be established. But I can't do it this week, for in the morning I'm off to Ely, Peterboro' and Norwich to see Cathedrals. You've never been to Ely, though it lies so close to your—and Milton's—Cambridge; but I've had the

[1] Probably *The Red Path*.

Cathedral in my mind since five years old, when I used to stare at a coloured engraving, all amber and azure. But you've never been, for all your Buicks: and I shall discover it to-morrow.

Speaking of Milton, I rejoiced in your final paragraph in *The Observer*:

"Fools will fools more confidently be",

in speculating upon the unknowable when it's a question of poets, than on any other question. Why should a mere gesticulating Frenchman touch on Milton and his blindness? *Who* is it that's blind? Don't the French owe us much, so much as to make them in decency humble before Milton?— The only retort should be, in fitness, A pox on you!

Ever

JOHN FREEMAN

Wednesday. 1927

MY DEAR SQUIRE

I ought to have thanked you before for sending me tickets for the Play, but I waited until I'd seen it. I enjoyed it nearly as much as my wife did, and that means a great deal. It's very seldom I go to the theatre—ordinarily I hate it, my puritanic blood made critical in an expiring spurt of conscience—and so I'm inclined to be cold in my mind yet soft in my heart: impressed by the very things that seem ignominious, easily swayed and angry at being swayed. The last play I saw was Pirandello's *Henry IV*, which overwhelmed me; when I saw yours I couldn't help recalling Pirandello, for something of the same painful urgency streamed over the stage and struck me sharply. It seemed mainly a painful play, even cruel; not simply in its acute emotional scenes (as with Kate and then with Helen) but in its general sense of men at war with time, snared by circumstances. It's common to be snared and teased by the senses, gross or fine: we're all subject to that more or less constantly; it's not so common to be aware of the *pressure* of time like an iceberg, annulling all motion and affection. What in fact it brought home was the coarse intolerable fact of death, *alias* time, *alias* fate—or what not. It was the *isolation* of man in time and space, the fact that his simplest and sincerest voice can't carry (except in the miraculous tones of poetry) across centuries or even decades or years—it was this that your play made so clear.

This afternoon I went to the lecture, and scoffed at all the speakers—heavy as pitch—until you spoke—This isn't flattery: you really had something to say that I liked hearing.

One day I'll come round and talk: I've not had a word with you for months.

Affly.

JOHN FREEMAN

Monday. 1928

DEAR JACK

I am tired and so, casting up my Sins, I remember I've not said a word (more than hasty "saying") of thanks to you for your part in my *Selected Poems*. You know they are due this Spring, and that I've actually had a spoonful of money from the divine Macmillans on a/c? I ought to have told you before: I ought to have typed you a letter all in Capitals, all in Red, with a huge "thanks" at the top; but being un-civilized, though not forgetful, I didn't. And thinking I *must* write I remembered that for fourteen or fifteen years you've printed my verse with such blind and incompre-hensible readiness as no editor has ever shewn to another poet. They are dozens, scores, hundreds—short and long, rhymed and rhymeless: you must be horrified to look back and remember.

If at the end of a long life you have to make your peace

with the Recording Angel (a malicious fellow, he!) and other virtues are dismissed with contempt and other charities declared folly, if then you speak of these many wise and kind indulgences, that Angel will be convinced you are the kindest of friends—and the best of critics. O rare conjunction!

This is nonsense: I *am* tired, as you will see.

Ever

J. F.

ERNEST TURNER

TO ERNEST TURNER

DEAR TURNER

It was very delightful to have such a long letter from you, settled at last—I suppose it is *settled*—in Australia, and to know that so far all has gone well with you. I hope nothing has occurred to diminish the pleasant excitement of new surroundings, except getting used to them and finding them still more attractive. Apparently a fatherly Government doesn't want you to regard your sojourn as a holiday, since you are invited to work as soon as you land, but that, I know, suits you. I never knew a man less prone to the contemplative life! I wish I could live it: I am prone to it, but it escapes me. You had six weeks of it, and were glad when it ended. Why does luck fall to the rich, and poverty beset the poor? The people that hunger after activities are lapped in idleness while they sail slowly half round the world; while the people that covet idleness—I mean only myself—are torn with work and fast-bound with Responsibilities.

Well, you've given me a brief diary (almost) of your family doings, but I can't pay you in kind. My wife will tell you of everything that happens—I can only talk of things that don't happen. She has the true diarist's mind: her weekly letters to her Egyptian friend (now in England for a time) are a marvel of narrative, and I can't attempt to follow her. You'll believe me perhaps when I say that nothing has happened, but then Gertrude will write a truthful letter which makes it seem that everything has happened. All that has, in sober truth, happened is that lately I've been to my fourth funeral this year, that I've been twice to Cheltenham (the last time with Gertrude to discuss family matters with my Aunt who has now left there), that I've been to Oxford to dine (or be dined) and read, that I've been drawn by a young artist for the *Bookman,* and that I've been continuously well. On Thursday I go to Paris and then to Brittany with the Allans, and shall be away about a fortnight; this partly because we've not been able to fix up a family holiday this year. Joy and Cathy go to Suffolk with an old schoolfriend, and Gertrude and I hope a little later to go away by ourselves.

Other people flourish. Joy and Cathy break up to-morrow, and there's great excitement because it's Joy's last term. In October she'll be at Oxford, and half lost to her bewildered parents and her sad sister. Meyerstein is away in Hampshire, I think: he's been moody of late, perhaps because he's working hard at a sequel to *The Pleasure Lover.*—But how does it sound to hear news so far away? Is it dream-like, or is it conceivable to you that your old house stands empty, awaiting your return, or our departure, since Dixon wants us to go? Is it conceivable that for some years you were within a few feet of this room? And is it conceivable that it has rained nearly all day and is cold, and that July is said to be the seventh consecutive month with a deficiency of sun? I can believe it if you can't.

Pray don't think this a mean letter. It really was a pleasure to hear of you all and I do hope that all will go well with you and that your health is giant-like.

Always yours

JOHN FREEMAN

P.S. Gertrude's letter will follow,—perhaps catch this up while the sun is napping over Tierra del Fuego.

ANERLEY
14th. November, 1926

MY DEAR TURNER

This is meant for a Christmas greeting, and would have been written by both of us but for a sudden misfortune, which however is now mending.

Gertrude has had to have an operation—Appendicitis. . . .

I hope you won't have any but good news to repay me for this mixed news. You are probably baking under Southern suns; we are drowned under Western rains. We've never had a wetter November, but all things end, even an English winter, which as yet has hardly started.

Joy is safe at Oxford. She has just completed her first month there and seems very happy. Partly because she is working hard, perhaps, for she has to take an examination at the end of the term and is doubtful of getting through in one bite. I saw her a fortnight ago and she was very happy walking round Oxford with me and looking into new places. In about another month she will be home again, and no doubt very glad to be among the old familiar surroundings, even if with a zest for new things.

Cathy is pretty well, though she has been secretly upset at her mother's forsaking her in this unmotherly and un-accustomed way. Her school has merged with the Hall School, in the Bromley Road, a fine old Georgian building with a sometime famous garden. St. Christopher's took over the Hall school, and moved into possession in September, but Cathy hasn't yet overcome her regret, for she dislikes change and would prefer the old whatever advantage the new had by comparison. But she has her own circle at school and defies Fate—I mean the mistresses she happens not to like.

As for myself, I am well but working cursed hard in town and have done little at home for some time. My office has

moved into its new building at Bloomsbury Square, where I
have a mahogany room overlooking the Square and all the
world. I feel very grand, but have a hankering for the old,
noisy, inconvenient little room in which I once saw you.
I've been hardly anywhere and seen hardly anyone. I've not
had even the whole of my summer holiday. Not because
we've had no summer—we had quite a fair allowance—but
because I could not get away for more than a fortnight,
which I spent in Paris and Brittany with some friends. On
the whole I liked the change, but was heartily glad to get
back into England.

I often wonder how things are going with you. I picture
you all as striding over immense pastures or arable lands,
clad in leather, with smiles of ferocious energy on your
countenances and saying to one another, "This is better than
poor old England." Well, perhaps so. Poor England has
strikes, taxes, fogs, and a patient necessity for acting as a
beast of burden to the whole world. Sunny Australia smiles
and sends her Prime Minister here for a holiday at our
expense. You are, I take it, the Complete Farmer, and begin
to know the difference between oats and wheat, and on close
consideration can determine between barley and turnips. I
suppose you ride kangaroos? The last time I saw a woman,
a fat woman, it is true, on a kangaroo she looked uneasy and
very ridiculous; partly because of her garters. But I suppose
one gets used to the motion. Is it true that people take a
sea-sickness dose (Mothersill's I think it is called) before
mounting, until they get used to the oscillation? And is it
true that the effect is often like the inebriation due to pleasanter causes? I'm ignorant on these points, and I've often
wondered why they don't have kangaroo rides at the Zoo.
Years ago one would have answered, "Because of public
decency"; but we have changed all that. Even grandmothers
no longer indulge in underwear, and indeed in very little

overwear. But you know all about this, for it is only eight months since you left these bewildered Shores.

I wish I could give you some news, but I'm better at inquiries than news. Bottomley is still in prison, thrushes are busy about the garden as I write, Cathy went to the Armistice service at Holy Trinity this morning and saw "millions of soldiers" in the congregation, Waterloo Bridge is still in pieces, we are still told that St. Paul's Cathedral (like this house, alas) is collapsing, and still (unlike this house) shows no outward sign of collapse; the Thames still flows somewhere between Westminster and London Bridge (although it is popularly supposed to have a longer course, but this is only the assertion of the steamer companies); our fowls still lay eggs only when they think fit—and nothing else happens that hasn't happened for a thousand years past. And so, by this time you will be convinced that I have nothing left unsaid but good wishes to you all, and the kindest of remembrances from those who are or should be here. Gertrude will write when she is well enough, but please don't shy at the trouble of letter writing when you've time and the faintest inclination.
Always yours

JOHN FREEMAN

ANERLEY
April 3rd, 1927

MY DEAR TURNER

Your letter came a week ago, and we were all very glad to have news of you. We felt that you were treating us badly in giving us such a mere rough sketch of your days, without very much detail, but I suppose you felt that it would be a monotonous story of labour repeated over and over again. I don't think monotony really uninteresting, for it leaves one's thoughts free—but this is philosophy. At any rate it was good to know that you were all well and that you

seem to have no special complaint against that common
enemy, Things in General.

Here we keep up a complaining spirit without much
difficulty, the main complaint, of course, being of the
weather. Do you remember the character of an English
spring? It is very cold, with strong north-west winds. The
barometer rises slowly and sinks abruptly, but the weather
remains undisturbed, I should say greatly disturbed—
violent, wet and semi-arctic. Weeks ago promised early
spring, and on the whole March was mild, but now we
think there will never again be mild weather. Ten days ago
I went down to Cornwall for the week-end, and last Monday
I returned. I went down by land, I returned—on the same
line—by water. Miles of country had vanished, and ocean
taken its place. To-day is sunny but deceptive, for a big fire
is needed to keep one moderately warm. But this is tiresome
news—my next will be in June to say that Spring and
Summer have gone.

As to our fresh news, my wife is going on pretty well, and
suffers only from the cold—a mere shift in the infernal wind
will make her infinitely better. I am well, though a few
weeks ago I was at home for a week with 'flu and a touch
of pleurisy. I recover like a rubber ball, that rebounds
without hurting itself or anybody else. Joy came home from
Oxford a week ago, perhaps a little more mature, a little
Oxfordian and certainly very happy in her experiences
there, though what she has been doing nobody knows, for
she is not communicative, yet is never silent. For once, it
seems, we shall not be having a spring holiday, owing to
visitors here and the difficulty of fitting things in. I am sorry,
for I think the change would be good for the seniors, at
any rate.

Your old house is still empty, and the landlord will not
say what he will do to ours or on what terms; and so it is a

tent rather than a house. There never was a landlord more lackadasical or one who so persistently did the wrong thing and so pleased neither himself nor anybody else.

I am very glad you liked Melville—I've pretty completely forgotten all about it. Only an occasional belated review from Fiji or Siberia reminds me of it. And I'm writing nothing at the moment, except occasional articles or reviews, for I work like a dog by day. And talking of reading matter, would you like me to send you the *Sunday Times* each week? It would be very old, but if it would interest you it would be a pleasure to send it.

Do write again soon. We all like to hear of your doings and fortunes. All kindest remembrances to you and all.

Ever yours

JOHN FREEMAN

ANERLEY

8th. January, 1928

MY DEAR TURNER

I hope you were not surprised or angry at not hearing from us at Christmas. It wasn't that you were forgotten, but that I didn't remember in time for the Christmas mail, and then put it off and again forgot. We all remembered you, with others, on Christmas Day, and I silently drank your health on New Year's Day, just after midnight, in a bowl of punch. You yourself are not blameless, for your letter didn't give us all the news we wanted. You said nothing of Phyllis, and for all I know by the time you get this you may be a grandfather; Marjory too may be married and several of the boys, and by the time you write again you may be able to tell me the names of several grandchildren. Your letter, meanwhile, was all about the dry weather. You are lucky. The papers will have told you of our weather, but the papers don't do justice to it. Papers couldn't. Before Christmas it was intensely cold; on Christmas Day there was a downpour of rain—a deluge. Christmas night it turned to a blizzard, and the next morning brought about eighteen inches of snow. Villages have been fed by aircraft, people have died of exposure, lines of cars, lorries, etc. have been left in the roads, and everybody wondered whether the good old-fashioned Christmas was such a delight after all. Then the thaw, gales and floods. You will see from the papers I am sending that the Thames has behaved cruelly, people being drowned in their beds and others ordered to leave their houses. We don't know what will happen next, but I suppose a plague of rats will follow, for the rats are said to have left the rivers just as the rivers have left their beds. I can assure you that only the rivers have left their beds very willingly of late. To-day, however, is a lovely spring morning, and I have just returned from my usual Sunday morning walk filled with delight.

You ask about the house. Both houses have been new roofed, and are completely water-tight, for the first time within living memory. Our house has been completely renovated, almost wholly at our own cost, and now looks decent. My study has been brought down to the first floor, and Joy and Cathy each have a large room on the second floor—much to their own pleasure. With all this, need I say, I work like a nigger, or rather harder than a nigger; but of this no reasonable being would complain.

Joy is down from Oxford until the 20th, and Cathy swears she won't go there. She is hoping to leave school at the end of the summer term—she will be seventeen—and wants to do NOTHING. But this we are resisting, yet don't know what she will do beyond going to France for six months for the sake of her French—an absurd notion.

Do you remember Felix? He still favours us at week ends. And that reminds me of sad news, which will interest Stuart.

Mrs. Hopper died some little time ago, and a few weeks later Hopper himself died. One of his workmen has spoken very highly of him, and it seems sad that two people, not very old, should pass away so suddenly, and leave derelict the place they had built up.

I spoke of the New Year. We thought that a holiday was due to us, or rather to me, so we all went to Brighton. The weather was better there than we expected, until the Sunday night when the gale simply forbade sleeping, and was followed by the worst of storms last Monday. But I could not get out, for I had hurt my foot slightly and spent most of the week-end in applying fomentations to the injured member. Nevertheless we had a pleasant time, and listened in to the service at York Minster, where a special celebration was held to commemorate the 1,300th anniversary of the church at York. Perhaps you heard something of this yourself, since the wireless seems to annihilate distance. I've not listened in to Australia, else it is possible that I might hear your voice.

Please write again soon and tell me how you and Mrs Turner and all are keeping. I am sorry that you have not been perfectly fit yourself; how anybody can be unwell in hot weather, while we can't possibly keep well in cold, is more than I can understand.

A Happy New Year to you all.

Always yours

JOHN FREEMAN

LYME REGIS
4th. September, 1928

MY DEAR TURNER

I was very glad to have your last letter, though it wasn't very full of news. I should have liked to have had detailed accounts (I means a/cs) of Phyllis, and Bob, and

Stuart, and Marjorie and all the rest, including your ox and your ass and your pet hippopotamus and everything that is yours. I should like to know more exactly the kind of habitation that has the duty and honour of protecting you from snakes, waterspouts and storms of wind: what society you have: what "Koleya" means and where the Burgundy comes from. But it's unfair to complain of what you haven't told me, when you write such long and interesting accounts of your New Life in the Bush. I only hope that the drought hasn't ruined you, nor the tempests, and that you find Australia more and more a true "home".

Our news is nil. Joy has just finished her second year at Oxford, and is about to begin her most strenuous year. Cathy has just left school and is trying to evade a choice of occupation. My wife seems better than she has been for a long time—perhaps because of the excellent summer—and I try to work a little harder each month and in fact seem to achieve a little less.

Here, at Lyme Regis, we are ending another holiday. The last fortnight (nearly) has been excellent weather, and we shall return with many regrets. I have had to do some trifling business at Exeter, Torquay and Truro, but yesterday we all made an excursion to certain ancient small towns, Beaminster and Cerne Abbas, with wonderful churches and ruins, delightful old houses and decaying populations. I've never seen more wonderful places, set in a lovely serene country of downs, heather and rabbits.

But all this will be put behind us when we return on Thursday. Everything then will be quiet and humdrum, or rather noisy and humdrum. Dorset and Devon then will be as far off as Australia and Botany Bay. Summer and autumn will be like dreams—it will be nearly winter when you get this—and it will seem that this blue quiet sea, and green shore, and broken cliffs, have never been anywhere. But at the moment—I write this on the shore—it seems real and simply true, and London only impossible. How would it seem to you if, by shutting your eyes, you could drop here on the beach and start talking again?

Please give our Dutiful Remembrances to Mrs. Turner and all the rest, down to the second generation.

Yours sincerely

JOHN FREEMAN

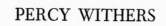

PERCY WITHERS

TO PERCY WITHERS

MY DEAR WITHERS

So friendly and kind a letter as yours makes me drop formality and get rid of a touch of distance between those who have been strangers until now.

Wilfrid Gibson had already written to me and to some extent prepared me for your letter, and indeed I meditated writing to you and only paused when—well, when I fancied it might seem anything but what it should seem. I was very glad indeed, therefore, to have a letter from you although perplexed and embarrassed (as I told Wilfrid last night in writing to him) at some of the things you said. But those things pleased me all the same, for you are one of the few to whom *Music* has not been a disappointment—or worse, a fulfilment of unflattering prophecy. So my thanks are due to you, if you think yours are due to me.

I should be very glad to come and see you, though I can't quite see when. In a week or two, if Spring returns, I hope to spend a few days with Robin Flower (whose name you know), and perhaps Wilfrid will have told you that I'm not generally my own master, any more than Charles Lamb was; I work in an office blessedly unrelated to letters and so live a double life of a kind which has come after so many years to suit me.—I don't say all this to raise difficulties. I will come and stay a week-end if you'll let me, and come as soon as I can. I am an unstrenuous person and "moon" about in the most completely lunar manner, but I hope that won't bore you.

This is all about myself—and so letters should be,

although yours wasn't; but perhaps your next will be. You say you are seldom in London, but if there should be a chance of seeing you in town, or at this house, it would give me pleasure. Meanwhile you have given me much to thank you for.

O, I ought to have apologised for delaying my answer. There have been reasons, but no reason is really adequate to excuse a negligent correspondent.

Ever yours sincerely

JOHN FREEMAN

ANERLEY
29th. December, 1922

MY DEAR WITHERS

It was so kind of you to send me Fausset's *Keats*, and a much longer letter than my fragments of letters deserve. I was immensely pleased with both, especially since they came in the very nick of Christmas Day. I've read a good part of the *Keats*—inevitably with a certain bewilderment, for the kind of criticism, the philosophic exegesis in which Fausset shines, is very hard for me to understand. So far as I understand and follow it I agree, and if these phrases seem scrupulously moderate you must take it that it is simply because of my numerous incapabilities, and that my mind will only let me look at such studies with a distant respect. Tell me of small technical points, show me why Keats used a comma here, an 'ed there, tell me the proportion of monosyllabic lines in various poems, shew me the beauty of his rhythm— and I'm your man; but these subtler interpretations of his mind, these cunning salts spread on his tail, are more difficult for me to apprehend than for most. I wonder, and admire, and only slowly understand. But I was very pleased to-day to hear an accomplished reviewer praise the book highly, both for matter and manner, and I heartily hope it will bring its author recognition and its dedicator gratification.

Our Christmas passed quietly—oh, you needn't fear, merrily as well. Both before and since, I've been busy with verse, one poem or narrative of 300 lines which I'm glad to have finished, and another a Wren bi-centenary poem which I'm almost sorry to have finished. And now I stagger to and fro like a hungry man, yet pleased to have done the things that have been on my mind, however ill they are done. You don't tell me of the fate of your own book and I'd like to know if Constable's have proved wise or stupid. Nor do you say if you have other plans, and I am hoping your health won't prevent your making and carrying out the plans that spring up thickly in an active mind. I fancy the mind grows more eager and exacting, the more anxious for expression as the body frets.

I wish you the most happy and prosperous of new years— the "you" including your wife and Monica and the rest.

Ever   ●   JOHN FREEMAN

ANERLEY
June, 1923

MY DEAR WITHERS

I've meditated upon a letter for a fortnight. Your welcome hand followed me to Cornwall, where I was spending my annual spring week with Robin Flower, and Conrad Aiken and Martin Armstrong making a quartette. We stayed at Gunwalloe, an almost inexistent village midway between the Lizard and Penzance. I fattened on cream, and if I'd been able to sleep I should have been perfectly content. I always have to come home to sleep. Both before and since I've been busy, but am now easier for a while. I've written but one poem since *The Grove*: I've not seen George Moore

for months, but mean to call this week; I've met Edith
Sitwell several times and have enjoyed the surprising
simplicity of her conversation; I've seen my bacteriological
namesake, and he's coming here on Tuesday; and I went to
the Handel Festival on Saturday. Such are my activities
during the few precious weeks of fleeting life!

Have you been to the Handel Festival? For years I've
lived within earshot of it (indeed it's difficult to live out of
earshot, for the choir and orchestra number 4,000!) but never
been until yesterday. I was dizzy but pleased: if it hadn't
been for polar winds I should have enjoyed myself dis-
creetly.

When I got home I found that Maurice Hewlett was dead.
I don't remember you ever speaking of him. I knew him,
mostly by letters, and liked him, admiring especially his
Song of the Plow, etc. and caring but little for his novels.
These deaths (my office chief and friend died lately) shock
and disable me, and Hewlett's particularly because of what,
it seemed to me, he meant. I liked his mind—the direct
honesty of it. I wish now I hadn't neglected to go and see
him for so long. I see there's to be a funeral service tomorrow
at his own village of Broad Chalke, a small place lost between
the downs. The old large house he used to live in until lately
was an old religious house, a beautiful creation of man and
time, with a giant tulip tree on the lawn and a pretty Italian-
ized garden beyond, with the Ebble (I think it was) flowing
between. Well!

When shall I come? As soon as I can, you may be sure.
Next week-end Joy (my elder daughter) and I meditate a
kind of lover's flight, an innocent escape to some Kentish or
Surrey hamlet, if this Arctic has passed by. The following,
my sister comes to complain of my long silence; the next
sees me hastening back from Scotland, whither I have to go
partly on business, meditating a call on Gordon on my way

back. Maybe one after then, unless a fury of work seizes
me—all this sounds rude, but you'll know it isn't meant so;
but I seldom spend week-ends away from home as you
know, and shall have to make some adroit adjustments first;
and all the time you say come, my wife and family say Go!
and I sit stolid or irresolute. Time flies, as it always does
with ageing men. Nothing is done, all's to do—and there's
that winged chariot, and my own little wheelbarrow
wambling on, loaded with weeds; a creaking wheel, dis-
coloured, top-heavy, with broken or strained timbers. No,
this isn't pathetic—it's so that life (i.e. time and I) run or
crawl on.—I think often of coming and remember our
delightful long talks and idle walks, and your books and
garden; and yourself.

I'm very glad about the book: I hope it comes my way
and then you shall see if I dissemble in dislike. But how are
you? Does Insulin or whatever it is renew your youth
and joy?

Is there a solder for a broken heart? Odd that the meta-
phorically broken heart mends with that gentle surgery we
all know of, but the physical heart nothing mends that we
know of now. This queer world—it perpetually amuses and
astonishes—bores never.

Adieu, a word almost English enough for my mood.

Ever

JOHN FREEMAN

ANERLEY
1924

MY DEAR WITHERS

I ought to have written before and meant to write last
Sunday, but the pen slipped from an idle hand, visitors came
to tea, talk flowed about them when they'd left, time passed,
sleep came, and your letter was undone. I'm very glad indeed

that you're so much better, but sorry you feel so much younger, for youth is an illusion and to re-enter one's illusion, to run back to one's prison and hear the gates fall softly to, to taste again the false medicines and liqueurs of that heady time, to be young again, having once been older and wished to be younger—what a misfortune, what a misuse. You are the bird that's blinded to make it sing, and self-blinded.

Immediately, I'll admit, there's a gain, since you are keen on Dorothy once more. Flower had told me that Binyon had spoken to him, but he didn't know who it was that wanted to rifle her quietness. Now I've talked to him again and he says the best thing would be for you to slip up one day to the Museum and he would discuss the project gladly and show you whatever they've got; for he's glad Dorothy is no longer to sleep in her alabaster chamber. I expect he'd be free to see you in the MS. room any day and he could bring you along to our daily luncheon party, even if you don't eat anything but figs and thistles.

Fausset spent a night here with some others this week and I was very glad to see him again. When shall I see you again? if not in town, I don't know: it's kind of you to ask me to come again but impossible for me to come. I'm extremely busy and if I can get away at all before Christmas I ought to go down to an aunt near Cheltenham; but even that I fear I must forgo.

I'm waiting for *The Grove*: alack, the whole edition has had to be scrapped because of the vile printing—I'm half angry and half indifferent. Actually I'm much more concerned with a long poem lately finished, *Prince Absalom*, which I'm anxious to publish soon but which I've not the least idea of at the moment. I'm waiting for a spark from heaven—it must be a spark from heaven because I think it is one of my best poems, perhaps the best. It isn't always pleasant to read things in typescript, else I might send it, but you'd better wait until it is out.

I'm busy, but don't pity me because I like work, even if it is prose. I love writing prose as I love watching a river; and prose is a river, holding the shadows of trees and clouds and the harsher line of the banks, with a snake waggling up and lifting his head above the water until I move. Imagination is that snake, and I have but to leave it alone and when it has gone to remember the furrow of its swimming and the bands of its back.   Affly.

                                                                J. F.

                                                        ANERLEY
                                                      June, 1924

MY DEAR WITHERS

Forgive my unmannerliness, I delayed writing until I could tell you all about Portfolios. Even now I can't tell you, for I'm waiting for information and shall have to write again; but I write to say how glad I was to be with you and to see you again, so active and happy. I'm glad, for myself, that the worst of the weather didn't come while I was at Souldern, though it must have been hard on Monica, as well as on Paul Nash. Yesterday's sun was so surprising and sudden that I walked with Joy at Hayes, we felt languid and content, and sat under enormous trees and discoursed of lyric poetry and sang old airs. The night before I had taken her to *Romeo and Juliet*. I don't like the theatre, she loves it and loves Shakespeare above all. She delighted in Romeo, and all the rest of the men speaking that divine verse in the best Oxford manner, when Mantua became Man-chewer, tune became choon, my lord became m'lord and my heart m'heart; and she even enjoyed a slim thin wisp of Burne-Jones shrilling over Juliet's magic lines. She delighted too, in the lavish "picture", the costumes so brilliant, the movement so bright and sharp; and even I, who could not endure the verse, could endure and enjoy the picture. Else it pleased me little to behold the sophistications of a play which I remember reading with joy and tears nearly thirty years ago, one night —alone—when the beauty and the freshness and sadness knocked at a young heart and opened it.

Well, you have something better to please yourself with than the traffic of a sumptuous stage: flowers, trees, woods, meadows, water, stone; and I remember how beautifully Juliet might—no, *must*—speak from the open casement of your stone chamber, looking out upon that small patch of grass and flower. That's where I might enjoy, and where it would be hard for verse to sound amiss; but these things can't be, and so I must be content with a London theatre— or with staying away.

I'll write to you again in a day or two; meanwhile all my best wishes and remembrances to Mrs. Withers and family.

Ever

JOHN FREEMAN

ANERLEY
22nd. March, 1925

DEAR WITHERS

I hope your silence doesn't mean that you're not so well, and I hope you'll forgive the irregular lines on this sheet for I can't see well, being too tired or too lazy to get a light and so sitting in the early dark of this rigorous snowy day. I'm writing now not because I have a headache—as I have, in this north-east wind—or because I've nothing to read and no one to talk to, but because I really should like to extract a line from your mute lips. My own "line" is full of complaint. I detest this weather, with the malignant north-east wind, for I can't stand winter coming when Spring should come. I've too much to do, I mean for bread and

butter, since my daily job is more and more exacting; and yet
I want to write a poem, the subject's all ready, and the
familiar nervous itch worries me; it's only time and energy
wanted, physical energy, to sit down with unembarrassed
head. I've just finished one long job and am dissatisfied,
being tempted to alter it so freely (on the top of a thousand
alterations) that I must refrain from touching it at all; for I'm
not sure that the dissatisfaction has very much to feed upon.
There's only, I think, the usual difficulty in reconciling p. 155
with p. 7, and the perplexity of eliminating repetitions and
trying to preserve the most elusive and magical effect—
Unity.

Well, and besides this I'm glad to say I've arranged with
Macmillan's for them to do *Prince Absalom*. I'm anxious to
get this out very soon, and after then, perhaps—perhaps—my
short stories—and after them, perhaps—perhaps—perhaps
—a series of unwritten poems that shape themselves thus:

I've no great reason, you'll see, to be dissatisfied, and it's
only a stupid head that's tired.—The stupid head, you'll say,
is more your concern: forgive it, and remember that your
own writing gives me the trouble as well as the pleasure of a
prize competition, with myself as winner.

But it's a selfish letter, I know, written on a selfish day; for
Sunday at Home is the Englishman's great day. Especially
this day, when we're looking for Spring that we thought had
come. How melancholy and how right the owl's note sounds
now! Our pear-tree buds stay as they were weeks and weeks
ago: a little wall-flower is out, and humbler, earth-crouching

things. Everything waits and shivers and seems on the point
of saying, I'm damned if I'll wait any longer. And at that my
heart almost breaks, though my head smiles.

One line will be enough to give me good news of yourself.
Ever

JOHN FREEMAN

ANERLEY
13th. April, 1925

MY DEAR WITHERS

Your last letter half amused me, but only half. I was in
fact a little surprised that you should demur to my article on
the Stevenson book. Most decidedly it wasn't, as you say,
clever. I'll admit it was carefully written—is that clever? it
was written with pleasure—is that clever? it was written to
welcome a poorly-written book because it served to put
poor R. L. S. in a human light—is that clever? it rebuked the
author for his attack on Mrs. S.—is that? it used the conversation form for sake of ease and manners—or that? It
wasn't written with any tongue in the cheek and a horrid
smirk at the reader—is that clever? I think it was gram-
matical, lucid and moderately readable, and I'm sure it was
fair—*must*, then, it be clever? Of course I don't manage the
conversational form well enough, and the ghosts of Landor
and Fitzgerald look smilingly over my shoulder as I write;
but am I clever or am I brave to follow them?—Come! what
you really meant was that you don't like the matter of the
article, and that I should say an honest good word of a book
whose sole merit it is to clear away the artificial mist that
dimmed and softened the natural features of his subject.
What else could I say? Half truths provoke whole truths.
I didn't know until I saw Colvin how much had been suppressed even in the letters, without a sign of omission being
conceded; and I suppose that when the letters in full are

"released" there will be further protestations and justifi-
cations and the rest of the plaster will fall.—One would
rather have the truth, even if one has to wait for it.

But I won't quarrel, least of all on a Bank Holiday, with a
quiet mild air without and a low fire within, and the mouse-
murdering cat on the rug and letters waiting for the post. I
hope you've had a pleasant holiday, which is to say I hope
you are feeling well, with no fresh occasion for discourage-
ment or philosophy. I could preach you a sermon, but
unfortunately all my sermons are "out" on duty to No. 1.
I've been too happy to philosophize, though, for I went down
for a couple of days to Charlton Kings, where I preserve an
aunt, and puffed up the steep paths of hills and looked down
(it seemed) on fine-edged Leckhampton; and then went to
Tewkesbury with her and rejoiced in all I saw, much in the
Abbey, but mostly, I think, in the houses—so comely and
comfortable, in their ruddy brick and timber, all smiling in
the strong April sun of Saturday. And in the evening I
returned in that wonderful hill-side way from Charlton Kings
to Kingham (which you know, I think) and was happy again
to feel myself flowing into those smooth bare hills and their
strength and smoothness embracing mine. To breathe the
air and sunshine of a hill, and then be suffused with the light,
shadow and silence of the valley'd spaces, was a joy. You
have it or the reach of it continually: I but seldom. Which of
us gets the more out of it, I wonder? I can't decide, and I
can't swear that it isn't myself.

I'm still trying a new poem, of which I'll tell you if it
comes near ripeness. At present it's a stem and a bud. I'm
passing the proofs of *Prince Absalom* and I'm waiting for
proofs of my prose work of the winter. Never was so
virtuous a writer! alack, never one so unappreciated. There's
a beautiful house empty at Tewkesbury—why isn't it mine?
There's a daily train to Devon and Cornwall—why not a

seat for me? Don't I write—stay: I had better refrain. *Never* was writer of prose or verse so unappreciated. I'm in despair! No, in truth, I'm ashamed or ought to be ashamed of not despairing. *I don't much care*; but tell it not in Gath, publish it not in Askelon. I think I hardly care at all, and Tewkesbury (lovely though the house is) may sigh in vain for me, and the Cornish train steam out dejectedly every morning. Base content, that finds its heaven in a smell of wall-flower and ecstacy in the evening's thrush.

No more. Our quarrel's done before begun. I pray for your health and may God give you better taste in prose. Happily your taste in verse is perfect.

Ever

JOHN FREEMAN

ANERLEY
Eleventh September, Nineteen twenty-five
Evening

DEAR WITHERS

> "I accept your admonition,
>   O solemn precisian,
>   And thee my Physician"

will follow, this time, in dating my letter and writing it better, and make you my debtor for legibility, not to say civility.—Forgive this imbecility—I swear I can't help it. Now—again! Your letter delighted me, for its news of your health, the best news of this kind for a long time. I congratulate you, your wives, families and that far flung line of your friends including myself between Souldern and Hell. I'm gladder still that your energies lure you to Italy, and my wishes shall follow you and yield whatever prayer and fasting can wrest from Fate.

But first, three small requests. First, can I have an *original* photograph of Bridges? You shewed me two, once, one all feet and one nearly all face. I'd so much rather have a direct photograph than a reproduction in the book.

Next, will you send me a card saying what is that Concerto of Hadyn's which I heard on your instrument? I remember the slow movement brought childhood back with its subtly reiterated and reinvolving refrain of *Hail Thou Once Despised Jesus!* I want to buy it, but forget what it was.

Lastly, if you are to be away in the potting season, will you arrange for your man to send me a few scraps of your brilliant orange wall-flower? I spoke of this in June when I was down.

And perhaps more than all: send me a line from Italy so that I may feel how much more I see by staying at home. All hearty wishes and congratulations.

Affly.

J. F.

ANERLEY
26th. June, 1927

My dear Withers

I will give you a song of Myself, but in a quieter tone than Whitman's, a purer (I hope) than James Joyce's and a less vulgar one than your Wells's. First to say that I congratulated Myself on receiving your gift of *Babel* and this further instance of your sagacity in choosing Poetical Friends. I took you at your word and denied Myself the pleasure of writing to thank you until I had read and thought a little of the book. It isn't an "idle" poem, and it has an intellectual conception which matches the aesthetic; and speaking for Myself it seems a poem which makes a double appeal, to the heart and to the head; and I'm not sure indeed if it isn't a virtue that the head gets more than that hyper-atrophied organ the heart. The only question I ask Myself is, if the influence of L. A. isn't too palpable to need the

suggestion of his preface: isn't, in fact, L. A. a little inordin-
ate of this poet's mind?

The theme is A'ish, but the style even more so: a deaf man
would recognize the sweep and roar of the blank verse, the
downward rushing impetus of line after line. But as I say,
I'm speaking only for Myself, who am not deaf to these
notes, and maybe have listened too curiously.

I have written no more verse since I last wrote, but
tremble with Expectancy, though teased with Business, and
so, while waiting, I've written certain articles and reviews,
merely to shew how these things can be done and how
soberly the Ass, Prose, can pull while the Mule, Verse, is
plunging in the hedge. I enjoyed writing, very hastily, an
article on Poe, and rather less another on an American book,
and soon, when I've written 2,000 words on Blake, in grave
yet elegant fashion, reconciling all his Irreconcilabilities and
smoothing every salience (until no one knows him from
Cowper or Whitman) when I've done this in the fashion
peculiar to Myself and despaired of by those that have no
Self (poor, petty worms that would be Dragons!) then, I
say, though you forget by this time what I was about to say,
I shall have nothing to do. *This* I shall say, Come back,
My Rhyme—but will the jade come back?

To-morrow I go to Edinburgh, not to see the Eclipse but
to Eclipse. Heaven be with me, and smite all rivals with palsy.
It's a mere business journey and of no importance except
for the quality of my bread and the freshness of the butter.

I was very glad indeed to hear that your *Friends* is to go
into Cape's *Travellers*. May more friends come with it, to
find in you renewed and renewing health.

Yours

J. F.

P.S. If you have read Wolfe's *Requiem* tell me whether you
admire it. And have you read *The Land*? I haven't, but must.

ANERLEY
Christmas Night, 1927

MY DEAR WITHERS

The hairs of your head are all numbered—by no needlessly expert mathematician; there's not a sparrow. . . . But why tell you this? Last week was a week of strange weathers and strange adventures; but one of the strangest was that of the policeman who broke his nose to please Cathy; other purpose there could not be when the effect was so ample and exact. The silver thaw, as the newspapers call it, provoked many mishaps, but the oddest precipitation was that of P.C. Smith, who fell in the street and broke his collar-bone. An ambulance was fetched and the insensible form of the P.C. was reposed within; and on the way to the hospital the ambulance skidded, and the victim became a victim anew, for the trick of the ambulance shook him to the floor, and he broke his nose while he still slept. Is there something funny in the episode?—the sleeping P.C., the ambulance hastening towards him and receiving his insensibility with a gentleness akin to love's; the sudden slide and jar, the P.C. falling on his nose and breaking it without feeling it? There must have been something funny as a relief from something pathetic, for mirth ensued and Cathy shook—not maliciously but with an acidulated enjoyment.

Did it strike you that the thaw and ice and thaw were sent to amuse Cathy?

But why do I mention this? To reiterate another instance of Design in the World. Among many gifts there came to us a flower from Selfridge's, with the card of Arthur and Florence. Who are they? we asked petulantly. We thought of King Arthur and Guinevere, of bachelor Balfour, Arthur Sullivan—all dead and gone, lady. We thought of Florence the fair city of your acquaintance, of Florence de la Mare as was, and Florence Nightingale; but it couldn't be one of these, for who was Arthur? In the absence of a clue it seemed not quite honest to keep the azalea, for it was the azalea in flower and some one unknown and benignant had sent it; yet if we sent it back it would die on Mr. Selfridge's hands. We *must* keep it, though Arthur and Florence went unthanked. Yet might not our thanks float out moth-like upon the mysterious air and sway into their ken? Perhaps they were readers of mine, choosing this shy but not ambiguous way of testifying to the pleasure of poetry.—Only at length did the truth come to me: that the azalea was sent to remind me of my first love, Coventry Patmore, and to repeat "first love's first cry" in my astonished ears. For, indeed, it was only an hour or two before that I had been re-reading, or re-glancing at, the Ode of that name; and so I could be reasonably—no, intuitively sure, that in the enormous cauldrons of Time and Chance this small and significant episode—coincident the godless might call it—had been caught in a swirl and snatched from the fume and scum of the world—for why? Merely so that I might get a miraculous savour out of memory! For this did Florence and Arthur buy an azalea and order it to be sent to their Aunt Mary; but Fate and Selfridge forbad. Aunt Mary is wondering why Florence and Arthur haven't sent this year—"they always send a flower, you know!"—and Florence and Arthur wonder why Aunt Mary hasn't written her usual half-waspish letter of thanks.

When, with the help of Michael and Gabriel and the stripling Abdiel, the mysteries of earth are made plain in Heaven, what a sudden lightening of darkness will be seen. On one side those severe Seraphs, with a look of infinite wisdom that only an editor can assume on earth; on another side, Florence and Arthur and Aunt Mary, and on the third side of the sacred Triangle, Coventry Patmore and Me. Bachian complications will rise and spread like swifts perpetually flying; geological fauns will issue from the bastions of eternity and disport themselves with nymphs and fays; and in the midst an Azalea will spring, fabulously fair, while all we bow down with humble delight.

Well, if you've read so far you may guess in what spirit I say *thank you* for the Binyon Anthology. It is a kind and thoughtful choice, and appreciated the more (that is, some way after the kindness of your remembrance of an unworthy correspondent who doesn't correspond) because it includes some of L. B.'s prose, which is *almost* better than his verse. Thanks and thanks.

I ought to have written long ago, but I have infinite excuses, though I scorn to recount them. I was glad to hear from you, and now I wish I'd said so before. But what will you have?

I've been well, though often tired, I hate this intense weather, which tries me too much, but May will soon be here and I shall be easy. This week-end I shall be away with my family—and then follows a series of horribly crowded weeks. I say this not boastfully; but just as Judge Jeffreys might boast to his wife of another fowl turned off to-day, my dear.

All my love and kind remembrances.

Affly.

J. F.

ANERLEY
6th. July, 1928

MY DEAR WITHERS

You must be prodigiously well to keep dumb for so long: only an abundant energy and preoccupation could restrain your agile pen. You are mute because you are so active. You dance and run, and cannot stoop to letters. Your wit sets your legs going and inhibits the graceful steps of the brain. It is roses, roses all the way in your garden now,

2 C

as you prune and water and hoe, and there's no time or thought for men jailed in London and bound fast to duty.

Of the latter I am the chief. Yet I've less cause for complaint than many have, for I've been frequently away. I have smelt primroses in Leeds, looked for daffodils in Manchester, peered among flowering rushes in Bristol, anticipated the bluebells in Glasgow and drunk water in Bath. And between these romantic places and the like—though there never was a like to Leeds and Manchester except Manchester and Leeds— I have stared at meadows and woods and running waters, seen again the stones of Avebury, delighted in a score of villages in a dozen counties, and drunk in the scents and sounds of infinite air and sea. The occasional use of my car has helped to bring the country to my plate: I have cut it— the country—to mincemeat and swallowed it ravenously.

So much for explanation—not excuse. I make no excuse, I accept none, Sir! You have not written because you would not write. I say no more.

Natheless, you will see from this literal recital that I have been so much everywhere as to have been nowhere, seen nothing, talked to no one, and no one talks to me. You don't even talk of Souldern and its Pool, and wonder if I'm never coming again. Talk not of Souldern: I shan't be able to dream of pleasure for months yet. In August I take a family holiday. After this I expect I shall spend two months in— making up for time lost: and then, Presto! is winter.

Write to me, then, and shew me what excuses you might make for your silence, if you could "demean" yourself. Stoop, that I may smile at your stooping. Tell me who has been with you, and where you have been: in return I'll tell you beforehand that my *Collected Poems* are just being published in Macmillan's best style, with a portrait by Laura Knight which makes me at once proud and contrite. And tell me above all, pray, when you do write, how the book strikes you, if it strikes you at all. Just Powers! to think I've been cherishing the thought of you for all these years, thirty or forty years, and don't know if you like my poetry. On what deceitful footing have I stood!

Resolve me this, and believe that I am—more than you are mine—
Yours ever
J. F.

ANERLEY
16th. May, 1929

DEAR WITHERS

How are you? I hear nothing of or from you. Silence has overcome your witty loquacity, no longer do your fly-mark characters tease my eye and intelligence. The postman never comes here: grass invades the garden path and the letter box hangs rusty on its hinge. Only duns haunt the step.

I'll not reproach you, however, I'll boast and say how I followed your footsteps, I think, hither and thither in Dorset a week or two ago, roaming from village to village, Minster to parish church, inn to inn, from one end of the country to the other. I imagine that you must have been to many of the places we touched—Wimborne, Charminster, Beaminster and a score of others; and if I'd had any decency, or a fraction less indolence, I should have sent you word of my roaming. My younger daughter drove us, and the four of us enjoyed it with scarce any differing degree of intensity of pleasure—which is a vile phrase to write.

That *was* pure pleasure, but I'm often away for pure business, but thanks to the car I find travelling endurable. Hail to thee, blithe Morris, agile Austin!—the latter being my daughter's midget, named Ozymandias and bearing the opening lines of the sonnet lettered upon the wind-screen. I

2 C 2

loll back and survey heaven, while I ponder upon verse and "progress" and mingle two personalities into one Inanity.

I've heard nothing lately from Wilfrid, nor for a long time from Fausset—men are very base—but this morning I was cheered by the *Times* announcement that L. A. is to be professor in London. I promise myself meetings!

Tell me what you are doing, how you are, what you think, how your garden looks and what I shall tell H. M. T. when he comes here again and urges me to write a book upon Doughty.

I shall be near you to-morrow, as we all come up to Oxford for dinner at the Mitre for a twenty-first. I wish I had time to come over and see you on Saturday but I've engaged to come home too early.　Ever

J. F.

ANDREW YOUNG

TO ANDREW YOUNG

My dear Young

I've already said thank you for your letter and now I'll say something more. You'll see we are here, and the prayers of the righteous have availed, both for himself and us; for the weather is superb and I take it you have it even finer—as you deserve, since it is your intercession with the Weather God that hath brought this abundance of sun and light.

You mustn't say too much about civilization and the Fall, unless you are prepared to say also that the Fall was inevitable, since civilization was. I too feel that the latter is a devouring griffin, insatiable and horrific; never was any seeming benefit so soon and so subtly diverted into an inner curse. Civilization has lent itself so easily to materialism—material development is so apparent when it is secured and seems so urgent when lacking—that the civilization of the mind and spirit is forgotten or ignored, or at best identified with education and education with learning things. One slips lightly into paradox and cynicism, else it might be only truthful to say that Democracy, as we now see it, is the chief enemy to civilization, confusing it with material prosperity.

But of course there is far more than this in the count, and it presents itself to me in a constant war between simplicity and complexity. I want things simple—sensations, delights, personal relations and the rest—yet enjoy them when complicated and enriched with all manner of variety. Nothing pleases me like a green hill or a grey stone, and the mere sparkle of water sends me crazy as it falls down between green grasses. But I yield to the temptations of material comfort and would ride in a car so as to get away from the people who live for cars; I admire pictures which are like the refined furniture of people who like their cars silent and speedy; and all the time I suspect the refinement I like or covet, and yearn more and more for the simplicity which is slipping away. Hence it seems to me, a false voracious civilization is the enemy of the true, and of the race of man; and when we are all civilized we shall all be dead at heart.— It is poetry and almost only poetry that saves one from this, and hence, again, one reverts to the past not because of a pleasant sentiment for past times refined of their grossness, but because the great Enemy was weaker then and it was possible to live unconsciously then, in a simple natural appetite for whatsoever things were true and lovely and of good report.

All this is platitude, a preaching to the preacher, which you'll smile at and dismiss. But tell me, how shall such subtlety as the restless mind is capable of consort with such simplicity as the spirit sickens for?

About the verses I sent you: I've done no more, or little more since sending, and probably the theme will rest while I am away. I thought of telling how Solomon subdued the Jinns, strange and fearful creatures: how he built the Temple with their reluctant aid; how others wondered at him— Sheba's Queen, to wit; and how he died in spiritual apostacy —Civilization already too strong. I fancy what you have will prove half the whole, and I see the whole as a pleasant book with illustrations to please the younger readers. You'll complain I've taken liberties, but I never mind doing that if I can justify the "taking" to myself.

I shan't argue with you about *Michael*; I prefer *Lycidas* and *Modern Love*. I admire *Michael*, but respect stiffens my admiration and makes it a little cold. I'd rather *Endymion*;

and many other poems by Wordsworth himself. But we needn't quarrel—nothing is here for tears. I'm dipping into Chaucer, and lapping up Trollope, all my mind having become lax and flabby.

Joy will write to Mrs. Young (to whom we all send love). I fancy she's in difficulty about a school-friend.

You'd like this beach—so would your family—rocks, cliffs, sands, tides, harbour, bay with great gray cliffs, heather capp'd, and lonely spaces. If the weather serves we shall betray ourselves by taking an expensive trip to Dartmoor on Wednesday; and then, for reaction, Joy and I shall go off for a night in a rural pub, after walking as much as we can.

I wish you'd write again as soon as you've the least inclination.

Yours

J. F.

ANERLEY
13th. September, 1925

MY DEAR YOUNG

I've treated you, as a correspondent, shamefully, as a friend not exceptionally, as a poet not jealously, as a spiritual master not reverently: I've not answered your letter though meaning to often and often. Your remarks about civilization interested me greatly, your complaint about the subject of our talks provoked me. As to the latter, whose fault is it that Letters attract us when we talk? Don't Letters, meaning books, give the essence of whatever intellectual energy and value may be found in conversation? I should be willing enough to talk of civilization, and isn't it what we are always talking of when we are not talking of purely creative work? I except that, because it doesn't seem to exist for the sake of civilization or anything else external to its own inscrutable impulse; but this apart the whole of literature is a civilized exercise and example (forgive these hasty cacophonies and snaky sibilations, and guess how I might write if I chose!).— But more seriously, your way of looking at a very hard problem, that faces us at every turn of modern life, seemed to me an easier one than I could follow. Evil seems a calamity that befalls one like a fever, or an accident; but worse than this calamity is that other and darker one which is involved —no accident or fever—in mortality. It's that that haunts one—to be, then not to be. There's the mystery that makes other mysteries insignificant. Life is so warm and so intimate that it seems real: one knows it cannot in one sense be real, yet it must at least be more real than the no-life after: no-life, in our human sense, because it is not informed as this life is, and is void of sensuous impressions. It is because this present life is perpetually thrilled with sensuous impressions that we take it as real; but with those impressions stilled, how can we live? The chair one sits in may be here when one is gone: another eye will stare at the grain of the wood, another ear listen to the ticking of the clock, another hand take that hand—is there any evil in evil to match this?

Forgive this melancholy note. It isn't quite directly answering what you say, but what you say provokes it, though it's better unsaid. I wonder if there's anyone who isn't haunted by this ghost? I fancy (though it's not wise or healthy to watch) that it has seasonable returns, and isn't always a near apparition; but is it ever far off from any? No more.

Solomon progresses. I worked at it while at Lyme Regis, and since, and I fancy it's two-thirds done. I didn't disregard your wife's demur by any means, but I've not found it easy as yet to remove what she disliked. Perhaps you'd care to see the rest when it's finished—*finished* it will never be until printed, but I mean when a fair copy of the whole can be read.—All else waits—*Melville* and *Absalom* and the *Six-*

penny Selections. I'm ashamed not to finish this page: I think I could finish it if I tried, but you'd notice the wheels creaking and I shouldn't catch the post. I'll leave off, then, smoke a cigarette while I post this, then idle with Trollope for a while. I hope we shall meet before November, but don't argue too closely with me on your own strong grounds.

Please, our remembrances to your wife and all.

Ever

J. F.

P.S. Your letters are as difficult as they are delightful to read: yet you complain that mine are illegible. Malediction!

ANERLEY
January, 1926

DEAR YOUNG

I've meant several times to write to you, and now an additional reason is that I saw your *Adversary* second-hand in Charing Cross Road yesterday! More seriously, you may like to know that I went to Doughty's funeral. I was shocked at his death, though his age prepared one for it; I was more shocked at his funeral. There were not twenty people present. D. G. Hogarth was there, and Colonel Lawrence, and one or two people representing Colleges and Societies; but of Doughty's contemporaries—not one, except myself. The greatest prose writer, the greatest poet, of our time— and not a single contemporary save the least of all could go as far as Golders Green to honour and salute him. I wrote a letter to the *T.L.S.* lamenting this, for it saddened me, but the letter was suppressed. I think of the fussy obsequies which will be prepared for lesser writers, and it seems a dishonour to our times that Doughty should have been so completely ignored. One needn't lament this for his sake—it is a stigma self-inflicted upon the country when the prophet is unhonoured.—I'm doing an article for the *Bookman*, but that isn't a serious critical organ, though it reaches people, who, happily, are impressed by what they are told if it is told with authority.

I hope you will be up soon. Tell your wife (that gluttonous theatre-goer) that Flower and Allan and Meyerstein and I went to *Dick Whittington* on Friday and thoroughly enjoyed it: here, we found, was the People's Theatre, all heart, no Art—simple, primitive, unsophisticated, clear of cant. Next year we shall go again—probably, in my own case, not to any theatre between whiles. Meyerstein is afraid of me: I've scoffed him out of many theatres, and now little but the Old Vic remains for him: soon that too will fall into disfavour.

Come up soon. All here send their Loves.

Yours

J. F.

ANERLEY
October, 1927

MY DEAR YOUNG

The sight of your slender web-like hand upon a sky-like paper was a true pleasure, and I read you eagerly. If my pleasure diminished as I read it was only because I was sorry that all isn't happy with you. Not that "all" is ever happy for anyone, until it is passed, for happiness, O Solomon, can only relate to moments and experiences which are gone but not dead.—But I must not metaphysicize in writing to a Scot. Nevertheless, while I can't follow all you say I can suspect the relation that is hidden between your references to Crabbe, churches, yourself, myself and truth etc., and I fancy—probably quite wrongly—that what troubles you is too much thinking. Thought, the power to think, is a gift to be used sparingly—not heedlessly applied to combustibles. You speak of me, but happily I have not a head for thinking.

Say if you like that I am dull and conventional, that my
mind is untrained and unlearned in "ologies"; well, should
I be happier—no, should I be *wiser* for thinking? It seems to
me that aesthetic is as potent as logic, as moving, as true;
that it is at least as divine as what you must needs call divinity;
and that the feeling—half pain, half pleasure and at its
highest all ecstacy—which a rhythm, a sound, a vision provokes, has as much to do with the immortal as any dialectic.
You speak of finding a church for me, and it will sound
arrogant to say that I have found one for myself, though I'm
not worthy or capable of entering it. I don't mean to tell you
where it is or what it is, for I can't describe it even to myself;
it is the church in which (to speak pretentiously) all my
poems have been sung, and all other poems heard.

I wish, then, that I could say something sensible and
practical in answering your letter and its pauses; but, as I
said, thinking isn't my strong point and it is yours—worse
luck. You have been tippling, you have indulged your
faculty, you have forgotten that the wanton use of a faculty
is worse than neglecting it. I speak seriously—give up
thinking, if you can.

Yet I'd like to see you in a country Rectory, with time for
versing. The English church is a handmaid to the Muse—
never was more blessed office more blessedly filled. The
Reverend George Crabbe, do you say? Why not? And why
not the Reverend Lord Byron, the Reverend John Keats?
Was Sterne the less delicious a writer for being a parson, or
the less worthy a parson, duly considered, for being a
novelist?—Thinking, and her jackal Conscience, have done
so much harm and so little good, have spoiled so many
whom God in His mercy would have spared, that I would
gladly see you knock them both on the head and retreat into
a living not too far from the centre of things, which is
Anerley, and write *The Aviaries* in six volumes.

Meanwhile, I'd like to see you. I'd like you to come here, but ever since our holiday we've been in the builder's hands and are reduced to a single room. Public decency forbids our entertaining even you. You've no idea what it is to wake one morning with no roof, the next with no floor, and again with no maids! We dress and undress surreptitiously, we eat like pigs, indiscriminately; our furniture is locked up or repairing; our money is spent; our tempers are worn; our spirits are exhausted. Far off and obscure, domestic peace is shaping and my study is nearly ready for occupation. But come to the Tibbald, and let us eat together one afternoon, only be sure to tell me first, for I've grown irregular. Changes have taken place in the World of Insurance which have fettered me, and indeed worried me, past endurance. I mean nobody can endure me. At a question I fret, at the gentlest remonstrance I rave; I have to be shaved at a barber's, my wife keeps the knives out of my reach; I'm not allowed to go to town by an electric train for fear I should walk on a live rail; I avoid water. In other words, the quiet path of my life has been crossed by new tasks not connected with Rhyme— or indeed Reason—and I'm not sure of turning up at lunch every day. But I want to see you after all these months, even if we find nothing to say to each other but, Well! and then, Must you go?

Our respects to your wife. I don't know if Joy has written lately, but I do know she has been trying to read hours and hours a day.   Affly.

J. F.

ANERLEY
Easter, 1928

DEAR YOUNG

A month ago you wished that Easter were gone so that you could write me long letters. When you read this Easter will be gone.

Doughty, Hardy, Science and Religion—your mind is indeed a serious one. I always knew it was, and now that Doughty and Hardy are both dead you can call them classics and give them all your mind, disregarding their successors as trivial and tame. And it *is* hard to believe in one's contemporaries, whom one may see and shake hands with, as one believes in those who shall never be seen. Every writer, when he finds a friend, loses a reader. The person who becomes a friend is not the person who wrote this or that which charmed the stranger and overcame the critic. The friend does not match one's conception of the writer. You see him at home, or walking, and you argue with him, thinking his mind narrow, his interest self-centred; and you no longer appreciate him, and wonder why he doesn't appreciate a single one among his contemporaries. How narrow-minded of Shaw, not to admire A. A. Milne! how obstinate of Milne not to revere Havelock Ellis! How insular of Kipling not to have loved Marcel Proust! How jealous of Moore, not to care for any one at all!

But you, now, with your serious mind so seriously bent, remembering:

We needs must love the highest when we read it—you, the austere Caledonian, may admire Hardy and Doughty without reserve: they can't write any more, and as for their posthumous works, why, of course they can't be worth printing: a mere unmerited piety alone is responsible for the publication.—Don't deny all this. Admit that it is true, and I'll admit that I share the common weakness.

But to-day I made a convert to Emily Dickinson! Tell me, have you done a good deed this year?

Where is Ladaig, where is Benderlock? I've looked all through Gulliver, and find them nowhere—not in Lilliput, not in those stranger Kingdoms. But I know where Arundel is, and I'm going to stay there on Wednesday for a week.

I too shall look for strange flowers—for the primrose and bluebell, and go down on my knees—not to Science or Religion—in delight. I shall bow to the Apothecary Sun who:

> "Gathered the blossoms that have no use
> Save to shine and smell
> For the mere delight of the eyes
> And the tongue to tell."

                                    Affly.
                                                J. F.

P.S. Addressing your envelope, I came near to putting "at" Bigwood Avenue, as though you were but calling there en route for Scotland and immortality.

ANERLEY
29th. August, 1928

MY DEAR YOUNG

Don't grumble that I haven't answered your last welcome letter. You didn't give an address in your remote island, and though I suppose you could have been found via Hove, I thought that if I waited I might have another letter, and then waited in sheer idleness. But not a word more came, and as I daily remembered that I ought to write, I grew daily more conscious that I ought to have written, and so accumulated sins upon sin's head.

Well! You have probably had wretched weather, and if so I am very sorry. But apparently you like atrocious weather. I remember that in winter, when I was shivering in the south, you went to the far north in order to enjoy severe weather, all the time pretending that you were ill. Prithee, where do you go when you are well? The Arctic must be too mild a zone for your strenuous spirit, the Antarctic too easy a trial. Wouldn't London do, in August? I suppose you are living on oatmeal, whiskey and herrings, and may the Lord have mercy on your stomach. But I pity your family. While you are rapt in commerce with the skies, I suspect

WORKS BY
JOHN FREEMAN

COLLECTED POEMS

With a Portrait by LAURA KNIGHT, A.R.A.
Crown 8vo. 8s. 6d. net.

LAST POEMS

With an Introduction by SIR JOHN SQUIRE
Crown 8vo. 7s. 6d. net.

PRINCE ABSALOM

Pott 4to. 3s. 6d. net.

SOLOMON AND BALKIS

Pott 4to. 3s. 6d. net.

HERMAN MELVILLE

Crown 8vo. 3s. 6d. net.
(*English Men of Letters*)

MACMILLAN AND CO. LTD., LONDON